Praise for *A Blue Hand*

"Baker's work is a piece of devoted scholarship and legwork dunked in the screwy, hyperintelligent, tragicomic essence of everything that drove Ginsberg to take a trip that not only changed his life but helped spawn generations of hipsters, hippies, writers, artists, rock stars, mental cases, and self-anointed medicine men."
—*The New York Times Book Review*

"Biographer Deborah Baker, wife of Indian writer Amitav Ghosh, has plumbed Ginsberg's poems, letters, journals, and diaries for *A Blue Hand*. . . . The result is a dense, exotic, intriguing saga—not just Ginsberg's but India's too: its lunatic saints and rugged landscape, its poverty and unrest."
—*National Geographic Adventure*

"[Baker] reminds us that the Beats were not marble statues but flesh-and-blood human beings struggling with their egos and their ambitions as we all do—albeit with considerably more audacity and intensity."
—*Chicago Tribune*

"In incisive and elegant prose, the book casts light on those who ended up as only minor characters in Ginsberg's and Snyder's versions of events. . . . By triangulating and supplementing the accounts in Ginsberg's *Indian's Journals*, Snyder's *Passage Through India*, and Kyger's *Strange Big Moon*, Baker offers a panoramic vision of the Beats' journey to the East."
—Steve Silberman, *Shambhala Sun*

"This literary travelogue illuminates the Beats' mythic fondness for India's sadhus, poets, and saints."
—*More*

"*A Blue Hand* moves through time with confidence and certainty, teaching as it inspires, enlightening as it lectures. Insofar as the plethora of books on the Beats that have been released in the last few years, this is one of the most worthwhile, for it reviews an important aspect of the Ginsberg lore that has often been ignored."
—*The Electric Review*

PENGUIN BOOKS

A BLUE HAND

In 1990 **Deborah Baker** moved to Calcutta, where she studied Bengali and wrote *In Extremis: The Life of Laura Riding,* a finalist for a Pulitzer Prize in Biography. Since then, her essays have appeared in a range of publications from *The New York Times* to *The Statesman,* Calcutta. With her husband, the writer Amitav Ghosh, and her two children Lila and Nayan, she now divides her time between Calcutta, Goa, and Brooklyn.

VIOLET

HAND

FORTH

A Blue Hand

THE TRAGICOMIC, MIND-ALTERING

ODYSSEY OF ALLEN GINSBERG, A HOLY FOOL,

A REBEL MUSE, A DHARMA BUM, AND

HIS PRICKLY BRIDE IN INDIA

Deborah Baker

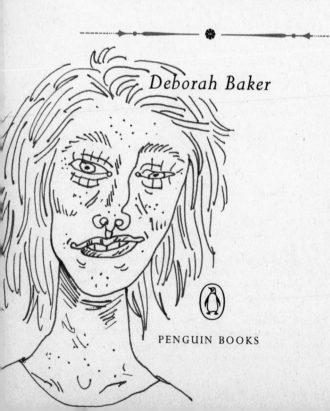

PENGUIN BOOKS

PENGUIN BOOKS

Published by the Penguin Group

Penguin Group (USA) Inc., 375 Hudson Street, New York, New York 10014, U.S.A.

Penguin Group (Canada), 90 Eglinton Avenue East, Suite 700, Toronto,
Ontario, Canada M4P 2Y3 (a division of Pearson Penguin Canada Inc.)

Penguin Books Ltd, 80 Strand, London WC2R 0RL, England

Penguin Ireland, 25 St. Stephen's Green, Dublin 2, Ireland (a division of Penguin Books Ltd)

Penguin Books Australia Ltd, 250 Camberwell Road, Camberwell,
Victoria 3124, Australia (a division of Pearson Australia Group Pty Ltd)

Penguin Books India Pvt Ltd, 11 Community Centre,
Panchsheel Park, New Delhi – 110 017, India

Penguin Group (NZ), 67 Apollo Drive, Rosedale, North Shore 0632,
New Zealand (a division of Pearson New Zealand Ltd)

Penguin Books (South Africa) (Pty) Ltd, 24 Sturdee Avenue,
Rosebank, Johannesburg 2196, South Africa

Penguin Books Ltd, Registered Offices:
80 Strand, London WC2R 0RL, England

First published in the United States of America by The Penguin Press,
a member of Penguin Group (USA) Inc. 2008
Published in Penguin Books 2009

1   3   5   7   9   10   8   6   4   2

Pages 243–245 constitute an extension to this copyright page.

LIBRARY OF CONGRESS HAS CATALOGED
THE HARDCOVER EDITION AS FOLLOWS:
Baker, Deborah, date.
A blue hand : the Beats in India / Deborah Baker.
p.   cm.
Includes bibliographical references and index.
ISBN 978-1-59420-158-5 (hc.)
ISBN 978-0-14-311483-3 (pbk.)
1. Ginsberg, Allen, 1926–1997—Travel—India.   I. Title.
PS3513. I74Z57 2008
811'.54—dc22
[B]
2007030500

Printed in the United States of America
DESIGNED BY AMANDA DEWEY

FOR AMITAV

There is an orientalism in the most restless pioneer,
and the farthest west is but the farthest east.

HENRY DAVID THOREAU
A Week on the Concord and Merrimack Rivers

PART ONE

The
Columbus
of Eternity

IT WAS WELL AFTER MIDNIGHT on December 11, 1962, and Allen Ginsberg, a thirty-six-year-old poet from Newark, New Jersey, had gone off to pee for the umpteenth time. Ginsberg, along with his sometime lover Peter Orlovsky, was hurtling north in a third-class carriage on the *Doon Express*. The train had started at Howrah station in Calcutta and would deposit the pair sometime the following day in Benares. Ginsberg had been suffering from kidney ailments for years.

In the tiny lavatory mirror, behind the heavy black frames of his spectacles, his eyes held a gaze of curiosity, magnified by the power of his lenses. There was his nimbus of thinning hair. There was the heavy woolen sweater over a lumberjack shirt. There was the familiar and worn expression of loneliness. Back in their compartment, Orlovsky was already fast asleep on his bunk, his dirty blond hair splayed across an innocent face, oblivious to the chill wind that came through the open windows. He was undoubtedly dreaming of the talkative Bengali girl who had come to see them off at the station. They would soon be reunited. Though he had been Ginsberg's companion for eight years, his feelings for him were now more filial than sexual. Orlovsky was twenty-nine.

They had spent the last seven months in Calcutta. In the final days of their stay, Ginsberg had sat on the muddy temple steps below the Howrah bridge, taking leave of the small shrine dedicated to the mother goddess. Above him, the traffic had roared its mantra hum as it rattled across the Hooghly River. As a young man, Ginsberg had formalized an intricate ceremony of leavetaking. So from the bridge he had walked north to the burning pyres at Nimtola, where corpses, serene on their flower-bedecked litters, patiently awaited his good-byes. His last evening was spent in a rowdy farewell to the Bengali poets he had come to know. Stumbling out of the toilet and swaying down the corridor as the train clattered away into the night, he returned to his seat to write down his thoughts in his notebook.

For twenty years Ginsberg had relished the ritual of pens and paper, the relief that accompanied the emptying of his thoughts and the satisfaction of notebooks with filled pages. There were the small spiral-bound pocket notebooks that he wrote in on subways and buses, and there were sturdy bedside notebooks for nighttime *cris de coeur* or an early morning dream. Returning to a notebook after a day's neglect, he would begin in the present and circle back, writing his thoughts and observations not as he had them, but as he recalled having them. Periodically he cast back through the pages, prospecting for the glowing seam of a poem, like a miner long accustomed to working in the dark.

As the years had passed, the notebooks changed. More and more, Allen Ginsberg used them like a blank tape, inviting the world outside and inside his head to inscribe its noisy jive of unlikely juxtapositions. In India he had several notebooks going, and one, designed for schoolwork, now sat open on his lap, interleaved with unanswered letters. On its pages the tracks of his thinking crossed the borders of day and night, past and present, waking and dreaming, poetry and prose. The rhythm of the train itself was inscribed in his handwriting and jagged line breaks.

He made a brief stab at a poem, but his thoughts scattered, his mind returning to the other figure on the platform at Howrah station, a young woman from South Carolina with the improbable name of Hope Savage. He had kissed her good-bye. Until meeting in India, they had seemed to circle each other in a *pas de deux* of travel. Ten years younger, she had arrived in Greenwich Village a year after he had left New York City for Cuba, Mexico, and San Francisco. They had come closest to crossing paths in Paris, but by the time he'd arrived, she embarked on a journey that would take her from the arctic reaches of the Soviet Union to the southern-most tip of Sicily. He had first heard of her in 1956 from his friend and fellow poet Gregory Corso. While working as a mer-chant seaman on a ship bound for Alaska, he had received a letter from Gregory, announcing: "She, Allen, is our Rimbaud and more today."

Ginsberg sat cross-legged on his bunk, coughing and chain-smoking as he wrote, his knapsack taking up the floor in front of him. Peter's new sarod was tucked under the train seat, as was his own striped umbrella and typewriter. As the lights outside be-came few and far between, the wheel carriages finally picked up speed and the rhythmic *doom doom* drummed a roll of finality into his brain. The *Doon Express* tracked the path of the Ganges back-ward, shadowing its pulse as it traveled from Dehradun in the Hi-malayas across the Gangetic Plain to the Bay of Bengal. Soon there was just darkness, broken only by the light of the illuminated windows skipping across the shallow banks of the train bed. The thought of the young woman left behind under the station clock dissolved into a more global anxiety.

According to the newsmagazines he'd bought on the station platform, the world was deeply imperiled, hostage to the cold war between Moscow and Washington and the recent hot one between Delhi and Peking. Scant weeks before, there had been a nuclear face-off over the missiles in Cuba, and nearly simultaneously, a border war between India and China had broken out in the Him-alayas. Was democratic communism or a capitalist republic the solution to the distrust afoot in the world? He refused to be para-noid. All over the train, blankets were being pulled up to chins, and reading lights blinked shut. People are afraid to intervene, he wrote busily, drawing up a five-point program for world peace. Point number four was a TV debate between Khrushchev, Kennedy, Mao, and Nehru, to be translated into every language and broadcast globally by the five-month-old Telstar channel, the first communi-cations satellite. His brain teemed with ideas—move the UN to the

Himalayas—and questions: Were the stories about the atrocities in Tibet really true? All this made its jumbled way into his notebook.

He returned once more to his last sight of Calcutta, viewed from the seat of a horse-drawn ekka-gharry piled high with luggage, their way eased by the team of water buffalo that parted the crowd before them. He never reflected on the immensity and variety of traffic over the Howrah bridge without recalling the Chaucer pilgrims en route to Canterbury. Each comb seller and watch repairer, each woman with a basket of fish on her head, carried a tale he would never hear. He returned, too, to the thought of the two girls who'd seen them off: the Bengali girl determined to live in the West and the American girl who couldn't leave it far enough behind. Had they stopped to ask, the fortune-tellers and astrologers lining the approach to the bridge might have helped them see their fates more clearly. He now asked himself what Shelley would have done, and his pen hung in the air.

Should he marry Hope Savage?

He'd been down this road before. It was the old shaggy dog story, and in his experience the punch line was more painful than funny. Somewhere on the train, a baby cried as if to remind him just how unlikely a prospect this was. In the end, in his rush to find their reserved third-class carriage, racing after the coolie as their luggage slunk away into the platform crowds, he'd added nothing more to his kiss than a wave good-bye. And as quietly as Hope Savage entered Allen Ginsberg's account of his Indian travels, she now departed. While his lone lit cabin sped along the rails, he put away his journal and picked up his book, *Journey to the End of the Night*.

From this distance, it appears that Allen Ginsberg was in thrall to a tired idea: Disillusioned Westerner goes to mystic East in search of . . . what, exactly? A guru? An unlimited supply of drugs? Young boys? Nirvana? A wife? Or, like every pilgrim, did he simply cherish the belief that beyond the known world there exists a place where ailments are healed, the heart is filled, and demons are vanquished? Whatever he hoped to find in India, Ginsberg retained the faith that on arriving at his next port of call, tiny checks from his publishers would be waiting for him in batches of forwarded mail. He had faith that no matter how unwashed, a poet would be welcomed. The discomforts, delays, and illnesses that plagued him from time to time were no deterrent. And perhaps just as the mysteries of train tables, currency exchange, and cheap accommodations were eventually resolved, so might others. Yet despite his passion for the idea of India, there was something improbable about Allen Ginsberg's pilgrimage there. Unlike many of those who came after him, he neglected to leave much of his past behind. Instead, he brought most of it with him.

SOME TIME LATER, with brakes hissing and whistle blowing, the train slowed as it pulled into the dimly lit station at Burdwan. The only passenger still awake slid his book into his pocket and peered out in puzzlement from the top bunk, his head grazing the ceiling. The man sleeping across from him groaned. The sudden calm, the settling of the rocking carriage, had him looking for a cigarette and his notebook to quiet this new unease, not yet fifty miles from Howrah. "Burdwan??" he wrote.

CHRISTOPHER COLUMBUS famously mistook the American continent for India. Were his calculations fudged to make the world seem smaller, more in reach of Isabella's coffers? Did it never occur to him that the shores he sailed along might yield, not some reach of the vast Indian dream, but every sailor's nightmare of the infinite abyss? And if not the abyss, what else was there to be found? Was it simply too difficult for Columbus to imagine that the world still held such surprises? On his fourth voyage, he hazarded that on the far side of this rather large island, a mere ten days' sail west, was the Ganges. For he had discovered men living like birds in the trees. How could they not be Indians? Columbus would reach the coast of Brazil before he turned back to die at home, discredited and dishonored, without ever fully appreciating what it was he had found.

It might be said that the journey from America to India had its beginning in this confusion. In a pamphlet published as an addendum to *Leaves of Grass* in 1871, Walt Whitman charted the cosmic journey he imagined a future poet might take, picking up where the dream of the Genoese had run aground. For Whitman, India was the place where the poet's woebegone questions— "Wherefore unsatisfied soul?" "Whither O mocking life?"—would be answered. It didn't matter to him that the sea route had long been navigated and Calcutta boasted as many trading houses as London. Looking west for East, Whitman held that the laying of the Union Pacific Railroad, the stringing of coast-to-coast telegraph lines, and the dredging of the Suez Canal would not only bind the wounds of a country riven by civil war, but herald a new enlightenment. Once American enterprise tapped the "primal thought" of India, he sang in prophecy and blind boosterism, nature and man will no longer be "disjoin'd and diffused" and the world would know itself at last. Even then he knew he would not be the One to bring back the spices and the jewels. "Passage to India" foretold the journey of another.

> *After the seas are all cross'd, (as they seem already cross'd,)*
> *After the great captains and engineers have accomplish'd*
>   *their work,*
> *After the noble inventors—after the scientists, the chemist, the*
>   *geologist, ethnologist,*
> *Finally shall come the Poet worthy of that name;*
> *The true Son of God shall come, singing his songs.*

ON JUNE 3, 1925, one year to the day before Allen Ginsberg was born, a young woman with an intelligent face gave birth to a son on 7A British Indian Street in Calcutta. The boy was named after the Emperor Ashoka, the Indian ruler who spread the teachings of the Buddha throughout Asia. When Asoke Sarkar came of age, his father told him the story of his family and the history of the region where they came from. It would be many more years before Asoke understood the significance of the birthday he shared with Allen Ginsberg and the fate that would bring them together. By then the story of his beginnings had acquired nearly mythic qualities.

With the Mughal invasion of the subcontinent, Asoke's father told him, all over India the lands of the Hindu rajas and zamindars were seized. Royal patronage of the Brahminical priestly castes ceased, and with their powers diminished, the faith of Islam began to spread. In the sultanate's employ as ministers, treasurers, and clerks, eventually the literate class of high-caste Hindu Brahmins and Kshatriyas resumed their position in society. In the course of their duties as administrators, they learned Pashto, Urdu, and Arabic. They took Muslim titles. The Bengali Sarkars, like the Chowdhurys and the Mazumdars, Asoke learned, were among them. The founder of Asoke's clan, a Bengali by the name of Dey, became Dey Sarkar. In exchange for the loyal service of his ancestral Sarkars, in the nineteenth century the Muslim rulers gave the Sarkar family generous landholdings in the district of Khulna.

Khulna was a sparsely settled region, then as much Hindu as Muslim, in the eastern reaches of Bengal. Mathura Nath Sarkar was the first of the Sarkars to stop using the Dey name. A devout Hindu, he farmed his lands and became a wealthy man. At the turn of the twentieth century, he fathered his first child, a beautiful boy with radiant skin. He called his son Nagendra Nath, which was one of the names of Shiva. The apple of his father's eye, Nagendra was groomed to inherit the estate and to shoulder the mantle of patriarch.

When still in his teens, the boy chanced upon a performance of a jatra company. Jatras were open-air theatricals that toured the countryside putting on dramas drawn from the Ramayana and the Mahabharata or reenacting the lives of saints. As on the Elizabethan stage, comely young men played the female roles. Entranced by the performance, Nagendra was determined to join them, and before long he had secured the starring role of Sakhi. Sakhi was the angelic maiden who appears before every scene of the play to sing and dance an introduction to the mythological drama to follow. Nagendra's embodiment of Sakhi brought forth waves of tears from the villages he traveled through.

In a fit of fury and shame, Mathura Nath disinherited his son and vowed never to see him again. He was certain Nagendra would soon return to him, begging his forgiveness.

Nagendra Nath Sarkar was Asoke's father.

· · ·

IN THE SUMMER OF 1948, Allen Ginsberg was twenty-two and living in a borrowed apartment in East Harlem surrounded by works of Christian theology belonging to the absent tenant. To reach there, he had crossed the lower Hudson from New Jersey and set his sights on a law degree from Columbia University. As Manhattan's office towers rose before him, he made a vow to become the voice of the huddled masses. Laden with every possible encumbrance, he stepped off the Hoboken ferry to meet his fate.

Instead, after five years' effort, with numerous distractions, diversions, and delays, he had yet to complete his course requirements and obtain his undergraduate degree. His entanglement with a motley crew of friends whose addictions, ambitions, lawlessness, and brilliant idiosyncracies had made the prospect of a sensible career following his graduation unlikely. Still, it was not yet entirely out of the question. While Allen Ginsberg hugged the Harlem harbor of Columbia University, his closest friends had already lit out for the territories.

Heartbroken for the first time in his life and jumpy about his future, Ginsberg had been reading Blake and masturbating dreamily when he heard an unearthly voice reciting the poem he had just finished. Was the voice inside or outside his head? He didn't stop to wonder. First, he looked up from his book to glance at the view outside his tenement window. There, in the silken heat of a July afternoon, he saw something that truly beggared description. He climbed out onto the fire escape, his eyes locked on the sky that surrounded him, his mind aflame. When the spell began to lift, he turned around to stick his head in the open window of a neighboring apartment. To the astonishment of the two young women living there, he screamed, "*I'VE SEEN GOD!*" before they slammed the window shut. That night, he paced the linoleum floor of his kitchen, reading Plato and reciting Blake over and over, trying to summon that ancient voice again.

Days later, still brimming with exaltation, he called his former psychiatrist from a pay phone to tell him what had happened. In the middle of his long-winded gust of description, the doctor told him he had nothing to say and hung up the phone. He took the train to Newark, where his gentle, devoutly secular, and respectable father despaired at the news, wondering if his son, who had only recently acknowledged his homosexuality, was now showing signs of his mother Naomi's lunacy. Either that or he had become a Christian convert, and who could say which was worse? Their visit ended in a nearly hysterical argument over the existence of God. Louis Ginsberg wasn't having it and suggested Allen begin another round of analysis.

William James's master work, *The Varieties of Religious Experience,* was quite likely among those books arranged in orange egg crates throughout the apartment on East 121st Street. One of the four qualities of a mystical experience, James maintained, was the impossibility of describing it. Ginsberg, however, was undaunted. To a Columbia classmate, he began describing his vision by alluding imperiously to Saint John of the Cross, Santayana, T. S. Eliot, John Donne, and perhaps Meister Eckhart and Jacques Maritain for good measure, interrupting himself only to light another cigarette or flash a beady, challenging look. His professors also heard him tell of it in such terms, as if the drastic import of his experience could only be conveyed in the shared vocabulary of their core curriculum. He saw himself as a saint. He saw himself fulfilling Whitman's prophecy as the "Columbus of Eternity." If he imagined anyone would be impressed, either by his mastery of the critical texts or by the event itself, he was quite mistaken. He watched as a look of pity bloomed in his classmate's eyes and recognized the face with which he'd once contemplated his mother's madness. Out of sorts and profoundly out of character, Ginsberg became huffy and dismissed him with an ungenerous remark.

Lucien Carr was the only one of his closest friends still in the city. Carr's caustic sensibility was completed by his unholy good looks. As a Columbia undergraduate, he had lived and breathed the fictional universe of Dostoevsky, aspiring to model himself on one of the novelist's nihilistic rebels. Consequently, he found himself serving two years for having stabbed his former scoutmaster with a Boy Scout knife. His lawyers argued that he had snapped, having been pushed to the end of his patience by the older man's relentless and depraved pursuit. Allen, having witnessed Lucien's wars on conventional pieties, knew it was not that simple but withheld judgment. After Carr's release from prison, Allen had confessed to him that he was homosexual and Lucien had winced, proceeding to lecture him that no good would come of it. Carr now kept clear of trouble, confining his adventures to drunken sprees in downtown bars. This is no doubt where Allen found him, his golden-boy face now obscured by a cautious beard.

Allen made it a practice to keep Lucien abreast of his every discovery, including nuanced developments in his thinking from the last moment of their previous encounter, as if he were yet another notebook to inscribe. Carr had often observed how Ginsberg was only momentarily nonplussed upon learning he hadn't read such and such a book, before droning on interminably. Lucien had introduced him not only to his touchstone writers, but—crucially—to William Burroughs and Jack Kerouac. Perhaps Allen was only hoping to repay the debt. Yet in the wake of the vision, Lucien noted that "Bebe" Ginsberg was carrying on with more than his usual intensity. Once again, it was impossible for Lucien to tell if Allen was serious. When his conversation was the most fantastic, he often seemed the most grave, and when he was talking plausibly, he acted as though he were putting something over. It was only when Allen came to the part about God that Lucien told him he was undeniably off his rocker.

Allen was not likely to attempt a similar conversation with that priapic satyr Neal Cassady, even if he had been in town. Just one year before, Neal had seemed to grasp his most tender hopes and deepest desires with a startling, miraculous keenness. And unlike Jack Kerouac, Neal had not shrunk from taking him, on more than one occasion, to bed for rowdy, ecstatic rounds of screwing. With Neal, Allen had come closest to the mystical romance with a boy he had fantasized about since childhood. Allen had even followed him to Denver like a lovesick schoolgirl, pining away as Neal reunited with his jailbait wife, LuAnne, and newest flame. Knowing that only the road held greater appeal, Ginsberg had paid their way to Texas to get him away, to introduce him to Burroughs, only to watch him find another girl the moment his back was turned. Neal's last letter had spelled it out: His new wife and forthcoming child were little more than an abstraction to him; he was a no-good shark who fed on the feelings of others but was incapable of generating his own. Nor was he the genius Allen and Jack imagined. He was nothing but a sick man who knew his own hollowness. Neal's real expertise was limited to girls and cars. And, of course, talk.

And then there was Jack Kerouac. Since leaving the city, Kerouac had struggled to appease both the demon of restlessness and the desire, when writing, for the comforts of home. Though he often spent weekends in the city, he had settled with his mother in Ozone Park, Queens, where she had a job in a shoe factory. By the time Allen told him the news of his vision, Jack had recovered from Scribner's rejection of his first novel, *The Town and the City*, and was in a fever of retyping the thousand-page manuscript. That summer, he had worked out a complicated algorithm whereby his typed progress was converted into batting averages. He was gunning to stay even with Ted Williams. He had little patience for Allen's ranting and told him that it made him look ugly. After Jack left, Allen began to imagine himself an incarnation of a Kafka character—the one who woke up to discover that he had been turned into a giant insect. His friends might shudder at the sight of him, but he remained trapped in the reality. Try as he might, he could not escape what he had seen.

Of them all, William Burroughs would have made the most sense of the Harlem vision. Thirty-four years old to Allen's twenty-two, Burroughs was anything but predictable in his response to reports of altered consciousness and the reality of otherworldly dimensions. He'd once looked into Theosophy at the New York Public Library and concluded that the idea of telepathic contact with Tibetan adepts was preposterous. He'd entertained a few mystical convictions when he'd taken up yoga but had ended up abandoning that, too. Still, he was known to reverse himself on seemingly ironclad opinions. But the question of what he would have made of Allen's vision was moot because he had left New York in the summer of 1946 after he was busted for forging morphine prescriptions. Unbeknownst to Allen, he had just been arrested in Beeville, Texas, for driving drunk and banging his common-law wife, Joan, on the grass verge of a public highway. He now preferred a more methodical mode of apprehending the infinite, involving controlled substances of various kinds. The world of junk, its gnostic codes and secret handshakes, had since claimed his full attention. It was only weeks afterward, in a distracted reply to Allen's letter informing him of his vision, that Burroughs confessed his ignorance and wished him luck.

Ginsberg was so absurdly conscious of the figure he cut that he seemed unfixed. He was all too eager to agree with every single personal assessment his friends offered him. Four years before, in Burroughs's book-filled apartment, he took turns with Kerouac submitting to Burroughs's withering Reichian analysis. In the course of these sessions, he'd been fully dismantled, and no one seemed capable of putting him back together again. At times, he would play up his emotional needs in a bid for attention; at other times, he cut a figure of Chaplinesque haplessness. He lacked either the wit or the sophistication to paper over his confusions or rein in his fantasies, something he imagined Bill, Lucien, Jack, and Neal had mastered. In this, he was absurdly mistaken.

As if to confine himself to some recognizable norm, he made an effort to be law-abiding. While Jack and Bill were arrested as accessories on Lucien's manslaughter charge, and Neal was busted for compulsively stealing cars for joyrides in Denver, Allen maintained an excellent grade-point average and was never without a clean pocket handkerchief. When he was facing expulsion for writing obscenities on the dirty window of his dorm room, he groveled before the dean. To them all, "Little Allen" appeared half-grown, a precocious intellectual with oversize horn-rims who'd read all the books but had little in the way of life experience.

Still, no one but Ginsberg would be knocked flat by a vision of God seen out the window of a Harlem tenement. In that brief moment, as the gears in his head slowed and temporarily disengaged, something miraculous occurred that would forever haunt him. Bathed in the light of that vision, he abandoned his hope of a mystical union with Neal and replaced it with a purer, more evanescent longing. Had Bill been paying attention, he would perhaps have talked him off the ledge he found himself on. Yet in the summer of 1948, he had it all to himself.

From that moment, Irwin Allen Ginsberg became a divining rod in the headlong and holy pursuit of God.

SHE SITS IN the Air India office in Delhi, wrapped in a shawl. In her hand is a letter retrieved from the American Express counter. She is beautiful, not even twenty-five years old, with light brown hair and blue eyes. It has been six years since she first left her home in South Carolina, and she is tired. Her letters no longer mention poetry. She is no longer in search of a revolution. Instead, she is paralyzed by indecision. It is April 1960, and the heat outside is nearly unbearable.

This is where I would begin.

There are other possibilities. The man whose letter she holds began his account of her in the early months of 1954. Yet stories might equally be told that begin in Paris or Tehran or Dacca or Aden or Kathmandu or any number of cities she passed through before she disappeared in Calcutta. She cut a memorable figure, even for those who met her once. In a traditional vein, her story would begin in late 1936 with the birth of the first daughter of Camden, South Carolina's leading citizen and landowner, Henry Savage Jr., and his second wife, Elizabeth. Had she met an untimely or tragic death, this version would undoubtedly lead with a photograph from the 1952 Camden High School yearbook, easily found at the local historical society. In it, she beams a dimpled smile and is dressed, like every other girl in her sophomore class, in a sweater set, Peter Pan collar, and pearls.

Three weeks before landing at the American Express office in Delhi, however, she was looking not for a beginning, but for a place to stop. She had set her sights on a protected Buddhist kingdom in the farthest valleys of the Himalayas. As it was in a sensitive border region where travel was restricted, she first tried to secure a travel permit from border officials in Darjeeling. They had sent her to Delhi, a thousand miles away. There she made the round of the national bureaucracies, tramping for three days from door to door in high-topped lug-soled hunting boots. Everywhere she went, she was told, "I have no power," and referred to another office. She was now systematically trying officials in the Ministry of External Affairs, looking to pin them down where they lived. She had yet to find any of them home. The lone official she did manage to speak to was the most lowly. Even he equivocated, suggesting that she come back in four days.

Nineteen fifty-two, when her high school yearbook photo was taken, was also the year she left school. Thereafter, she worked her way through the books in her father's study and the town library. When she came upon an author she couldn't find, she traveled to libraries in Columbia and Atlanta. She had to travel two hundred miles to find a library that would loan her the works of Friedrich Nietzsche. Though his work told her nothing she hadn't figured out for herself, through him she learned of the "infernal voluptuousness" of Wagner's "Prelude" to *Tristan und Isolde* and the morbid emotion of his "Liebestod" finale. Playing the LP at top volume in the den, she wore out the family phonograph.

Her correspondent, a southern writer named Jerry Madden, had long since learned not to ask her the obvious questions. How she came to leave home, what her parents had said and done the day she left. Back when they first began to correspond, she wanted more than anything to say she had no idea what he was talking about. Intending then to write deathless, prophetic poetry, she wasn't interested in narrative and pedestrian fact. When he had ventured to ask her of her plans, she mocked him. Was he an entomologist? Would he have the effrontery to ask a butterfly what it knew of flight before taking up his dissecting tool? Beneath her teasing, there had been an unmistakable edge. She expected him to read between the lines of her letters. She was standing at the gates of hell, she had told him, in the clutches of a fiend he had not the wit to imagine, and all he could think to ask was: When was she leaving and when would she return. For this she scolded him. Yet his questions were not so different from the ones she now fielded from Indian border officials.

For the last two years, Madden just waited for word from her. Even had he wanted to, he would not have known where to write. Before he received her aerogram from Darjeeling, her last communication had been a postcard from the Afghan border nearly a year before. Now she was suddenly grateful for his delicacy, and whether in reward for his patience or out of despair over her dilemma, she had finally felt the need to explain herself.

She had long ago found America to be an unlivable country. Europe, Iran, Ceylon, and now even India had also been tried and found wanting. The point all along, she suddenly acknowledged, had been to find a place where she would be free to live her life as she knew it was meant to be lived. Once she found this place, there would be no going back. Did he understand? Did the Indian border officials?

She told him she had settled on the remote Buddhist kingdom of Bhutan. Yet faced with the news that she would have to travel to Delhi for a travel permit, she worried that there was really no way of knowing whether, having made it to Bhutan, she would again be disappointed. That she would once again discover that it was the same story there as it had been in the innumerable cities and countries she had already passed through. Perhaps it hardly mattered; she fully expected her request for a travel permit to be denied. Despite the futility of it all, she still had to try.

With Madden's concerned reply on her lap, she felt compelled to explain herself further. From Darjeeling en route to Delhi, she wrote, she went to Nepal. Nepal came closer than any other place she had seen to pleasing her in most every particular. She nearly stayed there, giving up the dream of Bhutan. She careened between wanting to stay and wanting to go, unable to decide. Perhaps he'd be surprised to hear that Jean had been with her. Last spring, she had left him in Europe to hitchhike east alone, thinking it was the last time she would see him. But they ran into each other in Ceylon ten months later. Together, they had applied for permission to enter Bhutan from Darjeeling.

In Nepal, Jean had begged her to stay. He reminded her that

life was short. When she decided nonetheless to leave for Delhi, to make one more effort to obtain a permit for Bhutan, he left her for Afghanistan. Before leaving, he told her that she was like a man with but one bullet left in his gun, who hesitates only because he cannot afford to miss. But she was incapable of turning her back on what she'd already begun. Though Jean promised to return when she was settled somewhere, she was doubtful. It hardly mattered anymore. She no longer had any more time to waste. She had wasted enough already.

So she sat there in the Air India office, scribbling an anxious reply to a man she scarcely knew, half a world away, outlining the struggle of the past six years and the crossroads where she found herself. There was no one waiting on her decision but herself. She came to the bottom of the page and signed her name. Hope.

As an afterthought, she scrawled a final note in the margin of the letter. Perhaps she should ask the Air India manager for a free flight to Karachi. From Pakistan there'd be no difficulty in finding a ship to take her to Yemen. Yemen and the Maldives were two further possibilities that she had yet to rule out. She said she would let him know her final decision.

The letter was dated April 30, 1960. It was the last letter he ever received from her.

JACK KEROUAC didn't believe in plots. He thought they were absurd. Life has no plot, he said. Any story line could be broken up, shuffled like a pack of cards and dealt out in any order, and the story would remain the same wherever you began and whatever direction you took. So apart from changed names and a few details, his books were about what actually happened, beginning with a spate of time, chosen arbitrarily.

"Do you know what arbitrary means?" Without waiting for an answer, he barged on. It didn't mean willy-nilly. It meant "to judge fully." So you take two moments, one on this end and one on the other. Past to Present. Simple as that.

Does a story really remain the same regardless of the order in which it is told? Does a life have no plot? For me, Hope's story began with the entomologist's questions. Who was she? What did she look like? How did she end up in India? Did she find what she was looking for? Simple queries, yet whatever questions I found answers to led only to more questions. Some of them led to the phone directory, and some of them led nowhere. Still, I persisted, as if I could summon the truth of her from keen curiosity and the accumulation of documents, as Allen had once summoned God by invoking Blake.

But one question loomed above them all.

Where was she now?

THE FIRST EXTENDED DESCRIPTION of what Allen Ginsberg saw out his Harlem window found its way into print in a 1966 *Paris Review* interview conducted nearly two decades later, several years after his return from India. Ginsberg referred all future interviewers to this account when repetition had soured him on talking about it further. By then, he had abandoned the Christian references. By then, he was no longer "Little Allen." Now his bearded, bespectacled face and swamiesque figure was ubiquitous on college campuses and protests against the Vietnam War.

After hearing the ancient voice reciting Blake in his sublet apartment, Ginsberg described what he saw outside the window:

> I began noticing in every corner where I looked evidences
> of a living hand, even in the bricks, in the arrangement of
> each brick. Some hand placed them there—some hand had
> placed the whole universe in front of me. That some hand
> had placed the sky. No, that's exaggerating . . . the sky was
> the living blue hand itself.

Nor was this the end of it. The sense of exaltation returned periodically that week, like a divine mood swing. Gradually, his sense of panoramic awe downshifted to a microcosmic view of the wretched humanity surrounding him. One day, a bookstore clerk's long and vaguely horselike face suddenly transformed before his eyes into something out of Jonathan Swift. Astonished, horrified, mesmerized, Allen realized he was being granted access to the man's true nature. As he glanced around, an entire menagerie of souls began to open around him, revealing their lot of suffering and joy. Suddenly, too, he saw with pity the fears that held hostage those Columbia dons and friends who, however sympathetic, were unable to see the shimmering world he had beheld.

In 1948, in the immediate grip of his vision, Allen recognized that for him, as for Blake, poetry was key to sustaining this altered perception. Through some secret machinery, a poem might open the door to the cosmos. All spring he had read and reread the works of Dante, Saint John of the Cross, T. S. Eliot, and Donne, feeling for the first time that each of these poets was talking directly to him from the deepest reaches of their minds. His own poems, he realized, had only imitated the masters, and though they had been sincere, he had not yet found the right key. As the memory of the Harlem vision faded, he tried to bring it back. Here the story changed.

As he walked past the new Columbia library and intoned Blake's poem "The Sick Rose" over and over like a magic spell, the vision did return. However, it was not a blue hand that opened the door. Instead, an alien apparition, a fanged serpentine monster of doom, swooped down from the black skies of upper Broadway, malevolent and vast and intent on eating him alive. "The sky was not the blue hand anymore but like the hand of death coming down on me," Allen said, "and I got scared, and thought, I've gone too far."

This complicated the entire experience.

William James had described this phenomenon as well, ascribing it to the fact that mystical experiences and paranoid delusions arise from the same mental stratum. "Seraph and snake abide there, side by side," he wrote prettily. While Ginsberg had sworn an oath that he would "never forget, never renege, never deny" the "sense sublime" of his 1948 vision, a darker possibility had inescapably presented itself.

WHEN HE WAS a toothless old man in a baseball cap and tennis shoes, Gregory Corso, abandoned by nearly everyone who had once loved him, would show up at Allen's apartment in the East Village raging drunk and yelling like a spurned suitor for all that the world owed him. At Allen's poetry readings, he would shout insults from the back of the house, proclaiming to all that he was Gregory *Nunzio* Corso, a *poet*. When his entreaties would fail or the handout was insultingly insufficient, he would sit down and try to piece together the fragments of his life, scrawling out long slack sentences with a pen clutched by rough hands with dirty fingernails. Despite decades of protestations to the contrary, he was not writing poetry. That muse, along with several wives, had long ago left him to the clutches of a far more demanding mistress.

By the end of his life, he had been addicted to heroin for forty years. The details of his lifelong misfortunes were now indistinct, worn away like the face of a coin too long in circulation. His now humbled ambition, when Allen was tapped out, was to create manuscripts to sell so he could score drugs. He had long ago lost or sold all the letters and early notebooks from the time when he first called himself a poet. His juvenilia had been left in a Greyhound station locker. Boxes of letters given to girlfriends or wives had been misplaced. If the proprietor of the Phoenix or Gotham Book Mart or the 8th Street Bookshop wouldn't cough up enough money for a fix, having seen one too many "first" drafts of his early poems, he would head to B. Altman's Department Store on Thirty-fourth and Fifth, and perhaps nick a first edition on his way out.

It was once possible to take an escalator up from the women's coat department to the rare book department at B. Altman's to buy an autograph of a ballplayer or American president or an edition of Shakespeare's plays bound in Moroccan leather to accessorize a living room. Corso was so intent on scoring a fix that he would write his manuscripts directly on the department store stationery where a fellow addict—his "enabler and co-dependent," Allen would say bitterly—worked in the rare books department. Gregory would begin at the top of the page with a description of his poetic intentions. He would stake his claim to his own authenticity. He would finally set the record straight about the Beats.

Within a page or two he would lose interest, but it took time before the purveyors of rare manuscripts did. His stops and starts of recollection, self-justification, and self-assertion found their way to public archives and private collections, itemized, cataloged, and sandwiched in acetate covers: "Gregorian Rants," "First Suicide Note, June 12, 1991," "Autobiographical Fragments." In the 1980s and 1990s, he would go through several notebooks a year, sometimes filling up only the first and last pages, as if to obscure the empty middle. They still smell of cat pee.

He was born in 1930 at St. Vincent's Hospital and brought home to 190 Bleecker Street in Greenwich Village above Rizzo's Funeral Parlor. He had no memory of his mother, who, he was told, died when he was a baby. He had spent his childhood years in a succession of foster homes, only to be repossessed by his father at the age of ten, a changeling and petty thief who wet the sheets every night in fear of the beatings that would follow if he wet the sheets. He spent four months in a reformatory where he was sent after he stole a neighbor's radio and steam iron. There he learned not to cry and to play the clown to avoid being beaten by the toughs. After he put two fists through a glass windowpane in the reformatory, he was sent to Bellevue. There, the nurses were pretty and affectionate and no one stole his food, though he helped himself to the oranges allotted each bedside table every night. After hitting a patient in the eye with a wadded-up piece of bread, he was moved out of the general ward to the fifth floor, and it was then that he arrived at the last circle of hell. He was twelve.

Unlike the general ward, Ward D had no pretty nurses to make sure he gargled twice a day. Instead there were zombies staring into space, men talking to themselves and lying naked on the floor, covered in scabs. In Ward D, women screamed in locked rooms and visiting families sat in stunned sorrow. It was here that he realized he was completely alone in the world. On Ward D, he said, he became a poet. He moved to the streets after that, sleeping on rooftops and subway trains, keeping one step ahead of the cops.

Then, when he was seventeen, the year he was sentenced to three years at the state prison in Dannemora for robbing an army-navy store, his grandmother told him his mother wasn't dead, but a whore who had abandoned him as a baby to return to Italy with her lover. Suddenly, looking around at the hardscrabble and illiterate Italian immigrant community of Mott Street, the tenements strung with workingman's clothes and faded housedresses, he realized that he was more her child than theirs and that in leaving him, she had opened the door for him to follow her out. After he left prison, he did.

Woven into the regrets of his own life, however, were his reconstruction of another's. He was twenty-five when he first met Hope Savage, and she was nineteen. As he grew older, the effort to grasp the dimensions of her life seemed key to his desire to amend all the wrongs he had committed as a son, husband, father, and friend. At times he used her real name, at others he used the name she made up for herself. However generous the patience and patronage of the wives and benefactresses who had followed her, Hope Savage was his first love. He never lost sight of this fact and ascribed great significance to it.

In exploring her life, he hoped also to avenge the wrongs suffered by women at the hands of the Beats, as if her life might embody all their forgotten histories. "These pages, my biographical remembrances of my first true love." "She believed she possessed great talents." "Written When a Sad Young Girl Spoke of her Shock Treatments at the Age of 15." "On Having Once Loved." And in these pages, interspersed among the non sequiturs and indecipherable chicken scratching his handwriting had become, he would indulge in his memories of the angel who had once loved him as a god. In tracing and retracing the outline of her story, of all that he had known of her and all they had shared in their brief time together, he sometimes betrayed the anxiety of a man seeking absolution for a crime he could not bear to contemplate, much less name.

As if he still felt Hope's eyes upon him.

. . .

ALLEN GINSBERG'S ARRIVAL at the Columbia Psychiatric Institute in late April 1949, less than a year after his Harlem vision, had an air of inevitability about it. Ginsberg accepted an eight-month hospital stay in lieu of jail when the authorities discovered that his apartment was being used by thieves to store their loot. The specter that had haunted him the previous summer had been followed by the arrival of Herbert Huncke, a Times Square junkie of his acquaintance recently released from prison. Huncke had proceeded to strip the Harlem apartment of the absent tenant's theological works, flatware, winter clothing, and records, before moving on to Allen's few possessions, beginning with his typewriter. After being barred from ever again crossing Allen's threshold, Huncke disappeared into the underworld fraternity of Times Square hustlers and addicts and drug connections.

Writing Jack Kerouac of his woes from a new apartment on York Avenue, Allen summed up the months of effort he'd expended in his search for God. He'd moved on from his belief that Blake and iambic pentameter would lead him to heaven. Now heaven was in the hands of Sigmund Freud:

> If I did not have faith in the mechanical procedure of psychoanalysis as a way of making me find myself and God I would no longer wait here in the city for a vision but I would have despaired of life here and left—on an actual pilgrimage, as of old—across the land, would throw myself on the mercy of the elements and die out of this life of vanity and fear, give up completely, and wander without home until a home were everywhere.

In less than a month, Jack would find his own divine vehicle in a 1949 Hudson. In a mad seventy-two-hour dash from the West Coast, where his wife was expecting his second child, Neal Cassady had arrived unexpectedly in New York City on the arm of yet another blonde, with the aim of liberating Jack from his mother.

Allen, forever hopeful, imagined that his beloved Neal had heard secondhand of his vision and had come to New York to listen pop-eyed to his account of it. Perhaps they would enter heaven together after all. On one memorable evening not long after Neal arrived, Allen jumped in the back of his convertible and sailed through Times Square, declaiming W. B. Yeats's "Sailing to Byzantium" to the tourists with the "roar of a general." Instead, after New Year's Neal teamed up with Jack to tear up the highways between the coasts. Once again, Allen was left behind, spinning and bereft, going through stacks of books, coffee cups, and cigarettes while they careened around the country. He was incapable of objecting when Huncke reappeared, sick with withdrawal, his swanky patent-leather shoes crusted with snow and brimming with blood.

This time, instead of emptying his apartment, Huncke filled it. He began wearing Allen's clothes, and the bed was commandeered by Huncke's business associates, including a tall redhead who crowded the furnished cold-water flat with her perfumes and unmentionables. Allen had planned on quitting his job at the Associated Press after graduation and spending the summer with Bill and Joan. After everyone's arrest, it was something of a relief to be found mentally incompetent and to offer himself up to the white robes of the asylum. Perhaps he had needed, as Joan had put it, to blow his top. The stint at the psychiatric institute would signal the real completion of Allen Ginsberg's studies. When an insulin shock patient was wheeled into his room, Allen discovered an even more sensitive and heedless soul than his own.

There was a kind of comfort in that.

SHORTLY BEFORE HIS DEATH, the French surrealist and opium addict Antonin Artaud wrote of his shock treatment in a Paris sanatorium. Despite repeated glucose injections to bring him out of an insulin-induced coma, his body remained rigid, his breath still. Eventually, his doctor summoned two orderlies to remove the corpse. Only as they neared did his body give a small shiver. When he awakened, everything detailed to him of what had occurred, he wrote, was something he had also seen, not from this side but from the other. For the remaining months of his life, he remained stuck in this *bardo,* suspended between the world of the living and the world of the dead.

Not long after the death of his hero, Carl Solomon had presented his shaven head to the Columbia Psychiatric Institute, requesting a prefrontal lobotomy. At sixteen, AWOL from college, he had jumped ship from the merchant marines and ended up in Paris, where the existentialists and the surrealists were squaring off. He immersed himself in the work of Céline, Sartre, Gide, Michaux, and Artaud with the ardor of an epicurean tasting French cuisine for the first time. On his return to America, Solomon sought to fly his own surrealist flag, to be "suicided" by society. "A lunatic is a man who has preferred to become what is socially understood as mad rather than forfeit a certain superior idea of human honor," Artaud had written. A voluntary lobotomy, Solomon imagined, was the perfect gesture for the drama staged beneath his private proscenium.

Instead of performing the requested procedure, the admitting staff handed him over to the head nurse, and over a period of nine months the psychiatric institute gave Solomon fifty rounds of insulin shock before pronouncing him cured of the surrealist disease. Once he began his treatment, Carl Solomon's views did in fact change. He was dissuaded from Artaud's view of psychiatry as the invention of "a vicious society" in self-defense against the assaults of "certain superior lucid minds." Instead, he became convinced that his attending nurses and doctors were a species of seraphim. Through them, he had been inducted into a secret paradise where all manner of esoteric knowledge was granted. The fact that some patients never emerged from their insulin comas made him feel doubly blessed. "I had been handed, by skilled and provident men," Solomon insisted, still in the grip of amazement, "the very concrete void I'd sought."

Each insulin session began the same way. In the dead of night, muscle-bound angels would burst into his room, ring his bed, grab him by the arms, and carry him screaming to the elevator. He would descend to the insulin ward, where he would be strapped down and injected with a massive hypodermic needle. As the insulin snaked through his bloodstream, his compulsive pun making would cease while he contemplated the heap of his piteous belly under the canvas restraining sheet. His body then took on a kind of holy light, absorbing the full blast of a mind working furiously on infinite and simultaneous levels of association. As the grip of the drug closed on his brain, he perceived the world's impending annihilation, a vision that unsettled him only briefly before the coma descended.

The true terror would set upon him when, fifteen minutes later, he was brought back out of his reveries by a countering injection of glucose. At the vast edge of his unmapped mind loomed the Void. The first sound to penetrate his skull would be the sound of his own screams. The nurses would coo softly and ply him with sweets, raising his blood sugar and eliciting his gratitude and allegiance. Gradually, the vision of the Void receded. As the months passed, he would grow larger and larger and more and more forgetful. Gone was the mama's boy who loved baseball and fishing, the champion speller and earnest Communist who'd been born too late to fight the Fascists. Gone was the outraged fifteen-year-old who had seen the word *freedom* used to disguise white supremacy, to declare war on Korea and communism, and to suppress every spark of human hope. Gone was the nervous, hollow-eyed homosexual anarchist who, disillusioned by his own country's break with Russia, had transferred his allegiance to French surrealism. "I had quite simply forgotten the name of my universe," Solomon managed to recall, "though it was also true that this name rested on the tip of my tongue."

A characteristic of the shock patient's sick mind, Solomon insisted, was the belief that it was possible to reawaken in someone else's state of consciousness, most likely that of the previous occupant of the insulin table. At the same time, he insisted, there was evidence that this happened all the time. He swore that he saw a virtually illiterate patient arise fully conversant with the works of the Christian mystic and heretic Jakob Böhme, whose writing was barely known in America. These miracles of transmigration were the talk of the insulin ward, and all his efforts to come to an understanding of what befell him during his 1949 insulin season got stuck here. Even the doctors couldn't challenge their superstitions, he said, because their bible—the work that established the treatment protocol (Solomon had managed to sneak a copy while the nurses weren't looking by wrapping it in the dust jacket of *The Literary Origins of Surrealism*)—acknowledged that the workings of insulin were a mystery wrapped in an enigma.

After a coma two months into his treatment, Solomon awoke back in his room, having flitted through an infinite number of psychophysical universes without yet settling in one. In the midst of his panic, he heard a gentle voice at his side, telling him to submit and let go. After some minutes, he turned to the young man with the conventional haircut standing by his bedside.

"Who are you?" he asked wanly.

"I'm Prince Myshkin," Allen replied, testing Carl's literary sensibility by identifying himself as the angelic innocent of Dostoevsky's *The Idiot*.

"I'm Kirilov," Carl countered, thereby heckling Allen's presumption and settling his own consciousness neatly into that of the suicidal anarchist of *The Possessed*.

Solomon was released two months before Allen, a newly minted heterosexual, fully sane, renouncing all visions. Allen intended to leave on the same terms.

He could renege, he could deny, but he could never entirely forget.

THE PONY STABLE wasn't a high-profile establishment, but a lesbian bar on Sixth Avenue in the Village. On the small table in front of him lay a sheaf of typewritten poems; Corso hovered over them in a hunch, as if waiting to be caught. This was not where he found her. In the early months of 1951, Hope was still in South Carolina, a girl of fifteen besotted with poetry and horses. He had only just turned twenty himself, a compact and handsome youth with a squarish face lit by bright eyes and framed by an Italianate crown of black curls. With a job loading trucks in the garment district, he may have found the Pony Stable's outsider setting congenial, its women unthreatening. He had only recently been released from prison in upstate New York and may have felt something of a misfit among the Village's newly ascendant bohemians. Italians were fine for local color but were far too hot tempered for cool.

The bohemians had taken over the San Remo. Despite the fact that the bar was located in the heart of Little Italy and across the street from where he'd been born, it was hardly the place he'd known as a youth. The shifting tableaux of bespattered painters and sloe-eyed hipsters at the bar and in the wooden booths, the figures who arranged themselves around the black-and-white floor tiles, were as hard to read as a chessboard. And though they dressed like young Italian widows, the girls who frequented the San Remo weren't anything like the ones he grew up knowing. Like him, they would sneak glances out from under their bangs, their kohl-lined eyes taking in the scene behind a cloud of cigarette smoke. Silent, ghostly wraiths, they sipped their drinks and waited for the alcohol to embolden them.

"Consummatum est!" Allen had announced. Upon his release from the looney bin, he had finally lost his "virginity" to a girl and, to the incredulity of William Burroughs, was proving to be quite a Lothario. After paying the fines for drunk driving and public indecency charges in Texas, Burroughs had moved on to New Orleans until a drug possession charge obliged him to jump bail and relocate his family to Mexico City. There he received a stream of updates on Allen's conquests from Jack, who'd gotten married the previous November and had finally managed to publish his first novel. After a few middling reviews, it sank like a stone.

Amid his talk of girlfriends and the vagaries of employment, there was now an air of bewilderment about Ginsberg. To those who had sat out the mania of his vision summer, he felt obliged to explain himself. He was now completely sane, he would say, his eyes darting sideways as if to acknowledge sanity was no more real to him than any other state of mind. His fantasies of God had vanished into thin air, leaving him . . . And here he paused, wondering what, exactly, was left to him. "Thin air and solid objects," he said, smiling shyly. By the time Allen sat down next to Gregory

Corso, he was living in the Village with a girl named Dusty and working as a marketing executive out of the Empire State Building on Fifth Avenue. To all appearances a real man.

That first winter of Corso's freedom, there were nights when his attic apartment on West Twelfth Street overwhelmed him with its lonely, desolate air, seeming more like a prison than Dannemora had been. On those nights when he didn't go out, he would watch a dark-haired girl in the apartment across the air shaft. He would watch her move around, preparing dinner. He would watch her go to the door to greet her man when he got home from work. He imagined himself that man, stripping off his tie, hanging up his suit jacket or, in his eagerness to be in her arms, throwing it casually over the back of a chair. He would watch the man make love to her and imagine it was him. Perhaps it was to escape the grip of this obsession that he'd ventured out to the Pony Stable, packing his professionally typed poems like a real Greenwich Village poet.

After they had exchanged their entire life stories, Corso watched Ginsberg's eager eyes pass over his sheaf of poetry. Absorbing his praise and hearing the names of all the poets he had still to read, Corso calculated that this fellow would be good for a couple of bucks that night. He noted, too, that after handing over the loan, Ginsberg didn't say anything about paying him back. And when Corso confessed to him his secret desire for the dark-haired girl, Ginsberg took him back to his Village apartment and introduced him to her.

That it was Ginsberg who would finally welcome Gregory Corso to the world beyond petty thievery and prison would also stick in his grumpy-old-man throat. He was already a full-fledged poet, if unpublished, he insisted later, by the time Ginsberg sidled up to him at that lesbian bar. He longed to claim as mentor the mobster who had told him, "Don't serve time, let time serve you," but the man had only penny dreadfuls on his reading list. Corso had been left to read haphazardly in the prison library. On B. Altman's stationery, Corso made a careful accounting of his poetic balance sheet, set out in one of his favorite literary devices, an imaginary newspaper interview. Clearly, Allen Ginsberg owed *him.* In exchange for the gift of his own pure poetry, all Allen gave him was his "big homosexual eyes."

> *Are you suggesting that if it weren't for Gay lib*
> *He'd still be a neglected poet?*
> *On the contrary, in spite of Gay lib*
> *He's still a neglected poet*

So what if Ginsberg had introduced him to Seldon Rodman's anthology and Robert Lowell. In return for the poetry of Hart Crane, Ginsberg got Shelley. Corso had discovered Shelley in the prison library. And it was Hope who gave him Rimbaud, not Ginsberg. And Swinburne he already had. There wasn't time to type this all up, but he made an effort to be legible before completing his transaction at the department store register.

Dusty was, he boasted later, his first lay out of prison. In a necessary lapse, he didn't mention Allen, who seduced him as well, to their mutual regret and later fervent denial.

HOPE WAS SEATED by herself a good ten seats and several rows away in the auditorium at the University of South Carolina at Columbia. From his first sight of her, he knew that he'd never seen anyone more beautiful. And it was not just the beauty of her face that transfixed him. Her skin was of the purest, palest, and almost unearthly whiteness. At the time, most girls kept their hair closely styled. Yet hers was so long and so lovely, it reminded him of the print he'd once seen of Botticelli's naked Venus emerging from a clam. He couldn't remember the name of the foreign movie he and Kevin had gone to see that night but supposed he had it written down somewhere.

He and Kevin agreed that neither of them stood a chance with a girl who looked like that, so when the lights went down, they settled in. When the lights came up again, you could have knocked him over with a feather. In the course of the movie, the girl had left her seat and quietly taken the one right next to him. She was no more than a schoolgirl, but it didn't take him long to figure that there was more to her than her beauty. She had made the move, he decided, because she was lonely and they looked interesting. What she wanted, he saw right away, was to talk with someone who was likely to understand her, someone conversant, it developed, with the Greek plays and the poetry of Swinburne, Shelley, Keats, and Blake. To find such people in South Carolina in 1954 wasn't the easiest thing in the world. It wasn't easy in Tennessee, either, but the merchant marines and the army had widened his horizons. He'd not only been to New York City, but he'd seen Greenwich Village. It was his personal opinion that it wasn't all it was cracked up to be.

They took her first to an Italian restaurant with red-checked tablecloths and ordered a bottle of red wine. He told her his name was Jerry Madden, and he was born and raised in Knoxville. He was now stationed at Fort Jackson and trying to write his second novel, though his first had yet to find a publisher. Kevin was a year older, had gone to Harvard, and was also stationed at the base, working as a clerk typist because these Ivy League boys were supposed to be literate. Yet he had nothing to say for himself and spent the meal more or less gaping at her. Every once in a while, though, he would give her a shy and, Jerry supposed, charming sort of smile. Mostly he seemed slightly awestruck. But Jerry . . . well, he was happy to talk books and to get to know her. It wasn't long before she started reciting Shelley at the top of her lungs. At this, both of them kept trying to shush her, saying, Not so loud. Her voice was peculiar; there wasn't the hint of a southern drawl in it. It was high-pitched, orphic, and, he thought, strangely monotonous.

I am the eye with which the Universe
Beholds itself and knows itself divine

Before it got too late, they saw her to her bus for the thirty-mile journey home to Camden, exchanging addresses and numbers. The moment the bus was out of sight, he and Kevin started dancing around, jumping in the air and yelling goddamn, god*damn*, and, Can you *believe* it? They returned to the abandoned house they shared with two other recruits, sleeping two to a bed. The house, of course, was entirely against regulations, but it was close enough to the base to make it possible for them to appear for the six a.m. roll call. Just as he was falling asleep, Kevin in the other bedroom suddenly began yelling "Goddamn, goddamn!" in the darkness, and that got him started again. Their roommates told them both to shut the hell up.

He took the bus to see her the first opportunity he had. He figured he had a chance, being a literary man. Her name was Hope Savage.

GINSBERG CAME UPON JOAN as she sat in a chair in a sunny garden in St. Louis. She smiled as he approached, learning toward him, her arms relaxed on splayed knees. The wash of her intelligence, the beauty in her unfurrowed brow, gave him a feeling of enchantment. She looked so much better than when he had last seen her. He was reminded of how easily she had welcomed him to her apartment after he'd been suspended from Columbia. Jack had joined them, and Burroughs would come round, and despite his insistent queerness, she had become Bill's "old lady." She had overcome his reticence with her intelligence, wit, and a frank lust kindled by the Benzedrine-soaked pellets she'd extract from nasal inhalants and pop with chasers of beer. She bore him a son and took his name as her own, not asking for marriage.

In the St. Louis garden, Joan asked after old friends and lovers, as it had been nearly ten years since her stint at Bellevue to detox, and she hadn't been back to New York since. Allen settled in happily to gossip, telling her of the lonely fate of Burroughs, lost in Tangier, disappearing slowly into the four walls of a darkening room as the pages of his manuscripts rose around him. After the publication of his first novel, Jack had moved to Rocky Mount, North Carolina, with his sister's family and mother, partly to escape a wife who was dunning him for child support. His writing, far more carefully arranged than Bill's, was accumulating unpublished in his desk while he meditated on the Buddha in the dark backyard. Neal had found a steady job with the railroad and the love of a good woman, he told her, but was still straining at the gates of heaven. He supposed he still believed that. Lucien Carr was a brain and a hard-boiled manner behind a night editor's desk, sending and receiving cables, history feeding through his ink-stained fingers.

As for himself, he had finally left New York, traveling alone for six months of pure joy in Cuba and Mexico. Amid the ruins of Mayan empires, he had discovered a nostalgia for all the continents and ruins he'd yet to see. Nights in the jungle brought dreams of the iron passageways of ships, the farewells at dockside, the piles of luggage streaming up gangplanks, and the sight of Brooklyn receding across the waters. In these dreams, Europe was a fading monument toward which his ship ineluctably rolled, a caravan cresting across a blue gray expanse of seas. He had filled the pages of his journal with old world fantasies, "the pope and his carpets & desks & paintings and other treasures gilt or marble & theologic props . . ." His itinerary continued beyond Hemingway's Spain and Fitzgerald's Paris, past Eliot's London and Pound's Italy, venturing on to Ankara and Luxor and Angkor Vat. He wanted to circle the globe.

Heaven, of course, still haunted him. He kept track of the years that had passed since the vision, perhaps as a way of atoning for his faithlessness. In recompense, he collared editors at New York publishing houses with saintly, tireless, and fruitless industry, on behalf of Jack's unpublished novels, Bill's narrative of his addictions, and Gregory's poetry. He shared what money he had, even with those who stole from him. He paid the rent and utility bills and filled up his father's attic with the ephemera of his life. He found a new mentor in Dr. William Carlos Williams, a poet of neighboring Paterson, New Jersey. It was Williams who helped wean him from metaphysical conceits, irony, and the tyrannical pentameter, to hear the intonation and see the imagery of American speech. But he had yet to publish any poems in reputable literary quarterlies, much less a book.

On a farm outside Chiapas, he wrote his Harlem vision into a fragment of a poem. He struck a prophet's pose but had yet to find the voice.

there is an inner
anterior image
of divinity
beckoning me out
to pilgrimage.

O future, unimaginable God

Still, he worked and reworked the vocabulary of his consciousness and the intensity of his intimacies with as much attention as he paid to line breaks and diction. He seesawed between his affection for women and his attraction to men. After he crossed the border into California, there had been another hopeless interlude with Neal, but he'd finally moved on. His life seemed suspended in the expectation that the vision of Harlem would return. Resolved to be ready, still convinced he'd been chosen, on the advice of a new shrink in San Francisco, he eventually jettisoned his suit and tie and devised a poet's life. Not long after that, as if in reward for the leap, he met and fell in love with Peter Orlovsky. He paused, nearly breathless.

It was when he began to speak of love to Joan that he suddenly knew they were in a dream. He'd never been to St. Louis. The woman who sat smiling in the sunlight had settled into an early grave nearly five years before. He interrupted her talk of her children and asked her what happens after death. Do you remember us? Do you still love us? Forgive us? Before he could finish, she faded away, still smiling, folded into another dream of Mexico City.

In the wake of her death, Bill's account of himself had never seemed so insufficient, though Allen had let it pass in sympathy and incredulity. Bill's letters discussed his legal avenues, his plan to move deeper into the jungle to continue his hunt for *ayahuasca,* to take a heroin cure, to set himself up on a plantation of some kind. It was the newspapers that wrote of Bill's game of William Tell. While waiting to sell a man his gun in a Mexico City apartment, Bill had suggested the game to pass the time. Joan had taken up a glass from the table and set it on her head. Decades later, Burroughs claimed that he'd been possessed, overcome by the sense of fate bearing down on him, "a dead hand waiting to slip over his like a glove." But what dead hand lifted that glass? After the bullet passed through her brain, Joan lived one last hour with her thoughts.

In the dream, Allen watched as her smile faded into a glimpse of mottled tombstone, wet with rain in an overgrown foreign cemetery. Only now did he realize how she had shadowed him on his return the previous year to Mexico City, how she had dogged his steps on the dark wet streets, steering him to the house on Orizaba where he'd last seen her, two weeks before her death. Though the image that arose in his dream had the precision of something he had seen, in truth he'd never visited her grave. He had buried all thought of her until the magic of the dream brought her back.

That jump between Joan's smiling face and her grave gave him a simple solution to the problem posed by his 1948 vision. In his journal, he jotted down scraps of poems from memory, showing the jump cuts, the larger and larger leaps taken by a roster of poets, noting the *frissonnement* that resulted. This was the trick, he now figured, to distill visionary experience into a poem and convey it, through a kind of supernatural mental transmission, to the reader. Poetry might set off similar explosions in people's heads. Take away the "sawdust of reason" and the poem becomes a machine whereby the juxtaposition of real and unreal images, the telescoping of time, combines with the suggestion of magical emotions to release the fleeting "archangel of soul."

Kenneth Rexroth, the querulous and cranky doyen of the San Francisco poetry scene, was unimpressed by "Dream Record: June 8, 1955" and the notes that accompanied it. He suggested Allen lose his tricky theories and try to write something a little fresher.

"THE WAR DID HIM IN," Kate Orlovsky said of their father. "Left him in pieces and filled him with anger . . . made him the brute you boys knew." Raised on Long Island, the son of impoverished Russian immigrants, Peter Orlovsky was a boy in a young man's slim body, unworldly and ill at ease with the shadow he cast. His father was an alcoholic, perpetually hoping to make a killing on some mad scheme or another. One older brother was institutionalized, kept in a suspended state of catatonia. His youngest brother, thirteen-year-old Lafcadio, seemed destined for a similar fate, while his twin sister clung grimly to sanity.

In late 1954, Peter Orlovsky was discharged from the army with a small mental disability pension. His last post was in San Francisco, where he worked as an orderly at the sprawling Letterman Army Hospital complex on the bay, filled with wounded and dying soldiers evacuated from the front lines of the Korean War. Peter had joined the army to help support his mother and his benighted brothers, though he was barely able to look after himself. On weekend leave, he would wander about the streets of San Francisco, homesick and lonely, too shy to speak with anyone but unable to bear his own company. He was nineteen years old and still a virgin when a painter picked him up at Foster's cafeteria, had him sit for a portrait, and made him his lover. Eventually, the painter found Peter's clamor for attention, his spells of melancholy, wearisome. Seeing that a new acquaintance, Allen Ginsberg, just arrived in San Francisco, was eager to meet the "eternal boy" of the painting displayed prominently in his apartment, he passed Peter along on his way out of town.

Allen was avid for love, but he was older and more wary now. Peter struck him as a malleable and beautiful naïf. He wrestled with his desire, tempering and disguising it by imagining himself Peter's teacher. But he could not hide his calculation from himself. Their first night together, Allen held him and kissed him and then, surprising even himself, turned him on his stomach to claim him more forcefully, as if to extract some due for the years of heartache. When Peter began to weep, Allen comforted him, but regrets soon followed. On New Year's Day 1955, he wrote. "The first time in life I feel evil. . . ." Whatever its urgencies and imperfections, it was still love.

Was it the tenderness that accompanied Peter's good-bye when he left for New York? Peter hoped to save young Lafcadio from his elder brother's fate by bringing him to California. Was it the news that Carl Solomon had relapsed, that he would soon join the fif-

teen thousand lost souls at Pilgrim State? Perhaps it was the note
Carl wrote him soon after his commitment, in tiny handwriting
on a small scrap of paper: "I haven't met your mother at any of the
dances." Was it that message that flipped the current, split the
atom of his brain, and tore the howl from Allen Ginsberg's chest?
As one sifts through the journals, the letters he wrote and received, the mythologies and legends that emerged later, there
were any number of paths Allen Ginsberg might have taken to the
line that emerged from his typewriter as he looked out his window in San Francisco, sustained by cigarettes, coffee, peyote, and
the impossibility of love.

> *I saw the best minds of my generation destroyed by madness,*
> *   starving hysterical naked,*
> *dragging themselves through the negro streets at dawn looking*
> *   for an angry fix,*
> *angelheaded hipsters burning for the ancient heavenly connection*
> *   to the starry dynamo in the machinery of night*

In the grip of the grief that all love delivers, and a breathless
thrumming hyperbolic line, the vision Allen Ginsberg had so longed
to experience returned. This time, the voice that accompanied it
was no longer God's or T. S. Eliot's or Walt Whitman's or William
Blake's, though it bore the impress of all of them. It was his own.

> *Who howled on their knees in the subway and were dragged off the*
> *roof waving genitals and manuscripts*

IT WAS A REAL ANCESTRAL MANSION, Greek columns and
everything, Jerry Madden would later relate, describing Hobkirk
House at 1919 Lyttleton Street in Camden, South Carolina. A far
cry from the two-room railroad company shack he was born in.
Where his own father was a drunk, Henry Savage was not only the
town mayor, but also a very erudite and educated gentleman
farmer, the author of a number of books on politics and natural
history. Jerry couldn't keep track of all Hope's brothers and sisters,

there were so many of them. His own brothers were petty thieves and con men currently serving time.

When he arrived, her mother called her down. Hope was just as beautiful as he recalled, but when she turned to sit, he noticed that her dress was awry, that it was stuck and her underwear was showing. Of course, her mother was embarrassed and spoke to her, but if Hope cared, she didn't show it when she impatiently yanked it straight. This was further evidence to him that Hope Savage was an otherworldly sort of creature, oblivious of ordinary everyday things. Despite the white house and the big porch, she was no southern belle.

Though there was a graveyard nearby and thousands of acres of forested woodland, they stuck to the estate grounds. She told him little about herself, or perhaps she did and he was too full of himself to remember what she said. He tried to talk to her about his enthusiasm for Albert Camus, but she wasn't interested. He moved on to politics. He had refused to sign the loyalty oath. He thought of himself as a communist (theoretical) who had fought racism from a tender age. He was also against the death penalty, and the recent execution of the Rosenbergs had outraged him. She told him she thought communism was boring. At each turn, his effort to engage her, to discuss the writers he was most interested in, was repelled. She wouldn't budge from her love of the great Greek tragedies and Shelley and Swinburne and Rimbaud. That was it for her. And Blake. He returned to the base somewhat disheartened but eager to see her again.

The next thing he knew, Kevin had bought a car and gone to see her. And when he returned to the base, he made out as though he had kissed her. Jerry could scarcely believe it; he was crushed. How could she have chosen him? To appease his heartache, he decided to base the title character of the novel he was writing on her. Perhaps that would get her attention. One afternoon after he had really begun to write, she came by the house off the base. Without a word to him, she and Kevin went into his room. And that was it. Jerry knew then she would never be his girl.

She called him soon after and told him to meet her at such and such an hour at the Capitol grounds of Columbia. She said it was urgent. Or perhaps she wrote him a letter. The fall of 1954? It was a long time ago now, he couldn't really remember. It was nighttime when he arrived, and if she wasn't there to meet him, she arrived soon after. Despite the interlude with Kevin, there still seemed to be something otherworldly about her. She began to pace back and forth in front of him in great agitation. The way a condemned man might mark off his cell, he thought, beginning to look at her with the greedy eye of a writer. Still, he didn't ask her what was wrong or why she had needed to see him. He kept his hurt feelings to himself. To be completely honest, for a brief while he entertained the fantasy that she was wearing nothing under her trench coat. So her question, like so much else about her, was entirely unforeseen.

Her mother had told her that if she cut her long hair, she would give her $100. Hope wanted to know what he thought she should do. Should she take the money and buy the bus fare to New York City? Should she go and live in Greenwich Village? When she began again to recite poetry, pacing back and forth in front of him, her agitation caught the attention of a cop patrolling the Capitol grounds. Was the young man bothering her? She came to his defense, describing Jerry Madden in the most extravagant terms as the best and truest friend a girl might ever have.

His spirits lifted. Here he was, trapped in the army and being moved from base to base, kept out of Korea because he was a suspected Communist. Still, she saw he was wise to the ways of the world. Furthermore, he had actually been to Greenwich Village. Perhaps he didn't really believe she'd do it. Or perhaps he thought that if he couldn't have her, Kevin shouldn't, either.

Take the money, he told her.

SHE MET HIM one last time to say good-bye, but it was his own departure that was imminent. The army had decided that he wasn't the threat they'd imagined. Yet because of his obstinacy over the loyalty oath, Jerry was transferred again, this time to a base in Alaska. Nothing was said of her plan to leave the South.

Her family were nice people, very well-off, why would she? When he arrived in Alaska, he sent her a lonely letter reporting that when last seen, her boyfriend Kevin was dating a cow. He provided her with a melancholy list of reasons why she had been right to take no interest in him and half-jokingly, half-woefully, asked after her grave-digging romance with long dead poets.

While his letter wended its way from Alaska to South Carolina, rerouted to a post office box in Greenwich Village, Jerry worked and reworked his novel on a card table under a bare bulb in yet another illegal room off base. Her reply, when it came, found Jerry miserable. Up to his ass in snow, he had been detailed to chisel hardened cement out of the hold of a cement mixer. He was astonished that she had made it to New York City. When she made light of Kevin, describing him as a barnyard goose who fancied himself a swan, his heart leaped.

But her news of herself was less certain. She hadn't managed to write a poem in over a year, a situation she found unbearable. She asked him to write again before he tried to visit her. The light of her mind had grown too bright, she said. She longed to switch it off. As for her long dead poets, she found them better company than most people. From the bones of these heroes, she still hoped to fashion something colossal. She sent him a copy of one of the seven poems she'd written in 1953 and had once recited to him: "The Jungle."

As he read this letter, his true kinship with Hope became clear. They both claimed poetry as family, the page their only home. Of their families, they both "moved among them but were not of them," as Byron had so aptly said. As he sat down to write her a reply, he worked hard to amuse, tease, and flatter. But this was mere preamble. He wanted to know how she had managed to leave home. Had she run away? Did her parents know where she was? How would she survive? Brushing aside her melancholy intimations, he demanded details, descriptions, and explanations. He wanted to know everything about her now. He wanted facts. His novel required them.

My curiosity is keen, he wrote.

NAGENDRA NATH LEFT KHULNA with the jatra company, forsaking his father's land and love, leaving behind all he knew to sing and dance across Bengal, reenacting the lives of gods and lovestruck milkmaids. Several years into his travels, he told the eager young Asoke, he came upon a traveling mendicant who was a practitioner of an occult form of Hinduism called Tantra. With the same impulsiveness with which he had joined the jatra, he became this sadhu's disciple.

The essence of Tantrism, Asoke learned from his father, was the belief that there is an intimate correspondence between the macrocosm of the universe and the microcosm of the self. And within this microcosmic self, the dualities of human and divine, self and not self, reason and feeling, male and female, are dissolved—helped along by the dissipating powers of ganja. Unlike the orthodox Hinduism in which Nagendra Nath was raised, Tantric rites were open not only to the lowest Chandalas, but to women. For a man who had dressed as a woman, who sang heartfelt songs of love and danced as a woman danced, Nagendra Nath recognized the truth of these teachings

As the months passed, he absorbed the yoga practices and the magical rituals of the left-hand school of Tantra, wherein wine, meat, fish, parched grain, and sexual union were used to pierce the veil of illusion that shrouded the universe and unite a divided self. He learned of the secret *sadhanas,* those practices where temporary ecstasies led to the knowledge of the permanence of divine love. The highest ideal, the most intense experience of human love, he explained, was the love that exists between couples who are absolutely free from the material, legal, and social considerations of marriage. This love defies society, transgresses the law, and puts itself as the be-all and end-all of life. He watched sadhus drink country liquor from human skulls taken from the charnel grounds. He took his vows and became a sadhu himself. His son, Asoke, listened wide-eyed.

During the years Nagendra Nath was away, his father, Mathura Nath, grew old and blind, spending days sitting on the veranda of his house in Khulna, loyally attended by his only daughter and two younger sons. Though Mathura Nath could not bring himself to acknowledge it, he was waiting for the sound of his prodigal son's foot on the step. He could not bear the thought of dying without knowing his son once again.

In the end, Nagendra Nath gave up his Tantric vows, but he did not return home to his father. By his mid-twenties, he had settled in the householder stage of life, arriving in Calcutta from his years of wandering the countryside to sell fish and cooking utensils in the Bhowanipore market.

"YES, I'VE STROLLED through the dew-sparkled gardens of Babylon in the dawn of a summer morning. . . ." Stanley Gould's mellifluous voice, gentle and dreamy, seemed to transfix a girl, unspooling over her head like a saxophone solo. Every man in the room would surreptitiously take note. "And I've seen the birds of paradise stand at eventide against the white glittering marble of the Taj Mahal. . . ." His voice would rise and fall, coming fast, torrential, and then more slowly as he revisited his purported world travels. Slowly, the planes of his face would sharpen, his voice would take on an edge of anger, as if in memory of some outrage. Beauty had once walked the face of the earth, he seemed to say, only to be horribly betrayed, and he had yet to fully recover from the injustice.

Haloed by a cloud of pot smoke, Stanley Gould deflowered gardens of midwestern girls in flight from their parents with his orientalist hip talk and this melancholy reverie on beauty. Mason Hoffenberg, an aspiring poet, was a sidekick in Gould's routine, feeding him the straight lines. Hoffenberg lived in a furnished room on Macdougal and was something of a hanger-on at the San Remo and Minetta Tavern. A few years later, he and Terry Southern would write the international best seller *Candy,* a satirical picaresque about a Panglossian blonde who tries to save every depraved soul she comes across by submitting to their carnal desires.

For the Beats, however, Stanley Gould was the Village holy man and the slim, gentle pianist and painter Anton Rosenberg, its presiding angel. It was Anton who had given Hope entrée, after what she imagined was a rigorous initiation, to the nearly invisible fraternity of Village hipsters. Brooklyn born and the son of an industrialist, Rosenberg had by his mid-twenties jammed with Charlie Parker and Zoot Sims and hung out in Paris with James Baldwin at Les Deux Magots. He would die a heroin addict at seventy-one, having maintained the one sine qua non of 1950s Greenwich Village cool. As with Neal Cassady, there was something uncanny in Anton's and Stanley's ability to attract both men and women, despite their slow, junky manner and nearly ascetic air of detachment. Allen described Anton as hip without being slick, intelligent without being corny, and more than a bit Christlike. Kerouac would appropriate this comment as well as his coinage *subterranean* when he came to write a novel set in Anton's orbit.

Jack Kerouac, who viewed himself as a graceless hothead racked with lust, would sit in the corner nearby, his sulky eye on Anton and Stanley, wondering who was going to make it with which chick that night. The suspense generated by this question fueled every wine-soaked evening he spent in their company and whatever plot there was in *The Subterraneans*. The novel opened with a vision of Anton's unshaven, haunted beauty lounging against a car fender with Stanley Gould at his side. Jack's own brief and ambivalent affair with the beautiful black girl Stanley and Anton had once shared was his means of exploring their characters as well as his truest feelings about women and negritude. And when she slept with Gregory, he convinced himself that her betrayal, which he all but engineered, obliged him to dump her with the same cold dispatch Anton and Stanley had.

By 1955, Hope Savage tramped about in a long fringed shawl and worn saddle shoes among the Village bars and coffeehouses with a sense of freedom, secure in the knowledge that no one knew her real name and no one she cared about would ever think of asking. It was important to her that her parents had nothing but a post office box for her. Yet she also saw uptown plays, bought tickets for the opera, and visited the Museum of Natural History to educate herself on the flora and fauna of Jerry's Alaska. Until she met Anton, her closest friends were the lonely denizens of New York's underworld: unnamed petty criminals, the destitute, the drug fiends, and the drifters. She imagined herself their queen and toyed with the idea of moving to Paris.

Bill Keck, head cat of the downtown hipsters and freshly divorced, was not the first to think he might make this young southern belle. However childlike her affect, at eighteen she was old enough, a "chick." In an earnest effort to both seduce and enlighten, he grasped her icy hands in his own and tried to dampen her enthusiasm for Swinburne, suggesting she read the Chinese philosophers instead. She promptly turned the tables and laid down her own version of cool, flipping open his portable record player. These were somewhat ubiquitous in the Village; poets liked to "blow" their poems to the newest Bird recording. As "Liebestod" swelled in Keck's downtown loft, Hope began her pacing and reciting, loudly declaiming Swinburne's "*Dolores* (Notre-Dame des Sept Douleurs)."

> *Ah thy people, thy children, thy chosen,*
> *Marked cross from the womb and perverse!*

With Swinburne she now insisted that only the perverse were truly free. The lunatic's laugh would trump Sophocles's wisdom and grace. Her credo called for the flouting of all natural instincts. To forswear hunger and thirst and to deny desire any foothold. This was, she now believed, the only possible faith of a doomed generation. She planned to go even further, to give up all words, but particularly those of the poets she had once loved so vehemently. Hers would be a suicide of the spirit, not the irrelevant body. Forget poetry. The only spotlight that remained for her was that of a hollow-eyed Cassandra, wailing of an impending disaster.

Keck's effort to seduce her, persistent above the clashing racket of her recital, Swinburne's words, and Tristan's endless aria, was wasted. She merely raised her voice and quickened her pacing. *Enough* with the Swinburne and Wagner, Keck said fiercely. You and Corso, always going on about Rimbaud and Shelley and Blake! he shouted, working himself up. You all are nothing but a bunch of lunatics! You will egg each other on, right over the edge.

She laughed as she let herself out: poet, queen, oracle, doomsayer. Not anyone's chick.

IF GREGORY CORSO LOOKED OUT the window as the plane crossed the country, he would have seen a landscape marked off in neat squares of color. Next to him was his little brown army bag, and inside it was a toothbrush and razor, two pairs of trousers, three shirts, and thirty some poems. In the hold were his hi-fi, record albums, and books. He was keen on possessions, particularly watches. However, like much else about his life, what little he had was often swallowed up in the whirlwind that blew up around him. Once, his prize possession was a stamp collection. He treasured the names and evocations of the smallest and least-known countries. As a child, he remembered sitting on his bed in foster home number three or four, breaking open a new packet of a thousand stamps to survey his new domain like a tiny conqueror, much as he did now from his window seat. It was his first time on an airplane, and he was both terrified and proud of himself. He wore a black cloak with a blue silk lining befitting a poet and a traveler of means, as if to give himself confidence.

By the time a policeman handcuffed a bookstore clerk at City Lights for selling obscenity, Allen Ginsberg's "Howl" would be a famous poem. But it was the first reading of the still incomplete work in the fall of 1954 that gave the poem a life that leapt beyond the page, jazzed by his nervous and electric performance. Gary Snyder, a lean figure with a ready smile, was among the six young poets reading their work that night, and he marveled at Allen's transformation. From hyperintellectual neurotic to pure siren. Kerouac was there, as drunken instigator of Allen's soaring divinations. Neal Cassady was there, uncharacteristically diffident in his brakeman's uniform, a watch in his vest pocket. He asked Peter Orlovsky to stand beside him because he didn't know anybody. Only Gregory was missing.

The news of Ginsberg's "Howl" and a city turned upside down by poetry had eventually reached him, though when he boarded his flight nearly two years later, in August 1956, he had yet to actually read the poem that had so set everyone off. Gregory had heard all about Allen's adventures with volcanoes in Mexico and ruins in the Yucatán. He had heard about Peter Orlovsky, the mountain-climbing trips with Gary Snyder, and the book contract with City Lights. And, during a stint on a merchant ship to fill his pockets, Allen had written Gregory of a new plan to hitchhike south with Peter and Lafcadio to join Jack in Mexico City. From there, he would return to New York to say good-bye and set off on his first trip to Europe early in 1957. Suddenly, it was all too easy for Gregory to imagine Allen riding a wave of fame and fortune into the distant horizon, with himself supplanted by all these new West Coast poets. He had a list of their names in his journal.

With his keen and competitive eye sharpened by hearing of Allen's adventures, Gregory had made an earnest plan to travel to Afghanistan earlier that spring, but he was stymied by his four cats. When the cats inexplicably disappeared, he found that the expenses he'd incurred moving his belongings from the Village to a large house on Massachusetts Avenue in Cambridge, buying tins and tins of cat food, baked beans, and Ovaltine as well as a very fine hi-fi system, had greatly diminished the boat money he had set aside. He thought about selling the hi-fi but, as he explained to one well-wisher, doubted he could get what he'd paid for it. Then it occurred to him that perhaps the better plan might be to first go out to California and join Allen before heading off to Europe and beyond.

Upon his arrival in San Francisco, he found he was disastrously short of funds and alone in a city where he knew no one. He had booked the flight rather impulsively, not quite realizing that Allen wasn't due back from Alaska until the fall. One by one, he tracked down all Allen's friends and literary connections, and if a handout wasn't forthcoming, some creative outrage followed. He found Peter and Lafcadio equally lost without Allen, though he managed to cadge five bucks off Peter. Neal Cassady had family demands to meet, and Gregory had little patience for that. Snyder had shipped out to Japan, intent on Zen study in a Kyoto monastery. Gregory filled a notebook with self-portraits of monstrous distortions, too unnerved for poetry.

After waiting two weeks for Allen to return, he sat down to write him a letter, depicting himself as a loose cannon, raging drunk and on the brink of ruin. He told Allen he wasn't at all impressed by the city and was about to take off unless Allen returned immediately. Alternately piteous and swaggering, he littered the letter with the names of German poets he'd been reading—Novalis, Wackenroder, von Kleist, Rilke, and Goethe—as if to show he had moved far beyond Allen's reading list. The 1954–1956 Gregory, he announced, was a man who had fucked Wagner and, unlike the 1950–1951 Gregory, now disparaged *Les Misérables.*

In a final declaration of independence, he told him that the woman who had hosted Allen's first reading of "Howl" at the Six Gallery had also asked him to do a reading. He announced he didn't believe poets should read poems. Instead, he proposed to stand, wrapped in his cloak, and address the audience with the open fire of a tommy gun. Though he had few poems to show for it, the past year he'd also been busy, having

> met a beautiful Shelley with a cunt with Anton and she dug me and gave me a place to live and has been with me up till a month ago when I decided that I wanted to go to California. She went back home and expects to join me soon. She sends me money and delightful letters and I love her very much. Was she, who taught me. She has fantastic memory, only nineteen, can recite and feel all of Shelley, yes all, Prometheus, Alastor, Revolt of Islam and also fifty stanzas of Swinburne's The Triumph of Time—but more! She is going to kill herself in her twentieth year.

This was the first mention of a girlfriend to Allen, though he'd lived with her for a year and had even traveled to South Carolina to meet her parents. Corso was never clear how women figured into Allen's scene, and he did not want to risk losing his seat—which despite his bluster he often felt was precarious—at the boys' table.

Left on his own, however, Gregory was overcome with longing for the precious girl he had left behind. Not long after arriving in San Francisco, he called her collect, begging for money. It was actually Hope who had paid the rent on the Cambridge flat, bought the hi-fi system, introduced him to Wagner at the Metropolitan Opera, and come up with endless plans for traveling to scary places like Afghanistan, Mexico, and India. She had paid his plane fare and given him the cloak as a gift. The German poets were also courtesy of this girl, as she had recently taught herself German and was translating Goethe. Sanskrit and Arabic were next.

Gregory closed the letter by asking Allen to write her in South Carolina, swearing she was one of them. Truly.

IN HOPE'S EYES, it was not the birds who flocked around them who were the prey, but the hipsters themselves. Would-be bohemians sought out their bluesy haunts, hoping for a glimpse of cool cats and easy women and oblivious to the hustlers and hoods who followed them hungrily. Even out-of-town tourists began to arrive downtown. But it was not the pretenders who made Anton and Stanley skittish. They barely took notice.

The hipster revolt against the system was as earnest as her own, Hope told Jerry. Their attachment to one another was a question not of camaraderie—they all had solitary natures—but of unspoken fear. Like her, they feared a society that locked up its most gifted and troubled. They saw traps waiting for them wherever they looked. Their ears were sharpened by the anticipation of triple-locked doors clicking shut behind them. Anton had eluded the locked room by escaping to Paris. Stanley seemed to have once traveled all over the Orient. Now Hope, too, wanted to stand at eventide against the white glittering marble of the Taj Mahal and see what they had seen.

Within months of inviting Gregory to join her in her digs on Macdougal Street, Hope's letters to Jerry had become more playful and affectionate. Though she still signed her real name, she asked that he begin addressing his envelopes to "Sura." The new name was partly a means of eluding her parents and partly, she admitted with a lighter heart, to cultivate an air of mystery. While the surname she used was of French inspiration, "Sura" came from an archaic form of Spanish, meaning "from the south." She had developed a fascination for Mexico. A country whose founding fathers were outlaws and whose police force openly peddled narcotics would know nothing of the hypocrisy so rampant in America, she decided. There she could live fearlessly.

Finding Gregory reluctant to leave his cats, Hope invited Jerry to desert his post in Alaska and hitchhike to the Village. From there, they would travel to Mexico and South America, never to return to the United States. She seemed to know he would decline, given that he'd already been accepted into the Iowa writing program. Yet she cited Dante, Shelley, Byron, and Wagner as examples of genius in exile, and also the bearded Russian anarchists Bakunin and Kropotsky, as if to signal that she had advanced her political education since their last conversation. While American communism might be a bore, Russian anarchism was thrilling. She was intent on hunting down Trotsky's widow in Mexico City, who was said to welcome visiting revolutionaries. "Revolution is the solution" was her new motto. That Jerry had only one month more to serve in the army would make his escape a true act of subversion, she said. She even promised to commit a felony so that she too would be unable to return to the United States. Alas, she acknowledged, their rebellion would not serve any identifiable cause.

That was the difficulty. She reminded him that he had once told her everything in the world had a cause. She was still looking for her own, she said. But which way was it? Her prophecies smacked of a minor sibyl at best, one stuck among the rustics. She had vaster worlds to conquer. An Athenian wouldn't be taken in by such silliness, suggesting that despite herself, she still held out hope for poetry, for herself. She wanted to write something worthy of Alexander the Great. After a performance of *Lohengrin* at the Metropolitan Opera, she was ready to abandon everything. But where was she to look? She would gladly sacrifice health and reason to find it. If the result of all her sufferings was ten perfect lines, ten perfect *words* of poetry, that would be enough. If poetry continued to elude her, what reason had she to continue?

But to die having accomplished nothing was even more unbearable.

JUST WHERE SHE WAS TO GO was still uncertain. In late summer of 1956, Hope went home to see her family before setting off. While she was there, Gregory sent a box of his books and papers to Camden for safekeeping. In September, she attended Jerry's wedding in Knoxville, sending him a thank-you note with a drawing of his novel's title character, Cassandra, in her bed, translating Goethe, having already mastered Finnish, Sanskrit, and Arabic.

As late as November 1956, the three possibilities were India, France, and Mexico. Was she waiting for Gregory to return? To invite her to join him in Mexico? Corso's collect calls had been followed by letters and postcards, all with the same pleas for money, the same confessions of stupidity and incompetence. She had already wired him funds, but to get more meant asking her father. Her parents had met Gregory that spring, before the move from the Village to Cambridge, and whatever misgivings they might have had about him, they did not hesitate to send him what he needed.

Hope's letters soothed Gregory in the way a mother's bedtime story dispels a child's nightmare. She told him fairy tales in which he was both pirate and prince. His name was emblazoned among the stars. He had been robbed of the throne that was his royal birthright and true destiny. They would belong to each other until the end of time. She loved him unreservedly. Receiving them, he took heart and decided he would not have to choose between her and Allen. He wrote to Ginsberg once again, announcing his discovery of the Rimbaud of their age.

When Allen returned from Alaska one month earlier than planned, Gregory quickly recovered his equanimity. Not only did Allen rescue him from penury, but he arranged for him to read his poetry in front of huge enthusiastic crowds for the first time in his life. A radio station made a recording of his work. Lawrence Ferlinghetti, a poet and Allen's publisher at City Lights, agreed to bring out his first real book of poems. Robert Duncan said that while Allen Ginsberg may be the Elvis Presley of American poetry, Gregory was certainly the Frank Sinatra. He wrote masterful poems about Alcatraz and Coit Tower on which Allen rained praise. He began wearing his cloak everywhere. Suddenly bells were ringing in San Francisco! It was the greatest city in the world for poets! Everyone was young! Everyone shouts in the street! Overcome with excitement at being back in Allen's company, he again called Hope collect. Allen's plan was to leave San Francisco for Mexico. Gregory would go with him, and then he would follow Hope to Europe.

Allen is like a saint, he told her. He goes from village to village spreading the word of God!

THOUGH HE FOUND THEM hard to resist, grand gestures rarely served Gregory well. In Mexico City, he would spend all his money on a fancy hotel rather than stay in the dumpy flat with Allen, Jack, Lafcadio, and Peter. He would fend off a nervous breakdown while waiting alone for Hope's father to wire his airfare back to New York, though he might well have shared the car journey with the others. As it was, Gregory was still barricaded in his hotel (convinced Mexican thieves had their eyes on his new cashmere sweater) long after they'd arrived in New York City. Then, in December, he would dismiss Jack Kerouac's offer to sail with him to Le Havre or Marseille or Gibraltar. He said he would rather sail alone, directly to Paris, right into the arms of Hope Savage than arrive there for the first time on some "beat train." His stamp collection might have set his mind afire with dreams of travel, but it had not provided him a firm grasp of geography, Jack observed.

Hope waited for Gregory to return before leaving for Paris. They had three days together. For Christmas, Hope gave him a $25 Parker fountain pen. If he managed to secure a passport, she promised to send an international money order for his passage. If his prison record meant that he was not allowed one, she promised she would come back. Though she didn't want to return, before she left she made an effort to imagine what it would be like. She knew Anton and Stanley would be exactly where she had left them, in the shadowy corners of the San Remo or Minetta Tavern. Whatever beatific visions the wider world had once offered up, their heroin habits had narrowed their vistas considerably. Yet she knew she could trust them to withhold questions about where she had been. She knew they would acknowledge neither her departure nor her return. This was her idea of home.

Stanley Gould's reverie on beauty would always end on the same note, as if to acknowledge how small their universe had become. "But I have never seen *anything* . . . to *compare*," he stuttered, his eyes locking on the open gaze of a girl following him like a flower follows the sun, "with the *beauty* . . . of the . . . *human face*." Mason Hoffenberg would bring Gould's seduction routine with him to Paris in the late 1950s, with Terry Southern as *his* sidekick. When he wasn't paying out Gould's lines on the Left Bank, he pirated them for the character of Professor Mephisto in *Candy*.

At least that was the tale Hoffenberg told in a Woodstock bar twenty years later, behind a line of eight vodka martinis, finally clean of junk.

FOR THREE YEARS, India hovered over Gregory like a "necessary light." During that time, he wrote epic letters from various cities in Europe, begging Allen and Peter to decamp with him for India. Allen was growing old while adventure awaited, he said. As if Allen needed to be reminded, Gregory declared, "more than poetry is needed." In early spring of 1961, Gregory was suddenly threatening to book passage back to New York from Greece if Allen didn't come soon. "Hope Savage is there," he had stressed, "were it in me to pursue her and kneel at the very sight of her. She is something that I must finally face up to." For Gregory, Hope and India were practically the same thing, and he couldn't bear to face either alone. He added, "The monster in me was hideous to her."

Allen lay in bed, listening to the splashes of strangers in his bathtub. The Catholic Worker farm had refused to take Lafcadio off their hands so that he and Peter could finally leave New York. There was also the question of what to do with Gregory's cats and record collection and manuscripts. Everyone around him was strung out on amphetamines. Peter was often sick from junk withdrawal. Elise Cowen, a dark-haired Barnard graduate with severe butterfly eyeglass frames, hung around him like a shade. And Herbert Huncke, who had stripped his Harlem sublet, was back. His appraising eye was no longer on Allen's typewriter, but on Peter, who was working nights in a madhouse. Huncke wrote him love letters describing his sleeping body, begging Peter to ask him to die to prove his love. "You are much too fine for me Peter. . . . I look at you, hear you speak—feeling wonder in my entire being." It was hard not to recognize in these developments an echo of the hellish descent of 1949 that had precipitated Allen's stay in the Columbia Psychiatric Institute.

In the spring of 1961, however, Allen Ginsberg was not the obscure and unemployed seer he once had been. Allen Ginsberg was famous. Four years before, the mere rumor of some wild-eyed poet baying out in California had the East Coast literary establishment beside itself. Yet no longer did fame mean John Hollander decrying his "dreadful little volume" in the *Partisan Review*. Fame was not Kenneth Rexroth, the Daddy of what was now referred to as "the San Francisco Renaissance," defending "Howl" in the *Evergreen Review* from the attacks of "all the cornbelt Donnes." No sooner had the Bay Area acquired its tag, than the scene dissolved in resentment and hostility. Rexroth was now among Allen's most vocal detractors and keen to distance himself from his former protégé. He quipped: "An entomologist"—by which he meant himself—"is not a bug." Gregory's brief stay in the city had not charmed many.

All that had been mere preamble. Beat had now become fashion spreads on "beatnik" style, Jack writing on "the Beat Generation" for *Playboy,* to accompany a foldout of Yvette, a Beat Playmate; Jack making a drunken fool of himself on TV, in public readings at the Village Vanguard. It was square cocktail parties with Dad in Westchester featuring a "Rent a Beatnik" and ads in the *Village Voice* for houses to let in Tangier. Even the word *beatnik* carried the sneering suggestion that they were all Soviet apologists, if not outright Communists. And behind the curtains, vigorously working his carny machinery of ridicule and fear, the Wizard of Oz himself, Henry Luce, was brainwashing the country, trying gamely to forestall the nervous breakdown he himself had precipitated with *Time* magazine's alarmist talk of bomb shelters, drug fiends, and juvenile delinquents. Even J. Edgar Hoover had identified the beatniks as one of the three most dangerous threats facing the country. A police state was not far behind. Allen desperately wanted a one-way ticket out, and if he had to bring Peter's mad brother Lafcadio along to India, he would.

Who else would come? Cassady was in jail on what could only be a trumped-up charge of drug trafficking, Allen thought. *On the Road* had made Jack rich, yet he wouldn't even write Neal, much less send him a typewriter so he might write his own best seller. Jack's romance with the open road, high seas, and exotic lands had proved fleeting, one best reexperienced at a typewriter, after a breakfast of Wheaties in a tidy kitchen with a familiar smell. His orbit seemed to be drawing tighter and tighter to the sun of his particular solar system, his mother. The Northport ladies were not only conspiring to remove his novel from the local book racks, but were sharpening their knives to set upon Peter's long-suffering mother, who lived two blocks from the Kerouacs in a converted chicken coop. The local papers had it that Northport had become a nest of beatniks. Still, Allen held out hope that Jack would join them. He knew Gregory was in. Typically, Gregory had bought a white silk suit specifically for India and offered to buy one for Allen and Bill, too.

And what of Burroughs? Six months earlier, Allen had written him from a village in Peru after a deeply unsettling experience with *ayahuasca,* a vine that, like peyote and Dr. Leary's LSD, conferred extraordinary visions. After taking the drink, Allen found himself gripped by a nausea of cosmic dimensions, face-to-face with a fanged and bearded skull haloed by colored snakes vomiting up the universe. He named this wrathful deity the Vomiter. The Vomiter had made a simple offer. He would offer Allen all the knowledge of God he had so keenly desired. The sole condition was that his understanding would come at the cost of his life. Distraught at the prospect of abandoning Peter and his father, Allen's nerves failed him. When the Vomiter faded away, he saw the faces of his friends and was overcome by his own knowledge of their suffering, to the point where he felt he just couldn't continue. "I remember your saying watch out *whose* vision you get," he wrote Bill.

> but God knows I don't know who to turn to finally when the chips are down spiritually and I have to depend on my own Serpent-self's memory of merry visions of Blake—or depend on nothing and enter anew—but enter what?— Death?

Eventually the intensity of the terror let up, but he was left with the question of whether to travel farther down the river, deeper into the jungle, and up his dosage of *ayahuasca.* He begged Bill to write him from Tangier and tell him what to do, giving him a forwarding address where he would wait for word from him.

When it finally came, Bill's reply was unequivocal. There was nothing at all to fear. Enter the Void. Yet his letter was also impatient, as if they had already been down this road a hundred times before. First, Allen needed to forget once and for all the myth of "normal consciousness." Then, he had to actually *listen* to what he was being told to do. He spelled it out as clearly as it was possible for him to do.

> Take the enclosed copy of this letter. Cut along the lines. Rearrange putting section one by section three and section two by section four. Now read aloud and you will hear My Voice. Whose voice? Listen. Cut and rearrange in any

combination. Read aloud. . . . Do the same with your poems. . . . Try it. You want "Help." Here it is. . . . And always remember. Nothing Is True. Everything is permitted.

The rest of the letter was nearly ALL IN CAPITAL LETTERS. Allen thought Bill must have lost it, and he returned to New York, bereft.

Was he truly serious about his quest for God after all? Was he willing to risk everything? If so, why hadn't he taken up the Vomiter's offer? Perhaps he was essentially a coward and a clown. Chained to his UPI desk, his family responsibilities, and his "just the facts" manner, Lucien Carr had borne down on this point with pointed sarcasm. Carr had woken up the morning of this thirty-third birthday to discover he'd been taken down from the cross he'd been on since 1947. An ulcer had forced him to give up drinking, and he had now a personal pipeline to the Divine. The single commandment of his new religion was, "You don't mess with people."

So how much was true about Allen's vaunted search for God and how much was shtick? For all the media's mockery, Allen realized that he had played a part in the Beat caricature; he couldn't help himself. He took off his clothes at the drop of a hat and, egged on by Gregory and Peter, became a kind of provocateur, spouting nonsense in radio interviews. He lost sight of the God he had courted for so long merely by talking about Him so much. He had begun to think of himself as the Ancient Mariner, first his Blake vision, then "Howl," his albatross.

Looking around at the increasingly erratic behavior of his neighbors and flatmates on the Lower East Side, Ginsberg once again felt a deep unease, hardly daring to question just how they had reached this impasse. If Lafcadio was his bellwether, the signs didn't look good. Perhaps he had hit on something real after all. Perhaps, like Carl Solomon's account of the contagion of consciousness on the insulin table, the entire country was now having *his* nervous breakdown. Was Timothy Leary's psilocybin the seraph or the snake? His own pigeon-chested sensitivity, the longings, the nerve-racked queerness that had been the bane of his late teens and early twenties, had somehow become a source of uncommon power. But to what end? Heaven or hell? He was too lost himself to know. This was his deepest fear: that he would pass along this nightmare, this rogue demon over which he had no control, to others. Like Peter or Lafcadio. He couldn't be their teacher any longer. He was out of his depth and needed a teacher himself.

Not long after he returned from Peru, he had met an Indian woman named Pupul Jayakar at the home of Dorothy Norman, the American photographer and a friend of Gandhi's. Wealthy and well connected to the Nehrus, as head of the hand-loom board of the Gandhi-inspired cottage industries movement, Jayakar was working to open the American market to Indian textiles. She looked upon the Beats as trendsetters. A few days later, she and Dorothy joined Allen, Peter, and Elise Cowen for dinner at a Chinese restaurant. There Allen poured out his anguish over the state of his warmongering, materialist country. All three women listened patiently as he spoke of his sense that India, in spite of its poverty, had continued the search for God. He told them he felt India held the answers. Peter's attention wandered. Allen was like a broken record sometimes.

"But India may have lost its way," Pupul Jayakar countered. "While you look to her to find answers, the young in India look to the West. What do you expect to find?"

He wanted to touch real poverty. He wanted her help in finding a guru and moving closer to God. He wanted to experiment with drugs, he told her.

Jayakar admonished him. Drugs were not the means to God. Drugs were not the path to truth. Drugs sustained the illusions spiritual wisdom sought to dispel.

"There is no compassion in drugs," Dorothy Norman added.

"But where is compassion?" Allen asked, his voice tight with tension and unhappiness. Elise looked at him with the fixed stare of unrequited love. America dropped the bomb and was applauded, he continued. America executed the Rosenbergs. America supported Franco in Spain. America destroyed domestic radical opposition. America financed France's war in Algeria. America used foreign aid programs as weapons in the cold war. America used obscenity laws to censor Burroughs, Miller, Genet, D. H. Lawrence. America chased out homosexuals and Communists from all government posts. America attacked the Cuban revolution and ran South American governments according to American self-interest. In America, moneymaking was the only index of social status. Finally, weary of trotting it out all over again, he told her of his Blake vision and the unsympathetic response it had met.

A teacher would help him open the doors and windows of his mind, Jayakar said, but he needed to see that drug-induced ecstasy was not the same thing as illumination. He readily agreed. Still, he wasn't ready to accept that drugs were not somehow part of the answer. He joked, "After all, God is very funny, and He might even accept drugs as a way to Him." Jayakar didn't think God was funny.

He shifted slightly in his chair. If not ecstasy, was it asking too much to ask for love?

"Can you help me find a gay guru?"

"An eccentric guru?" She looked at him, perplexed.

"No, a gay guru," he insisted. "I do not want to be grasping, but I feel it is essential that I find God through a guru whom I can love."

Jayakar was nonplussed. She was a follower of Krishnamurti, and he was no ascetic, no Gandhian Brahmachari. "Listen to desire as you listen to the wind amongst the trees," he had taught her. Still, she wasn't sure where to go with this. Peter then piped up, as if the sudden silence had startled him from his reveries:

"We are like little children. We need guidance and help." He'd heard Allen say this before. Then he asked if either of them would like to try some peyote or mescaline, as they had lots on hand back at their apartment on Second Street. Lots.

The plan now was for Allen and Peter, and possibly Jack, to meet up with Burroughs in Paris and journey from there to pick up Gregory in Greece, then travel together through Turkey to the Middle East. After that, they would make their way overland through Iran, Afghanistan, and Pakistan to the Indian subcontinent.

And somewhere along the way, they would all meet up with Gary Snyder and his wife, who, felicitously, were planning a trip to India at the same time from Kyoto. However many in his entourage, only in India, Allen Ginsberg now decided, might he be "aloner than before." In India, he would find his teacher.

ONCE OR TWICE A WEEK the Bengali poet would wend his way to Washington Square Park. In the midst of a worldwide lecture tour to celebrate the birth centenary of his compatriot, the great Nobel laureate Rabindranath Tagore, he had agreed to teach a semester in the city. He found himself drawn downtown, as if he might find a little bit of Calcutta there, tucked away in an obscure corner of Greenwich Village. In 1961, Buddhadev Bose was a vigorous man of fifty-three, with deep-set, intelligent eyes and a sensual mouth, and, in the dimple of his chin, something of his whimsical nature could be divined. He wore his learning and his gifts lightly, as versatile a traveler as he was a writer.

South of Washington Square, the regularly numbered streets and avenues of Manhattan descended without warning into an incoherent jumble. When the ordered rows of avenues, flanked by the monumental buildings of banks and corporations and the grand apartment buildings of the rich, gave way to this maze of obscurely named streets, Bose insisted that even the most seasoned New York cabbies became disoriented. He had once suffered such a predicament while trying to locate an address in the Village's fickle geography. He'd had an appointment to meet e. e. cummings at his home on Patchin Place for tea and went round and round in a near desperate game of blindman's buff trying to find it. The driver had never heard of such a street, nor had any number of pedestrians they stopped to ask. By the time they found the address, a miracle in and of itself, as it was tucked away in a hidden mews off Greenwich Avenue and Sixth, it was near dinnertime. Doubtless, he reflected ruefully, the distinguished poet had long before concluded that Orientals lacked all understanding of time.

Otherwise, he found the Village quite congenial. Like College Street in north Calcutta, the Village had book publishers and avant-garde magazine offices. And there were far more book-stores than could be found elsewhere in the city, and many of these establishments stayed open until midnight. It was here that he had discovered America's true gift to the world, the paper-back. In glass storefronts, in rows upon rows of bookshelves there was a wealth of sought-after treasures inconceivable at home. For those with limited means and unlimited curiosity, the classics of world literature, the controversial books of the day, the esoteric philosophies, novels in translation, and obscure poets all could be had for no more than the price of an ice-cream cone.

In the Village, he was reminded of the illicit thrill he'd known in the Calcutta of his youth, when he ventured there from Dacca in East Bengal to make his name in the world. The village coffee-houses were filled with painters and writers of all persuasions, the intellectuals, the scholars, and the penniless poets who had left their families behind. Among this assembly, he had had no trouble distinguishing the members of the Beat Generation, whose nefar-ious doings had sparked such a hullabaloo in the press. The females were particularly striking, for they nearly all wore thick black stockings, had long untamed hair, and eschewed lipstick. Except in deepest winter, the men forswore hats and coats. Yet their true consanguinity was to be found not in their outer appearance, but in the faraway look in their eyes and the way they ambled down the street, as if they had no particular business to attend to. In cafés, they might be found stirring their coffee distractedly, a copy of Li Po at their side.

Perhaps it was no more than a passing craze. With his char-acteristic generosity of spirit, he decided that any enthusiasm that elevated spiritual illumination and bookishness over grasping capitalism was to be welcomed. At an uptown society party, he had chanced to meet the Beat Generation's premier poet. Though his shoes lacked polish and his trousers were rumpled, he was as clean shaven as a banker. His hair, too, showed careful grooming. It was parted neatly in the middle, with a small bald spot visible only when he bowed, which he did on their being introduced.

Mr. Allen Ginsberg was a slight fellow with copperish skin and prominent eyeglasses. Their conversation began at cross-purposes, as is often the case at cocktail parties, with Mr. Ginsberg holding forth on bhang while he had tried to explain the impossibility of writing Indian poetry in English. Mr. Ginsberg asked if he knew the identity of the sacred psychotropic referred to as "soma" in the Rigveda. Since Sanskrit was first discovered by Europeans in the eighteenth century, the precise identification of this plant had long been a mystery. As described in the sacred texts, soma was used in religious rituals and was believed to confer divinity on Brahminic "living gods." To his suggestion that perhaps it wasn't anything more transforming than a fine Italian or French wine, Mr. Ginsberg seemed noticeably unsatisfied.

He soon learned that Mr. Ginsberg was due to depart for Europe the following Wednesday, and from there he was intent on setting off for India, even if he had to walk there.

"Five of America's greatest writers are now bound for India," he had announced. "Kerouac, myself . . ."

Alas, Buddhadev was unable to remember the names of the other three when he came to write of this meeting. Yet there was something in Allen Ginsberg's large eyes and mischievous, cherubic expression that prompted him to invite him to dinner the following evening. He asked politely if he might bring his friend Peter Orlovsky, with whom he seemed all but conjoined. Mr. Orlovsky was rumored to be the primitive of the group, and indeed, his conversation proved entirely innocent of grammar and enunciation.

At dinner, Allen Ginsberg once again returned to the subject of illicit substances and professed his amazement that Buddhadev had never once smoked ganja.

"What? Never?!"

He then was off on a tear about his experiences with various hallucinogens on his visits to Latin America and Tangier and, more recently, his experiments with psilocybin with Dr. Timothy Leary of Harvard University. The active ingredient, it seemed, was now available "for research purposes" in pill form. Allen had seen to its selective distribution among his writer and musician friends. He found it shocking that in the United States whiskey, which he considered a noxious poison, was legal, while marijuana, that nectar of the gods, was outlawed. The young man was so intent on challenging his low opinion of the weed that Buddhadev ventured to ask if that was his sole reason for traveling to India.

"You want to know what I'm seeking? I'm seeking inspiration! I want the heavens to open up before me. I want God! I wrote 'Howl' at one sitting, beginning Friday night and ending Sunday morning. I did not delete or change even one word. I refuse to labor over the text; when it comes, it comes."

Ginsberg then launched into a description of having once heard the voice of Blake while reading his poem "Ah Sun-flower." Three poems he heard from the dead poet's mouth! When he told his friends about what had happened to him, there had been an uproar, a sensation! He'd been sent to psychologists and priests. Ginsberg's conversation seemed, at times, a series of exclamations.

"The academics decided I was insane! They had me locked up for eight months!"

After Ginsberg left, Buddhadev Bose had a look at the books he'd left behind. He had inscribed a copy of a work called *Kaddish*—he was unfamiliar with the word—and an anthology of Beat poetry. Bose found the poetry difficult to follow, but he'd listened eagerly to Ginsberg's conversation, taking in the way he spoke as much as what he said, which was often overstated in the familiar manner of young poets. The caricature of the Beat was certainly there, but in the end he decided the portrait was insufficient. His own work had often been hauled off to court on charges of obscenity. He was certain that the heart of this Russian Jewish American youth was lit with the holy fire that had been so evident in the young Rabindranath. He went so far as to imagine there was something nearly Oriental about Mr. Ginsberg.

Buddhadev Bose hoped he would make it to Calcutta.

THREE DAYS LATER, a contingent of family, friends, and roommates from their East Second Street tenement accompanied them to the wharf. There would be hell to pay with the neighbors after the rowdy send-off at the Orlovsky home in Northport, but there was no turning back now. Among those on the wharf, Lafcadio was there with a frozen half smile on his face, not quite understanding that his brother was leaving him behind. Peter stood at the ship's rail and saluted him by taking off his Russian cap and holding it over his heart in the freezing rain. Louis, Allen's father, was there, as was his brother, Eugene. Carl Solomon, once again released from the madhouse, also came to say good-bye. Peter's pretty, teenage girlfriend Janine Pommy stood there, forlorn. She had wanted to go to India, too, or at least be asked to go once she'd saved enough money. Instead, she had been saddled with looking after Lafcadio. For three years.

Elise Cowen would help her, though her own grip on reality was far from certain. For some time, she had nursed the fantasy that she and Allen were twin souls. Others had remarked on their resemblance to each other, but for Elise, the fact that she had also met Carl Solomon on an asylum stay clinched it. In service to her devotion, she had typed up endless drafts of "Kaddish," Allen's poem about his mother's life and death in an asylum, and joined him in his studies of Jewish mysticism and Zen Buddhism. When Allen could bring himself to acknowledge her adulation, it unsettled him. This was the second time he had left her. Even the methedrine-fueled busyness, the zealous cleaning of the flat after all the packing and bill paying had been done, did little to disguise this basic fact.

The melancholy on the wharf dampened the Whitmanesque spirit of the occasion. To Jack, who'd said good-bye at the going-away party, not quite ready to join them, Allen wrote that it felt as though they were leaving for another planet. Peter hoped America would still be there when he got back.

Cut the hawsers—haul out—shake out every sail!
Have we not stood here like trees in the ground long enough?
Have we not grovel'd here long enough, eating and drinking like
  mere brutes?
Have we not darken'd and dazed ourselves with books long
  enough?

Contrary to Whitman's prophecy, Ginsberg did not board a train west across the plains or take a steamer through the Panama Canal. Instead, on Wednesday, March 23, 1961, the SS *America* left its Manhattan docks, bound east across the Atlantic on but the first leg of Allen Ginsberg and Peter Orlovsky's passage to India.

> *Sail forth—steer for the deep waters only,*
> *Reckless O soul, exploring, I with thee, and thou with me,*
> *For we are bound where mariner has not yet dared to go,*
> *And we will risk the ship, ourselves and all.*

The trackless seas awaited.

THE FARTHER EAST Hope traveled, the happier she became. She found Iran was as much an improvement on Europe as Europe had been on America. Writing Jerry from Mashhad, the holy city of Shiite Islam, she saw no chance that her travels would ever bring her back west again. Hitchhiking alone for the first time, she fell in with a number of other girls thumbing it all over the Orient. In August 1959, Afghanistan was in her sights. There were no more obstacles, there was nothing left now to stop her.

PART TWO

The
Mandala
in the Clouds

FIFTEEN MONTHS BEFORE, in the spring of 1958, Iran was where she stopped.

Hope had spent her first month in Paris waiting for Gregory to arrive at the end of January 1957. Then she went south by train to Toulouse and Marseille and north to Vienna at Easter to see a performance of Wagner's *Das Rheingold* from a standing seat at the opera, before continuing on to Hanover, Oslo, and into the arctic circle of the Soviet Union. When she hit water, she took boats, and where the rail ran out, she hitchhiked. When she could go no farther north, she turned around and traveled south again, through Scandinavia, Berlin, Munich, Rome, Naples, and Malta. From there she returned to Paris, but only briefly. From France she crossed the channel to London, traveling north to Edinburgh and then east across the Irish Sea to Dublin. Winter found her driving to Turkey, where snowdrifts soon overwhelmed the Volkswagen she'd bought for the trip. Somehow she made it to Athens, and from there she continued to Baghdad. In Tehran, spring had arrived; the roses were in bloom, and the air was rife with CIA conspiracies. And there she stopped.

It was as if she needed to be certain before she traveled any farther east. Had she, in her haste to leave for Paris that December, forgotten Mexico? And what of San Francisco, the city where

poetry was shouted in the streets? She returned to America. After a brief visit with her family, she bought a 1938 Chrysler for
$50 and drove to New York City. She met Anton in a Village coffee
shop before continuing on to Washington, D.C., to visit her older
brother. From there she went to Boone, North Carolina, to surprise
Jerry Madden. Six months earlier, her mother had written her to say
that he was asking about her. When Jerry stuck his hand in the door-
way to hit the light switch after an evening out, he felt a hand on his
own. His first thought was that the Christian fundamentalists were
after him, since he'd recently written a critical editorial in the local
paper. Instead, in the light stood Hope. With her was "this short
slender little guy in a trenchcoat, some French guy with a gun."

Gregory Corso did not accompany Hope on her travels. Instead, her companion was a French Vietnamese youth named
Jean. Corso would refer to him, in acid disbelief, as "Shelley's
grandson." Gregory's arrival in Paris coincided with Hope's discovery of Jean in a sanatorium where he'd been committed by his
parents for refusing to go to school. To Jerry, Hope had called
Jean a *ghelman*—everything she ever dreamed of incarnated in a
human being. Just as Muslim men believed they would be greeted
at the doors of paradise by *houris,* she explained, *ghelmans,* boys
with black curls and shining faces, awaited Muslim women. It was
also said that if a girl tried to use her imagination to summon the
features of these boys, she was condemned to perpetual dissatis-
faction with her earthly choices. Hope had been on the verge of
writing Jerry a fifty-page letter describing what had happened
when Corso arrived in Paris. She had stopped herself, loath to relive it. This was the reason for her long silence. As for Jean, she
admitted that poetry was not the first of his interests.

"Jean wanted to come to America," Hope told Jerry. "We are
on our way to Hollywood because he thinks that everyone in
America carries a gun and he will have all the women he wants
when he gets there, just like in the movies."

Through the thin walls of the guest room, Jerry heard them
making love. Four years before, Kevin had brought Hope back to
the shared house off base while he worked on his novel in the next
room. He would have understood Gregory's confusion, if not his

rage. In the morning, Hope appeared in the kitchen in a black head scarf, white raincoat, and pumps, like a black-and-white film still. Her beauty was no longer that of an overgrown schoolgirl, but of an elegant young woman. She was still a mystery to him. He worked up the nerve to ask her about Jean.

"Sex doesn't mean anything to me," she said simply. "My body doesn't really mean anything to me. It is merely an envelope."

Mexico, Los Angeles, and San Francisco followed in quick succession. In San Francisco, she found Rexroth fulminating on his pet topic: the plague Allen Ginsberg had brought on the city. And at City Lights Bookstore, she found a note addressed to her from Gary Snyder. Though Gregory had yet to meet Gary, when he heard Hope had returned to the States, he wrote to him and suggested he meet her. She was an old love, he said, who "has studied Chinese and is really a pure angelic mind." Some months later, Gary wrote him back, describing Jean and Hope's two a.m. arrival at his Mill Valley cabin, just north of San Francisco.

. . . she talks, with that mad Carolina voice, about Iran. She does have a beautiful, pale pure pale skin and a sort of weird serenity. Haven't seen her again.

By the end of 1958 she was back in Paris, with plans to hitch-hike to India, alone.

THOREAU WROTE THAT to be truly free in this world, "free as birds in the air," then one must be free from every kind of claim. Writing from Concord in November 1849 to a young admirer, Thoreau counseled that to live such a life required setting out on a long journey to a distant country. Only when surrounded by unfamiliar landscapes and strangers, he wrote, was it possible to live a truly free life. Relieved of all claims, you are not merely traveling. You are in search of a setting that will reveal your truest self.

Every traveler must then decide what to bring and what to leave behind. To pack wisely, you must ask: How long will I be away? How far will I go? What is necessary? What is there no room for? Home, family, a sense of belonging, and the habits and claims that accompany such things would appear to be among the first items you have to abandon. Like the most earnest world renouncer, Hope Savage was intent on traveling with as few possessions as possible. And the very first article she set aside in her packing was any notion of home.

Yet though she had abandoned the claim of home, her parents did not abandon their claim to her. When she told them she was leaving, she said she would rather starve than work for a living. Believing her, they agreed to send her a weekly sum of money. They once asked her older brother to check on her in the Village, giving him the name of one of the friends she had mentioned in a letter home. From this man, he learned where she lived and the name she lived under. Sitting in a coffee shop across the street from her Macdougal Street apartment, he sent a street kid up with a slip of paper on which he'd written a telephone number and a time for her to call him. After satisfying himself that she sounded happy, he didn't trespass further.

For every traveler there are those who are left behind, those for whom the idea of leaving home is all but unthinkable. Apart from attending law school in Virginia, Henry Savage Jr. had spent his entire life in Kershaw County, South Carolina. The summer before his eldest daughter departed for Europe, however, his circumstances changed. Under the sponsorship of a local Methodist church, an interracial group of teenage youth decided to spend the summer working and studying together at a local private school for "Negros." A bomb threat and a fiery cross on the school grounds convinced Savage the students needed his help to find a more tolerant venue. In 1956, however, the Klan was the final arbiter. After a cross was burned on his own lawn, Henry Savage moved his family north, settling in Cambridge, Massachusetts. It was here that Hope returned in the spring of 1958, before setting off for Mexico and California.

Her father undoubtedly knew the Klansmen who set the fire as fellow members of the Rotary Club or from one of the many civic organizations to which he belonged. But for a naturalist and historian, for a pilot and amateur botanist, home lay with the ground itself as much as with the people on it. His daughter would have felt not only the sting of the town's betrayal, but also the shame of her father's retreat. Perhaps, too, the burning cross would have reminded her how little her parents had grasped of her own plight in the bigoted and genteel confines of a small southern town. Intent on her escape, Hope did not see in the cause of integration the calling she had long sought.

JOANNE KYGER WAS a nearly perfect foil for the highly organized bundle of contradictions that was Gary Snyder. In 1960, she boarded a ship bound for Japan, to join Snyder at the First Zen Institute of America in Kyoto. She understood before leaving that there would be no question of living together. On this point, the diktat of Ruth Fuller Sasaki, the seventy-seven-year-old American founder of the institute, was perfectly clear. Still, she let the question of marriage hang fire, suspended in the daring of packing up and setting sail. Less than a week into her sea journey, however, Joanne Kyger decided that she was *not* going to marry Gary Snyder after all. If need be, she would cut short her visit to Japan and return home to California.

She had heard of Gary Snyder before she met him. Joanne had arrived in San Francisco from the University of California at Santa Barbara in the midst of the 1957 "Howl" obscenity trial. Not only had he been one of the poets reading at the Six Gallery, but in Jack Kerouac's novel *The Dharma Bums,* published on the heels of *On the Road*'s instant success, Snyder was portrayed as a sage in Salvation Army clothes and expert on all things Buddhist related. Upon her arrival in North Beach, Joanne began a meditation practice with the Zen master Shunryu Suzuki Roshi. The East-West commune where she lived was filled with talk of Gary Snyder's imminent return from Japan. When he showed up at her poetry group one Sunday afternoon in 1958, the romance was launched.

Joanne Kyger took pains with her appearance, with a marked fondness for nice clothes and an eye for good jewelry. This set her apart from those North Beach free spirits who looked askance at coquetry and makeup. Yet it was hardly a straight line from love to Kyoto, as Gary had another girlfriend, equally gifted, equally beautiful, and living only a few blocks away from Joanne. Exactly one year before she took ship for Japan, Gary wrote Allen that he couldn't manage to choose between them and upon giving them both up found himself under siege by several more. He was obliged to return to the "relative simplicity of two." He was fairly certain to leave them both, he wrote, because neither struck him as a wife who would be happy collecting firewood and making meals over cow dung fires in his envisioned future journey across Tibet. Nonetheless, he did concede that in Joanne Kyger, he had found "America's great future woman poet and a remarkable person in her own right." When he left California in 1959 to return to Japan, it was with the understanding that she would follow him.

From the outset, then, there was something of the Zen master in Gary Snyder and something of the wayward student in Joanne Kyger. Snyder had been meditating for eight years, had studied Oriental languages at Berkeley, and had already completed nearly two years of intense study at the institute. He was a published poet and translator of the eighth-century Chinese poet Han-Shan. Though he had already been married once, he aspired to a nearly brutal self-sufficiency. Han-Shan, who had retired from the world to live as a recluse in the mountains, dressing himself in tree bark and writing poems on the walls of the cave that sheltered him, was for Gary Snyder something of a model soul.

A Zen master's goal is to open his student's mind. One of the principal tools in this task is the koan. Translated literally, koan means "public statement." In particular, a koan is a statement precisely tailored to the Zen student's level of spiritual perception. A koan can also be in the form of a riddle or a question that by its mere proposition will unsettle habitual modes of thought, particularly those modes of thought imposed by society or grained with logical reasoning, or those preening, knee-jerk-like reflexes that enhance the ego. Of the two-thousand-some koans, Gary had answered forty.

In late August 1961, several months before they left Japan to travel to India, Gary had a long and rambling letter from Allen Ginsberg in Tangier. In the letter, Allen presumed to compare what William Burroughs was now up to with what Snyder was trying to achieve through his Zen practice. Allen claimed that William Burroughs's new "cut-ups" were "verbal mind breakers" in the manner of koans and that Bill had already succeeded in liberating his consciousness from both his mind and his body by projecting it far into space. Dr. Timothy Leary had just arrived from Cambridge, he said, and was planning to include Bill in his experiments with mushrooms. Harvard opinion had it that the cortex was in charge of "arbitrary conceptualization," Allen informed Gary, and if the cortex could be defused by mushrooms, the brain would be left wide open. Gary was left to imagine the possibilities of *that*.

Allen's account of Burroughs's breakthrough exasperated Gary with its naiveté, but Joanne copied parts of his letter into her journal. Non-Western cultures had been dissociating their consciousness for thousands of years, Gary countered, providing examples of similar yogic, ascetic, and shamanic practices. Allen had somehow convinced himself that between Burroughs's cut-ups and Harvard's scientific research techniques, drugs and electrical wires were destined to prove a far more precise means of transmitting ecstasy than his recent efforts at poetry. Gary adamantly disagreed. A poet's place is not to transmit mind or free himself of language, but to free language itself and challenge its listener's own "mind of words." He didn't expect poets would be out of business with these new developments. His certainty on this point was, as was quite often the case, cheerfully bracing.

"Don't you want to study Zen and lose your ego?" Gary Snyder had asked Joanne Kyger upon her arrival in Japan and learning of her decision not to stay. "What!" Joanne had replied with koanlike economy. "After all this struggle to obtain one?" When he nonetheless convinced her to put on a black dress with a scoop neckline and marry him three days later at the American consulate in Kobe, it was hard not to conclude that they had both entered into a riddle far more rigorous and perplexing than either might ever hope to master: What is marriage? This question occupied Kyger far more than her meditation practice at the institute.

Yet the end of a koan is not to give a correct answer, but to reach a mental precipice where the usual train of thought jumps the tracks and heads for the cliff. If you are able to contemplate this vista before you without shrinking, you will tumble over the precipice into an entirely new existence. The student of Zen is led to believe that this new existence will bring him or her closer to what the Zen master will call satori. There were any number of other names for it. Gary explained to Allen that it was the project of Hinduism and Buddhism to not merely explore the "intricate byways of Mind," but also to change them. His practice was an effort to adjust the whole web of his selfness to this other realm. Then he would move there permanently.

Joanne had, perhaps, already moved in. If marriage was a strange and unexpected place to find herself, then living as a foreigner in a country where she knew no one but the man she had just wed proved to be a spiritual knot of confounded ingenuity. An American sense of entitlement in a country struggling to recover from the devastation of war was suddenly problematic in a way she had never stopped to consider. Her conversational gambits in the company of Ruth Fuller Sasaki were unfailingly misunderstood. Initially, at least, Kyger was too mortified by the stares of people on the street to leave the small cottage she lived in with her husband. And once she worked up the courage to go to the market, she found herself fearful of getting lost, as she was unable to ask directions. And when she did, eventually, find the courage and the market and succeed in making her purchase (for there is a kind of relief, if not triumph, in conducting any social transaction, however small), she discovered that the shopkeeper, whom she imagined friendly and kind, had shortchanged her.

In the midst of this disorientation, there were dinner parties where the conversations were in English. She delighted in telling stories; her syntax was elegant and provoking, her humor bright and unexpected, as if conversation were her true métier. Yet in her wordplay, as in her poems, there was a serious intent. She pared away the fat of obtuseness and the loose flesh of sentiment to expose the bone of unadorned truth. Inevitably, however, in the exhilaration of wearing high heels, her lithe figure swathed in

Japanese silk, in the electric spar of rash confessions, she would drink too much sake. The next morning, unable to rise in the bitter cold, hung over and nauseated, she would reach the first of the many precipices that were to come.

This moment of clarity, when all her ideas about who she was and what was owed her disappeared, did indeed transform her. She became, in a casual twist of devastating simplicity, a woman who has begun to study the Japanese art of flower arrangement with a view to surprising and pleasing her husband when he got home. Even more unsettling, Gary proved to be a solicitous nurse. This clarity would, with the slightest agitation, devolve into murk.

While Gary Snyder was unwaveringly intent on approximating the life and spiritual practice of a monk, Joanne Kyger gradually discovered that a cloistered marriage was not her ideal. When she got cranky, her husband expressed his disappointment. This naturally made her more so and became further grist for instruction. She needed to learn how to take criticism. To learn humility. To sit cross-legged for hours. Her husband's own fiercely guarded independence, his self-discipline and sparse economies—indeed, his own study of tea ceremony and Japanese—served nicely as both an example and a chastisement.

"It seems to me half the time our relationship is involved in a battle to see who is going to get the upper hand. But when we balance, all is beautiful, then I forget how dreadful living with him can be. Is his own masculinity threatened that he must fight so hard to assert himself and show no regard for my desires or identity?" Between teaching English and his sitting meditation practice at the Daitoku-ji temple, Snyder was away for long stretches of time, leaving his new wife to fend for herself in the sincere belief that this was salutary. "Is the woman who waits the woman who weaves?" she asked her journal, reflecting on the perfectly Zen myth of Penelope at her loom, trapped in the web of weaving and unweaving her own designs.

When spring finally arrived and the sun warmed her kitchen and her bed, coaxing the tiny blue daisies from a garden she hadn't imagined, in the dead of that first winter, was even there, she returned to writing. She scrutinized her many vanities: She was

moody, difficult, bad tempered, and foul mouthed. She asked her
husband what if she didn't *feel* like doing the dishes right after a
meal. What if she put off the dishes because she was absorbed in
doing something else, *not* reading a detective story, but actually
writing a *goddam poem,* what would he say? It was the possibility of
freedom that she craved, she insisted, imagining a work that would
fill up the loneliness inside her. But if it was a question of freedom, what was the point of asking?

And if Gary Snyder considered her question, it was only briefly.
He had already found the answer, and by his lights, it was the only
one possible. He lit the heater in the morning, she did the dishes.
Warming to the subject, he drew her attention to the jar she put
the clean silverware in. Hadn't she noticed that it was too small to
hold the utensils and that dirty water collected at the bottom?

The possibilities for perfection were, she could now see, infinite.

> *I'm sure*
>   *you can see me better*
> *than I can.*

For nearly two years in Kyoto, she waited for him and the
dishes waited for her. And then they left to meet up with Allen
Ginsberg in India.

HE STAGGERED FROM ONE END of the small room to the
other, shouting in his nasal cowboy voice that poetry was done
for, gesticulating with one hand and holding a drink with the
other. Every few steps he would stop and pick up one of several
kif cigarettes going in various ashtrays around the room, take a
deep drag, and then resume his circumambulation and his rants.
Bubbling over on the stove was a batch of his special hashish
candy, which, in his lone gesture of hospitality, he offered to anyone interested. He attacked Allen's parries from all sides while
two simpering young Englishmen looked on agog. Both had ap-
propriated many of his mannerisms.

For years, William Burroughs had lived alone in a small damp room with a single door that opened onto the garden of the Villa Muniria in Tangier. There were occasional trips to Paris and London and two ill-fated returns to the United States, all in efforts to kick dope, make money, or see Allen. Still, it was to the Muniria he kept returning, first as an exile on the lam from the manslaughter charge in his beloved South America, then as home. One wall of the room served as a shooting gallery, and on another he posted the snapshots from his trip to the headwaters of the Amazon. An orgone box held pride of place in a corner. He would sit in that, doubled up like a large bird, to smoke kif. In the early years, he imagined that the expat community had taken a violent dislike to him. He felt himself to be a kind of ill omen. Pages of his novel, in constant revision, lay strewn on and around and beneath the desk he worked at. After *The Naked Lunch* had finally seen print in Paris, leftover fragments found themselves under siege by scissors, joining the montage of the Amazon trip. They were now part of the vast project of cut-ups.

The writer Paul Bowles had first seen him in 1954, walking along a back street in the rain, strung out on heroin. On getting to know him, Bowles had concluded that the sole organizing principle of William Seward Burroughs's life were his addictions. At various times he was addicted to heroin, Eukodol, methadone, paregoric, Demerol, codeine, then kif, *majoun,* and drink. When in the advanced throes of an addiction, Burroughs studied his drug connections with a sharpness that suggested at once a predator's hunger and a prey's fear. Initially, however, Burroughs had portrayed his use of these substances as part of his scientific investigations. He saw himself as a latter-day Amazonian adventurer hacking through the deepest jungles of his own mind for the Inca gold he was certain was there. The practical outcome of his quests was unclear. Perhaps he required drugs to maintain the equilibrium of a temperament that was, in its sober essence, wildly off the rails. Whatever the underlying reason, his hunger for drugs tended to impose a far more tenacious discipline on his life than that generally afforded by willed efforts alone. This was partly because his addictions had often landed him in desperate straits, which he then needed all his faculties to navigate himself out of.

In Tangier, his monthly stipend covered his drug needs, bought him boys, and provided him one last chance to salvage something of a shattered life. Though he gave no outward indications of struggle, he confessed to Allen that he constantly weighed writing himself off with a one-way ticket to the East, "where I can get junk, live with it and for it from here on out." Yet his reticence was such that Bowles concluded Burroughs quite pampered himself and suffered no visible pangs about it, or indeed about any of the other giant missteps in his life.

Yet Burroughs routinely freaked himself out turning over his dark thoughts. His fantasies tended to involve unspeakable sex acts, obscure but nasty criminal enterprises, rare viral complaints, and parasitical infestations. He would calm himself, confirm his own grip on a more lighthearted, fact-based sanity, by writing them down in a voice that was a parody of the dime-store crime novels he'd devoured as a boy. The effect was weirdly compelling. The effort to organize these "routines" into some fiction of artistic unity, however, was excruciating. Instead, in an outlandish yet touching courtship, he sent them to Allen, and Allen, in a deep and doubtless freaky way, became his connection. The manuscript gave Jack nightmares.

Back in New York, Allen had sent Burroughs his dates, expecting him to travel from Tangier to Paris to meet up. But when Allen and Peter arrived at their usual hotel on rue Gît-le-Coeur after a week at sea, there was no sign of him, not even a letter. Instead, by the purest chance they ran into Gregory on St.-Germain. Having waited in his finely decked-out Greek rooms for over a year for Allen and Peter to show up, Gregory finally gave up and traveled to Paris to meet them. That first day, as Allen wondered at Burroughs's whereabouts, Gregory warned Allen that Bill's newest kick had changed him far more than any drug ever had. Gregory had briefly suffered the delusion that Burroughs was God. And not a funny, loving God, he told Allen, but a wrathful, fearsome, Catholic one.

After they'd spent April in Paris, a letter from Bill inviting them to Tangier eventually arrived, and the three of them made their lackadaisical way south. They stopped at Cannes for the film festival, staying in a Saint-Tropez hotel on the French Riviera and frittering away the entire month of May nodding off in a sea of junk and movie stars. They were guests of a wealthy addict named Jacques Stern. Stern was related to the Rothschilds, and both Gregory and Burroughs had often mainlined with him in Paris. A hunched, spidery man dressed in a black silk smoking jacket and confined to a wheelchair by polio, Stern claimed he had spent fourteen months in India, meditating for ten hours each day until he reached a "nirvanic void." When his reverie was interrupted by insistent voices demanding to know, "Why? Why?" his guru dismissed him as not yet ready.

Stern's accounts of Indian cremation grounds and con man gurus made both Peter and Gregory all the more intent on enjoying his hospitality, as if to fortify themselves for the heavy Indian scene to come. There were rich meals ending with strawberries and cream and, Peter wrote, endless cups of "caffey o-lay." Gregory spent his time wheedling Peter to share his carefully husbanded supply of heroin and then scarfing it all up. "Oh Peter I would love just to get some shit—I'll be yr friend the rest of my life—come on baby." When Peter wasn't shooting up, he ogled the sunbathers strewn upon the beach, candy-colored bottoms to the sun, longing to poke his nose into each one. He entertained a fantasy of becoming a film star like Peter Lawford or, failing that, a gigolo who made girls for money.

"All you want to do is fuck," Gregory yelled at him, annoyed at Peter's single-minded preoccupation. "You just want to fuck a girl and that's all—no wonder you can't get any girls." Flustered, Peter stammered, his protest stopped in his throat by hurt feelings. Unlike the rest of them, Peter was always at a loss for words. If Gregory or Jack weren't shouting at each other, they were making literary talk. What they were reading, what they were writing. Then Gregory would read Allen's poems, and Allen would read Gregory's or Jack's, and then there'd be more words; they were up to their necks in them. And if they weren't talking or reading, they'd be sitting and writing more. Jack wouldn't even have to sit; he could stand and write on the street if he had to. They were at it all the time, and though he had recently begun writing poetry himself, he found it hard to keep up.

Peter, however, counseled himself to not be intimidated, to stand up for himself. Was saying a girl would be "a great lay" and such-like any better, he wanted to know, than saying you wanted to fuck her? *He* didn't think so. Gregory made out that he had more love to give a woman than Peter did, which was not true. He had taken Janine's virginity, and he talked her through it, made her open her eyes to see what he was doing. Gregory had taken her best friend in the next room, and the girl emerged sobbing. Next time, Peter vowed, he wouldn't get mad; he would just throw a bucket of water over Gregory's fancy white silk suit. The new one.

Peter's lack of guile seemed to bring out Bill's most withering asides when they finally arrived in Tangier in early June. "What if we cut up Peter?" Bill ventured. Since Peter liked girls so much, he cracked, they were likely to find a girl of some kind inside him, an alien "Venusian" controlling his every thought and action. Burroughs's two devotees snickered. Peter staunchly defended his love for women and for Allen, too. But it wasn't Burroughs's whinnying ridicule that finally got to Peter. It was Gregory. July 6, 1961, Peter wrote Jack, was the day "the shit was in the fan." It was also the day that the plan to all travel together to India foundered.

Perhaps it was the sight of Peter gliding through the surf, attracting appreciative looks from sunbathing beauties, that set Gregory off where he sat with Allen at the café on the beach, deep in his cups. It often took less than that. Though he'd rained flattery on the subject of Peter's recent turn at poetry, today Gregory looked Peter in the eye when he returned to the table. He didn't think Peter's poems were actually any good, he said. Ignoring him, Peter took out his sketchbook. Gregory persisted. Peter should just concentrate on swimming. Or baseball.

Where Allen's response to Burroughs's insults was weak-kneed at best, he was outraged at Gregory. He began an accounting of all that Gregory owed him. The white silk suits, the train fare from Paris, the money for his gambling hunches, were all brought to bear. Peter continued his sketching. Gregory Nunzio Corso drew himself up as if he were filling himself with air and prepared the shit for the fan. Allen didn't support him!

"All right, if that makes you feel better," Allen said. Gregory's rants generally turned on the honor that accrued to those who threw money his way. His outrageousness goaded even the most unflappable into tempers. Allen knew better than to respond, so Gregory turned his blast on Peter.

"Drop dead," Peter mumbled under the spray, then said a bit loudly, "I am not here; you are not talking to anybody." His voice was hoarse.

"Yes, I am talking to you, you shit."

"No, you are not because I am not saying anything to you now." Peter continued sketching, sullen and burning, deciding that Allen and Gregory were a "creepey cancer" to his soul and he would take off for Istanbul as soon as he could get a ticket. Gregory stalked off to rest in his room, and Allen decided to go for a swim.

"I may not come back alive," Allen said morosely before leaving. Peter didn't even look up. Somehow, it was always about *him,* he told Jack. Unlike Allen, *he* didn't need anyone to come with him. He would travel to India alone. And two weeks later, still weak from dysentery and hepatitis, Peter left Tangier for the Middle East (passing Timothy Leary at the docks) while Allen stayed behind and "vomited off the roof."

Before Allen could begin to absorb all the nuances of Burroughs's cut-ups and Leary's manic plans for the mass dissemination of hallucinogens, one bleak fact stood out. William Burroughs—his onetime master, the linchpin that held together his soul and all his ideas about art and a holy life—was now a complete stranger. "And if I don't know Bill, I sure don't know myself, because he was my rock of tolerance and friendship and true art," he wrote, trying to fathom what had happened to the plan to all travel together to India.

And what was he doing with his art? He was cutting it up with a razor as if it weren't no sacred text at all. Just as he was cutting up all known human feelings between us, and cutting up the newspapers, and cutting up cuba and russia and america and making collages he was cutting up his own consciousness and escaping as far as I can tell outside of anything I could recognise as his previous identity.

Gregory left not long after Allen did, having done little but drink, take drugs, and argue since leaving Paris. He'd written his new publisher, James Laughlin, that "the only girl I ever loved" had unexpectedly returned to America after a year in Yemen. Though he hadn't seen Hope since 1957, he wanted to return to New York to find her. He thought he might sort out his relationship with his long estranged father and get "clean of the past" while he was there. Allen had once advised him that if you are going to love, you have to start at home. He was going to love. He hadn't been ready for Hope in 1957, it seemed. She had overpowered him, like a visitation, he told Allen. Now he was ready for her. Only after that might he join Allen in India.

To that end, he restarted a correspondence with a manuscript collector in hopes of securing some loot for his passage. As for Burroughs's cut-ups, he no longer felt they had anything to do with him.

"What can cut-up the true felt emotion, idea, dream, vision, love? What measure, what science?"

TRAVELING ON ALONE TO GREECE, Allen couldn't quite admit to himself that Gregory and Peter were in a frankly mortal contest for his attention. That they took far too many drugs. His own fate preoccupied him. He might survive the loss of Peter. But what of the loss of love? What of poetry? Had poetry itself become a block? Did further awakening lie in forsaking language itself? Were words the medium of consciousness or, as Burroughs and Leary now jointly insisted, cunningly placed obstacles? While he still went everywhere with a notebook, littering a trail of letters marking his inward journeys with as much attention as his outward destinations, he had found himself at a standstill.

One morning in Athens, he was thunderstruck by yet another

notion. All his life he had waited to hear back from God. The God who to him and him alone had once recited:

> Ah, sun-flower! Weary of time,
> Who countest the steps of the sun;
> Seeking after that sweet golden clime.
> Where the Traveller's journey is done.

This ancient authority, this monotheistic "Pater Omnipotens Aeterna Deus," he realized, was a far cry from the Shakespearean and pagan "wide angel consciousness" Bill had once schooled him in. That Bill was gone, replaced by a truly Old Testament megalomania. And with that realization, the nagging uncertainties that plagued him as a youth settled back on his slight, stooped, middle-aged shoulders like a raft of vultures.

God had left his universe. And what of that sweet golden clime? Was India, too, only a dream?

THE EARLY 1920S found Nagendra Nath working as a handyman for a Calcutta company that manufactured a popular brand of pressure cooker. To make his way in the world, he told his young son Asoke, he began taking English lessons. It was not long before he fell in love with the young Jewish heiress who was his teacher. Marie was also the director of a precious stones and leather goods export company left to her by her father.

One day in the company offices, Nagendra Nath's eye fell upon a package from London lying on a desk. The arrival of such a package, the novelty of the postage stamps with their engravings of the English king, had a near magical effect on him. Boldly, he slipped the package into his shirt and brought it to Marie. Inside was an illustrated catalog and price list of medical electrical instruments, including a mechanical massage device and miniature sauna. The brochure promised that with this new technology, one could cure a variety of common ailments, including lumbago, gout, muscle pain, and all varieties of paralysis. Still a vigorous young man in his early twenties, Nagendra suffered from none of them. But with the theft of the package, he had once again determined his fate. This was the beginning of the Massage & Bath Clinic Ltd. of 59 Bentinck Street, Calcutta.

As Nagendra Nath was making less than seventy-five cents a month, it was up to Marie not only to fund the purchase of the equipment, but to import a beautiful English clinical nurse and masseuse to administer the treatments. She arrived from London accompanied by the apparatus. With advertisements in the Calcutta *Statesman,* they attracted the wealthy and sophisticated elites of the city. Bengali babus, rajas and maharajas, ministers, barristers, and high-ranking raj officials in the government and police all came to know Nagendra Nath, contributing greatly to his fluency in English. The spa was a tremendous success, and Nagendra Nath—zamindari son, chanteuse, Tantric sadhu, merchant, janitor, and entrepreneur—became a wealthy man.

And then he lost her. Marie fell in love with a wealthy European. She sold all her property and left India forever. To Nagendra Nath she left both her father's export company and the Massage & Bath Clinic, making him sole proprietor of two profitable concerns. But he was devastated. Despite the years of close partnership, he waited months for a letter, but he never again heard from her. In a fit of dejection and loneliness, he put an advertisment in the newspaper for a bride. He received just one reply.

Her name was Umashasi, one of the names of goddess Kali. She was a tall, dark woman with large liquid eyes and a long nose. Unlike Nagendra, she was well educated and had already published two books, among them a translation of the short stories of the American writer H. H. Munro, better known by his pen name of "Saki." The combination of her dark skin and advanced education had doubtless contributed to her difficulty in finding a suitable husband, leaving her somewhat bruised and wary.

Once again, Nagendra Nath fell in love, and from the marriage of Nagendra Nath–Shiva and Umashasi-Kali, Asoke Sarkar was born. As was the custom, a horoscope was soon prepared, siting the stars against the time of his birth. From the chart, the family astrologer prophesied that the boy would grow up to be a great sage.

. . .

THOUGH GARY SNYDER'S India itinerary allowed for some flexibility, it was clear from his letters to Ginsberg that the principles that shaped his route did not. The first was economy. Gary did not expect to spend more than $5 per day and he hoped to pick up some extra cash giving readings at universities en route. Unforeseen expenses were to be avoided like the plague (for which he recommended Allen bring his own bedding as well as water purifier tablets). Writing from Kyoto in the fall of 1961, he warned Allen that he would not be staying in hotels, as he had heard they were absurdly lavish. He also held that it was unbearable to travel during the summer months and impossible during the monsoons. This meant that he and Joanne had three months in which to cover the Indian subcontinent. As the date of their departure approached, Gary wrote Allen in greater detail the course he'd sketched in previous letters. By November, he'd learned that universities didn't really have money for visiting lecturers. He still hoped they might meet up in Ceylon to celebrate New Year's Eve, so as to take on India together. Perhaps they could join Paul Bowles there, Allen suggested in his reply.

In a brief respite from the hothouse in Burroughs's rooms, Allen had accepted Bowles's invitation to travel to Marrakech. Bowles found him to be a perfect traveling companion, easy to get on with and, unlike Burroughs, who mystified him, filled with a rare and nearly unnatural sweetness. Bowles thought he might be in Ceylon for the winter, staying on the island he owned off the south coast. Ceylon was boring, he said, but made up for that with its natural beauty, "if you find that useful." Allen did not. He remained focused on traveling overland to India from Greece, up through Turkey, and across the Middle East.

Bowles had traveled to India a decade before, and though his stay was short, he had been overwhelmed by the smell of shit. He described to Allen how Bombay's streets were thronged by millions of unsheltered refugees, where "every nook and cranny was filled every night with sleepers." Bowles sketched out the cornucopias of disease that awaited unsuspecting tourists. If Allen insisted on traveling there, Bowles advised him to do so first class, under the barricades of mosquito nets, staying in colonial-era hotels, where servants still prostrated themselves at the door before entering and went about in bare feet so as not to disturb the sahibs' repose.

When traveling in the North African desert to write his novel *The Sheltering Sky,* Bowles was accompanied by an entire equipage of tweed jackets, silk ties, dressing gowns, oxford shirts, and cashmere vests, with perhaps one djellaba for lounging about with a pipe in the evening. Beyond the perimeters of a well-tailored white suit lay the invisible plagues of Asia. Dysentery would riddle your intestines with bloody holes that would fester for years. Smallpox and loathsome skin diseases will pursue you with medieval virulence. And should you be so feckless as to sleep with a prostitute, it was said that there were venereal diseases lurking in the flophouses of Bombay and Calcutta capable of consuming your genitalia within the space of a few days. But the most dreaded specter was that of typhoid, a disease that Bowles once suffered from and to which a character in *The Sheltering Sky* falls prey. The nightmare that Bowles honed with such cold exactitude begins innocuously with a slight fever, a tiny stomach cramp after a day in the sun or perhaps a momentary lapse of caution with a glass of water. The novel, a 1950 best seller, provided postwar America with an excellent reason to stay home. Listening to Bowles, Allen was thoroughly spooked.

After studying the weather tables and talking with experienced India hands, Gary outlined his plan to work their way north from Colombo up the eastern seaboard of India to see the coastal cities of Pondicherry, Madras, and Calcutta. From there they would turn west inland, following the Ganges up to Bodh Gaya so that he might meditate under the Bodhi tree where the Buddha achieved enlightenment. Along this route there would be side trips to Nepal and Dharamsala to dig the Tibetan Buddhist scene. Then there would be trains to Benares, Delhi, and Agra, with more side trips to hill stations where all the famed Yoga Vedanta ashrams were. Gary had it in mind to get as close to the peak of

Nanda Devi as possible, even going for a tentative hike into the Himalayan foothills. And no doubt there were yoga and Tibetan meditation practices to pick up en route. Finally, he wanted to make a careful study of Hindu and Buddhist art and temple architecture. Allen received Gary's itinerary in Greece, and suddenly India began to lose its fantastic and fearful qualities and take on an actual geography.

As for Allen's news that he and Peter had parted ways in Tangier, Gary wasn't really sure what to say; homosexual love remained something of a mystery to him. His *roshi* would say that if he were to search for the right words, they would be the wrong ones. Gary settled by writing him that change is "usually right."

Joanne offered her two cents in a postscript:

"I think change stinks."

ALLEN HAD DREAMED of Bombay three months before he set foot there, sailing into the nighttime harbor past the Gateway of India. In the dream, the boulevard that fronted the Arabian Sea shone like the French Riviera at Saint-Tropez, its fancy hotels lit up like costume jewelry. From there, he passed through a fairytale gate to discover a middle layer of cheap apartments where he might live for a pittance in Gregory's white silk suit. Beyond the layer of cheap rooms, he sensed the hovels of his bleakest imagining and shivered with fear at the prospect of exploring them. He then came upon a door jauntily inscribed, "Well it's too bad, but goodbye." This he took as a sign he had finally reached the end of his search for a place beyond death, the heaven where man, rich and poor, lives in awareness that life is only a dream. Writing down the dream in Israel, he noted the irony of writing of the real Promised Land from the supposed one.

Allen had soon discovered that traveling overland from Israel to India was an impossibility, owing to the overlooked fact that India and most of the Middle East refused to recognize Israel's existence and it was impossible to obtain an Indian visa there. He had gone to Israel in the hope of tracking down Peter, who had seemingly disappeared from the map. He sent letters to Petra in

Jordan and Damascus and Jerusalem and one to Northport in hopes that Peter's mother, Kate, had an address for him. They eventually found each other on a street corner in Tel Aviv and were promptly reconciled, for the time being shaking off whatever had happened in Tangier as a bad trip. They spent a month in Israel and all their remaining funds going from pillar to post trying to secure a boat out, leaving Allen completely sour. "A ratty looking Bronx, amazingly full of jewish people who all think they're jewish, under a jewish sky with jewish streetcars & jewish airplanes & armies . . . so after awhile I felt like an arab." After receiving a $500 check from *Playboy* in exchange for a promise to write about India, they booked passage to Mombasa, Kenya, where a boat was leaving for Bombay in early February, nearly a month away. By then it was far too late to join up with the Snyders in Ceylon. Allen subdued his anxieties with ganja bought from a shoeshine boy in Mombasa and spent the crossing in a cloud of smoke, reading the Upanishads, the Bhagavad Gita, the Rigveda, and Kipling's *Kim*. His fellow passengers in the hold lay faint with seasickness while Peter picked his nose and played his guitar. Though relieved and overjoyed to be back with Peter, Allen wondered if their relationship would survive the journey.

Filled with Indian refugees fleeing the expected persecution that would follow East Africa's pending independence, Allen's boat arrived in Bombay on February 15, 1962, one month short of a year since he'd left the New York City docks. Allen spent their last dollar on a taxi, making a beeline for American Express to collect both his letters and his year-end royalties from City Lights. Walking around the city for two days, Allen discovered that Bombay looked less like what he had dreamed and feared and more like a shabby, Victorian-era London with some Art Deco edges. At night, gangs of boys with goatskins filled with water raced to fill the water tanks atop each building. At his first opportunity, Allen wrote Bowles that his description of India couldn't have been more screwy.

After a preamble relating the morning ablutions of Indians, "they scrape the roots of the tongue . . . and make monsterous vomiting and coughing noises for an hour every morning," Ginsberg went on to describe the vast array of cheap Indian hotels with clean water and nontoxic vegetarian lunches available to the economizing traveler. The *dharamsalas* were like YMCAs set up near temples to provide lodging for pilgrims and business travelers. Ashrams also had inexpensive food and lodging but could be found only where a holy man once lived. If he was still living, you could sit with him and ask him questions. Finally, if you wanted to go the English route, you could stay in the bungalows or circuit houses generally available near every rail junction. Formerly, raj officials stayed in them when they made the rounds of their jurisdictions. These rooms even came with a servant. Train travel was equally blissful. If you brought your own blanket and air mattress and reserved one day in advance, it was possible to stretch out with a book and doze comfortably on a three-tiered bunk not unlike a luggage rack.

Not having found any letter from Gary at American Express, Allen and Peter booked such a journey on an overnight express train to Delhi. Even the dining cars charged less than fifty cents for a huge Western meal and less than ten cents for a vegetarian tray, Ginsberg crowed in his letter to Bowles.

"I must say, you made it sound as if a westerner would die of rat poison if he stayed anywhere but Taj Mahal Hotel," Allen said crossly.

A WOMAN MARRIED in a red-and-gold Benarsi silk sari is a well-married woman. The rooftops of Benares are dotted with cross-legged old men at spinning wheels who, like latter-day Rumpelstiltskins, spin skeins of gold thread onto skeins of white silk. The city's crooked alleyways are filled with the sound of massive looms rhythmically clapping elaborate patterns into silks behind old wooden shutters. Yet on a cottage porch not far from the entrance of Sarva Seva Sangh headquarters above the Rajghat, Gary Snyder discovered a bare-chested old man with a neatly trimmed beard working a *charkha* with simple khadi cotton.

Gary had just polished off a lunch of South Indian masala dosa, idli, and pickle at Ayyar's café on the ghats. Perhaps this contributed to his feeling of contentment and expansiveness. Next to the old man, too, was a beautiful Indian girl with a bored expression on her face. When Gary approached, the man motioned for her to get a cushion. She retrieved one from the cottage, tossing it carelessly by the wheel on which Mahatma Gandhi spun both his politics and his faith.

Gary Snyder had not come to India to find a guru. His *roshi* awaited his return to Kyoto. Yet countless stories are told of how an unsuspecting traveler meets an aged crone or wandering mendicant and is suddenly transformed by the encounter, inspired to follow this sage in simple clothes and learn what needed to be learned. Benares provided auspicious ground for such encounters. Hindus believed that if you met your end in Benares, you would forgo the misery of countless reincarnations and proceed at long last to heaven. Consequently, the ghats of Benares were crowded not only with the aged and infirm, widows and beggars, but with the sadhus and saints who helped them navigate this final passage. Still, Gary Snyder did not imagine he might require heaven, much less an old Gandhian, to show him the way there.

Or a Tibetan lama. The day before, Gary and Joanne had stayed overnight in Sarnath, a mere six-mile journey by pony cart from Benares. After his enlightenment at Bodh Gaya, Shkyamuni Buddha was said to have gone to Sarnath to give his first teaching in a grove of trees now called Deer Park. While circling the stupa, a massive bricked tower that marked the spot where the Buddha had stood, Gary had noticed an elderly lama trotting around ahead of him. The lama was one of the thousands of Tibetan refugees who flocked to Buddhist pilgrimage sites in India in the aftermath of the Chinese invasion of Tibet.

Every day, the mountains emptied themselves of Tibetans smelling of yak and old leather. Initially, some had believed the promise that the People's Liberation Army (PLA) was there to free the Tibetans from serfdom. After Mao's initial invasion in 1950, the Chinese began building roads and permanent settlements. As the grip of the Chinese settled on each province, edging toward Lhasa, some Tibetans began to join together, organizing uprisings armed by shipments of guns provided by the CIA; but the Chinese had already made deep inroads into the regional bureaucracies. So the Tibetans began to leave lands they had lived on for as long as anyone could remember. First they retreated toward Lhasa. They arrived there in a steady stream, surrounded by pack animals, flocks of sheep and goats, with their valuables tied up in the knots of their clothing. Then, with the arrival of the PLA in Lhasa and the disappearance of the Dalai Lama into Indian exile in 1959, the Tibetans followed, leaving for India, Nepal, Bhutan, and Sikkim. The women had babies in forests en route, and elders died as much from grief as from the strain of the journey. As they moved across Tibet and their sacks of food got lighter, they sold their pack animals one by one. Families crossed vast snowfields, climbed mountains, and fought off brigands.

In the early years, when they reached the Indian border, the Tibetans would just say "Dalai Lama," because he was the only point of reference they had for the world outside their village. The Indian border guards would take down their names and let them pass. When the ticket agents on trains and buses and ferries asked for their tickets, they would repeat, "Dalai Lama, Dalai Lama, Dalai Lama," with their palms together at their forehead, and they were granted passage. Some were farmers, some were nomads, some were lamas and *rinpoches* and opera singers, but by the time they got to India, they were all refugees. Refugee centers in Kalimpong and Dharamsala sprang up to orient them and school their children or, if they were too old to learn, put them to work carding wool and knitting sweaters or clearing forests and building roads, living in tents alongside. Later, they were given a choice to move to settlements elsewhere in India or return to Tibet to join the insurgency.

When Gary's circumambulation was complete, the bewhiskered lama approached him. Was that his own heart slapping about in his chest like a landed trout? Having read the work of the French explorer and Tibet scholar Alexandra David-Néel, including her electrifying account of the secret teachings of certain Tibetan Buddhist cults, Gary suddenly became aware of an ache for magic practices he scarcely knew he had. Would he be initiated? When the lama pulled out a handful of Tibetan coins, offering to sell them, Snyder mocked himself and withdrew, his sensibilities offended that this holy ground had become a marketplace for lamas hawking souvenirs. He and Joanne returned to their ashram in Benares, his world once again fixed in its place.

THE OLD MAN held the cotton batting in his left hand while he turned the wheel with his right to feed the whirling spindle. Gary watched the procedure closely, impressed by the intricate but simple machinery. After a few minutes in silence, the old man finally spoke.

"This is an Ellora *charkha*. Gandhiji named it. He used it a lot."

In six weeks of travel, this was the first time Gary had witnessed someone actually using a *charkha,* though the emblem of the spinning wheel was ubiquitous as the symbol of the Congress Party. After picking up some guidebooks in Madras, Gary had proceeded to amass a wealth of information about India's social problems, ancient history, art, and religious iconography. He became unfailingly well-informed on nearly every subject save perhaps the byzantine byways of contemporary Indian politics. His opinions about what he saw kept pace with what he learned. Quite often, too, Japan and Zen Buddhism became the reference point by which he might profitably compare India and Hinduism. His reflections found an outlet in his journals and the letters he wrote to his sister.

Their first stop after Ceylon had been to the formerly French outpost of Pondicherry in South India. The main attraction for foreign visitors was the presence there of an exceedingly well-organized and clean ashram. Though the word *ashram* means "resting place," unlike those serving Hindus on pilgrimage, these modern ashrams maintained a core group of permanent devotees. If spiritual instruction was provided, it was generally provided in English, though European languages were said to be ill suited to the subtleties of Hindu philosophy. The first modern ashram in India was undoubtedly the one at Adyar, outside Madras, site of the funereal headquarters of the Theosophical Society.

Founded in the nineteenth century by a mesmerizing Russian named Helena Petrovna Blavatsky, Theosophy eventually attracted a worldwide following among those interested in everything from vegetarianism and the "Orient" to Freemasonry and table rapping. Like Alexandra David-Néel, Blavatsky had acquired her special powers at the feet of an order of mysterious Tibetan sages. Despite accusations of fraud and public scandals, Theosophy had had a decided influence on Indian nationalists. Adyar was only the first of its chain of ashrams, each providing a rich source of revenue for the society and a business model for enterprising gurus.

The ashram at Auroville in Pondicherry was founded by a man named Sri Aurobindo Ghose. The son of a high Bengali official, Aurobindo had been educated in England. Upon his return to India in the 1920s, he became a convert to the nationalist cause. After he was condemned to death by a British court, he was obliged to escape to the French toehold in India, where he spent the rest of his life studying and teaching Hindu philosophy. His opus *The Life Divine* was on every bedside table. Gary readily placed Aurobindo's ideas in the context of esoteric spiritual traditions. "It is not truly monistic, as vedanta is, but rather belongs, it seems to me, in the class with anti-matter dualisms like Manichaeism, Nestorian Xtianity, and some sorts of Gnosticism, Catharites."

Decades before Aurobindo died in 1950, he had left the project of running the ashram in the hands of a French Lebanese woman who had initially come to India to meet Alexandra David-Néel, whose best-selling books on Tibet had doubtless captured her imagination much as they had Gary Snyder's. Upon meeting Aurobindo, however, she ditched her husband and gradually became the resident divine presence, referred to as "the Mother." Under her watch, sex, tobacco, alcohol, and politics were strictly forbidden and members had to donate all their worldly goods to the ashram, providing her a captive audience. Sitting on her balcony each morning, her feet in a basin filled with lotuses and wearing a filmy and flapperesque silk scarf, the Mother would bless the devotees with her silent presence before going into a meditative trance. Spiritual benefits accrued to her devotees through mere proximity. This was known as *darshan*. "Another big Indian thing," Gary noted.

"They all believe that the Mother is a divine incarnation," he wrote to Allen, strongly urging him to check it out, "representing a new step in human evolution." Pondicherry would be at the center of this transformation, achieved not only by self-realization, but by a sudden transformation of matter itself. Human beings would become sexless immortals glowing with light. Gary's initial enthusiasm, however, soon gave way to a sense that Pondicherry was actually a rather sinister place. *Darshan* alone, he felt, did not constitute an authentic spiritual practice. Meditation seemed to consist of middle-aged devotees in uniforms walking vigorously up and down the beach or contemplating the map of Mother India for a quarter of an hour. And despite the plethora of teachings that the ashram was constantly churning out, Gary did not see anyone studying them. At least the Theosophical Society at Adyar was a center of Sanskrit studies. Critical exegesis of sacred texts became another of Gary's core principles. The POINT is, he wrote, there was no evident *practice*. If Aurobindo's teachings had been accompanied by useful meditation techniques, he was prepared to overlook the shortcomings of the doctrine. One clear benefit of their stay was unassailable. In their five days there, they managed to eat well, do their laundry, and get their bearings for the trip ahead, all on very little money. The breezes off the Bay of Bengal were also quite pleasant.

Their next stopover was at the Sri Ramana Maharshi ashram in Tiruvannamalai. Like Han-Shan, Maharshi was said to have lived for many years in a mountain cave. When he died in 1950, he left behind not only a pet cow named Lakshmi, but collections of his teachings, including one book in question-and-answer format that had been wildly popular in Europe in the 1940s. The book was said to have been compiled and translated anonymously into English by the Gandhian and Krishnamurti follower Maurice Frydman. In his 1939 introduction, Carl Jung wrote that Maharshi's goals were no different from those of Western mystics. He perceived him to be an uncompromising prophet of the modern age. Maharshi, for example, was quick to dismiss any prospect of a hereafter, insisting that reincarnation exists only so long as there is ignorance to give it credence. This was clearly something Jung was happy to hear. The belief that Lakshmi, Maharshi's cow, achieved liberation upon her death, Jung left unchallenged.

Maharshi's principal teaching was that the self and God were one and the same, and all one's efforts must be directed toward this realization. He taught his followers how to shift their focus, in specific and incremental stages, from the I to the self, and from man to God. Maharshi's work of introspective expertise, Jung wrote, was emblematic of the riches of an Eastern mind-set, "almost unattainable to the western human being." Maharshi also cautioned his followers not to forget the soul amid the Western onslaught of technology and commerce. This became something of a mantra in India's encounter with the West.

Snyder did acknowledge that as an adept of the wisdom (*dhyana*) yoga tradition rather than the devotional (*bhakti*) yoga one (as the Mother was), Maharshi was perhaps more worthy of study. He portrayed his mode of teaching as straightforward, if rather minimalist. To anyone who asked Maharshi a searching spiritual question, he would reply, "Who asks?" Gary allowed that such a question would eventually result in insight, particularly for those individuals who were "existentially bugged." Yet somehow, the Maharshi's inability to speak English seemed inseparable from the simplicity of his teachings. His enlightenment, too, Snyder imagined, arose not from his ascetic practices, but from his naturally sweet disposition. Not unfairly, Gary concluded that disciples rarely matched the insights of their masters, so Maharshi's true measure, so long after his departure, was difficult to take. As with Pondicherry, the stop in Tiruvannamalai was a pleasant enough interlude, but as they were on a fairly tight schedule, there was no time to contemplate the divine subtleties of the self. Ancient Hindu temples and Buddhist pilgrimage sites were next.

Madras, Bhubaneswar, Konark, Calcutta, Bodh Gaya, Nalanda, Patna, and Nepal passed before Gary's well-informed eyes like the Stations of the Cross. Calcutta was a horror, and his heart went out to those poets he met, starved for international intellectual gossip and still so hung up on Rabindranath Tagore. To their insistence that Tagore's poetry was incomparable in Bengali, Gary replied, "I should hope so." Despite their high spirits and fondness for whiskey, Snyder imagined that Buddhadev Bose and his son-in-law Jyoti Datta must at times harbor some nostalgia for the British, overwhelmed as they were by the social problems besetting their city. To Allen, he wrote that Indian intellectuals were square, filled with patriotism and anticipation of progress, but with only vague ideas of spiritual values. The concept of hip eluded them entirely. Gary was convinced that hipness constituted the next step forward in the evolution of the human spirit.

By the end of the second week in February, halfway through their allotted twelve weeks in India, Gary Snyder and Joanne Kyger had, with uncanny exactitude and a few revisions, covered half their itinerary. This midpoint found Gary contemplating the bleak and shimmering shore across the river Ganges at Benares. From there they would return to Delhi to pick up their mail before diving into the foothills of the upper Ganges. There, he wrote Allen, they would stay at the Yoga-Vedanta Forest Academy and hang out with singing yogis and cave-dwelling ascetics of all stripes. While he had periodically dropped notes to Allen keeping him abreast of their progress, it seemed increasingly unlikely that they would be able to meet up.

At Ayyar's café on the ghats, polishing off the large crisp masala dosa, Gary had taken up his journal. The real tragedy of India's beggars, Gary thought, considering the lineup before him, is that they made lives of their infirmities. Whether fingerless, legless, or eyeless, they "refused to be human." Their faces were screwed into permanent expressions of misery. A blind beggar sat nearby, weeping to no one in particular, his genitals carelessly exposed. Snyder's unsentimental catalog of the physical deformities and open sores his brief walk along the ghats had uncovered seemed calculated to curb his appetite.

Much like the beggars who preyed on his sympathy, on those short lifts from railway station to tourist bureau, museum, or *dharmasala,* rickshaw drivers had consistently tried to overcharge him. Gary paled at the thought of how easily the unwary tourist was routinely taken advantage of and fiercely refused, on principle, to be cheated *too* much. There were great intemperate scenes when he declined to pay more than the agreed-upon price. Tired and dirty, Joanne would stand in the heat listening to Gary's trembly, rage-filled voice, in thrall to a fantasy of ending the fuss by coolly decking the driver.

Gary was eventually able to formulate a coolheaded answer to the moral dilemma posed by beggars in particular and India's poverty in general. The cheating-fawning-bullying-whining pathology of beggars and rickshaw drivers was typical, he felt, of the complex of habits that served Indians under the British. Eventually, Indians would outgrow these behaviors. Until then, he refused to give alms to healthy adults or children, favoring instead the deformed, crippled, and aged. He gave India a decade in which to outlaw and eliminate professional begging altogether. In the meantime, he would be doing them no favor by reinforcing backwardness with money.

Gary's equally ironclad decision to travel third class, however, met an unforeseen complication that he never resolved to his own satisfaction. Third-class travelers had to force themselves on the train, fighting off all comers in an unseemly contest for a seat. Failure meant standing instead of sitting, sweating in crowded corridors while naked babies in the arms of old ladies peed on one's feet. To make it to the inevitably appalling toilet, you had practically to be passed, arms crossed on chest, over the heads of your fellow unseated passengers. Technically, third-class tickets also meant doing without the privileges that came with a second-class ticket, including reserved seats and access to the railway station retiring rooms. These rooms were clean and well lit, separated by gender, and often supplied with hot showers and comfortable beds. Despite the fact that they held only third-class tickets, the Snyders soon discovered that stationmasters would grant them access not only to the retiring room, but to unoccupied seats in the second-class carriages.

Gary hated the fact that his white face afforded him privileges he hadn't paid for. The idea that he was provided this hospitality as a foreign guest was doubtless as difficult for him to imagine and accept as the idea of a Westerner traveling third class was for his Indian hosts.

ALMOST IN SPITE OF HIMSELF, the old man often attended the talks Krishnamurti gave when he came to Benares in winter. Krishnaji had often teased him about his devotion to the *charkha*. He had tried to get him to ease up on his austerities, to enjoy life a little more, but the old man resisted. This was what he knew. Still, he would return again and again to hear Krishnaji speak, at once attracted and repelled by Krishnamurti's lyrical evocation of the primacy of love and beauty and desire. Quite recently, Krishnamurti had given a talk on Zen. Having heard Gary had come to India from Japan, the old man asked him about his practice. He listened carefully as Snyder spoke of his teacher, the rigors of *zazen,* and the subtlety of koan study. Once Gary finished, the old man returned to his spinning.

"I have been spinning since I entered public life," he said after some time. "After I graduated from college, I went and asked Gandhiji what I should do. He says, 'Can you spin?'"

The old man stopped there. Perhaps he was suddenly unsure of a story he had told many times. For the past year, he had been consumed by fears of his own death, and the code by which he had lived his life seemed to provide no consolation. He turned to Gary. And what, he asked, were his thoughts on Gandhiji's Satyagraha, his philosophy of nonviolence and noncooperation?

Uncharacteristically, Gary found himself at something of a loss. He sought to convey, as diplomatically as possible, his disinterest in purely social causes. Fortuitously, an article he had read in *The New Yorker* the summer before came to mind. The reporter had shown how the Negro movement was beginning to use Gandhian methods of nonviolent protest in their effort to desegregate schools in Durham, North Carolina. Joanne had been so moved by the article's portrayal of the quixotic and dignified resistance of the Negro community, she had been tempted to return to the States to join their fight. Gary, however, had raised several pointed questions. After freedom is gained, then what? How can the method of nonviolence discipline one's life afterward? It was insufficient.

"Some Americans have gotten a lot out of nonviolence from Gandhi," he began. "The Negro movement in the South . . ."

The old man interrupted, impatient and curt. One doesn't *get* something out of the philosophy of nonviolence. That was not the way it worked. The practice was to the philosophy as the warp and the weft were to the cloth.

"Like India," the old man continued, trying to keep the bitterness from his voice, "when she *got* independence, she threw Gandhi away."

THERE WAS A RETINUE OF LAMAS from the Young Lamas Home School, as well as a cluster of foreigners in yellow sannyasi robes and absurd-looking turbans. The Indians in attendance at the Delhi auditorium maintained a dignified air through the entire ceremony. After less than two weeks in India, it was beginning to dawn on Allen that nearly everyone he met was on to some sort of *sadhana* (spiritual path) and that every family had their very own guru or Brahmin pandit. The idea that the entire universe was an illusion seemed universally agreed upon, and not much was made of it. "It really is another Dimension of time-history here," Allen wrote Jack.

At the center of attention that evening was an earnest young man with very long hair who had pledged an oath of perpetual silence in honor of his guru's birthday the following day. This guru, Meher Baba, would later achieve mass market fame on a poster depicting his smiling visage above the legend "Don't Worry, Be Happy." Born a Zoroastrian at the turn of the century in Bombay, Meher Baba had himself taken a vow of silence as a young man and now communicated through his writings and with the aid of an alphabet board. One of his great projects was to identify the hundreds of thousands of "masts" living anonymously beyond the pale of society. These masts, he believed, were spiritually advanced souls who were so intoxicated with their love of God, they appeared to be completely mad.

It was the promise of a performance by Chatur Lal, the famed tabla player, that had brought Allen to the hall, and the music he and the lady sarod accompanist provided was indeed celestial. Yet while Peter was mesmerized by the music, Allen was enrapt by the public drama of the vow itself. On the train, Allen and Peter met another gentleman who had taken vows. Arriving in Delhi, Mr. Jain, a jeweler from Jaipur, had invited them both to join him at the Jain *dharamsala,* adjacent to the Jain temple complex, so that they could continue their conversation. He related to them how, after establishing himself in business, raising a family, and seeing his children married, he had become a Brahmachari. He had vowed, like Mahatma Gandhi, to abstain from sex for the remainder of his life. "You see, you must not give away your jew-els," Mr. Jain explained gravely. "You must retain your jew-els." Every Hindu was expected to eventually retire from the world, he said, to take vows of poverty and chastity and wander all over India. Allen tried to imagine his father, lost in thought, wandering around Newark in saffron robes.

Mr. Jain introduced Allen to all his jeweler friends who were also members of the tiny but ancient Jain Hindu sect. They were also named Jain. For Jains, the ultimate aim of their religion was salvation, and that could be achieved only through a succession of vows that would slowly divest the soul of the dust of its sins. A Jain will vow to never harm another living creature, to tell only the truth, to never steal, to contain lust, to speak gently, to take full control of his body, speech, and mind, to forgive, to be humble, and to meditate on the real nature of the world. The Jain idea of renunciation proceeds step by step through vows of bodily mortification, delivering the layman far beyond the shores of advanced asceticism. For Jains, old age is timed precisely to conclude with a fast unto death itself. Alongside the vows of the Jains, Allen's own vows to labor on behalf of the workingman, to keep true to the Harlem vision, and to never read poetry for money seemed trite and ill conceived.

Jains were atheistic, but Allen learned that some did accept the need to worship one or another of the Hindu gods. At the summit of the Hindu Olympus was Vishnu, the cosmic king;

Shiva, a great yogi and ascetic; and his feminine counterpart, Shakti, or divine energy. Shakti might be worshipped both as wife and consort of Shiva, but like Vishnu and Shiva, she also had many other names and avatars. Devotees of Vishnu or one of his avatars (Krishna and Rama being very popular) were known as Vaishnavites. Shiva worshippers were known as Shaivites, and followers of the feminine divine were called Shaktas. Mr. Jain explained to Allen that all gods are unreal, but most Hindus choose one and use the image of that god (either a picture or a statue) to focus on during prayers, to quiet the mind and soak the heart in the gentle vibes it radiated. Or, after taking your measure, your guru might assign you a god. Apparently, there was a personal god for everyone, Allen reported to Jack, tailored to your temperament, desires, or inclinations.

For the highly cultivated aesthetes or students studying for exams, there was Saraswati, the goddess of music, poetry, and learning. She rode on the back of a swan and carried a sitar. Lakshmi was the goddess of wealth and beauty, ideally suited to those obsessed with Bollywood movie stars. The rivalry between these two goddesses went some way toward explaining why the wise were never wealthy and the wealthy were never wise. Peter had already become a devotee of the elephant-headed and potbellied Ganesha, taking particular delight in how his trunk was always immersed in a bowl of goodies. Ganesha cut a debonair figure and was the god to apply to when faced with an obstacle and to thank when blessed with good fortune. Allen noted wryly that Bill would find Durga, the goddess of destruction, or her bloody avatar, Kali, downright companionable. With her necklace of human heads and belt of severed hands, Kali had taken the cut-up to its karmic extreme. Then there was the trickster cowboy Krishna "for cocksmen-cayote types" like Neal Cassady. Finally, to Jack he offered the compassionate Buddha, who was generously given a home on the Hindu Olympus. Allen hadn't yet found a replacement for his Blakean God, but he might have recognized something of his younger self in Radha, filled with yearning for absent Krishna, perpetually straining to catch the sound of his flute. In Hinduism, it seemed, a flute was rarely just a flute.

Meher Baba taught that it was through love that man became God. Sri Krishnaji's final hour-long talk on silence struck a similar love-struck note, his discourse delivered in a gentle but serious manner. Allen listened intently and decided that it seemed a somewhat naive philosophy, at least to the uninitiated, but not at all overwrought. Krishnaji offered a parting kernel of wisdom for the visiting foreigners:

"Silence would be good for America."

SHIVA SITS IN SPLENDID ISOLATION on the lonely summit of Mount Kailash in the Himalayas, his ropy hair piled high on his head like the towering mountains at his back. His posture is perfect and still. His mind glitters within the mirrored void of his own divinity. His lean, ashen form bears witness to his ceaseless austerities. Of all the Hindu gods, Shiva is the arch ascetic. His rocklike heart is untouched by offerings of food or flowers. His meditation is not broken by tearful requests for intercession. Those who petition Shiva must first endure the most extreme self-inflicted sufferings. Only then might he be roused. It was in response to the prayers of a saint who had fasted for years on dry leaves, standing on one foot with both arms in the air, that Shiva relented and slaked a dry land with the roar of the Ganges. Worshippers of Shiva perform similar feats of willpower and godlike detachment, believing that in so doing, they accumulate a store of psychic and physical energy. Storing this energy and wielding it in magical practices is said to be the foundation of the most ancient form of yoga.

"Holy Hindu town," Joanne wrote in her journal. "It stinks." After Benares and the Taj Mahal, Mathura seemed to offer little in the way of sightseeing or spiritual uplift. Suddenly, the momentum of their travels across the subcontinent seemed to stall, precipitated by a nasty fight with a rickshaw wallah. Gary, somewhat defensively, assured Joanne that the reason for the stopover was that the Mathura museum was the center of first-century Kushan Buddhist art and provided the only extant example of temple statuary where women's vulvas were on vivid display.

A crowded train compartment en route to Delhi did not improve their moods, as Joanne had yet to acknowledge the karmic benefits of needless austerities. When they were met at the door of the fearsomely pink Birla Mandir *dharamsala* by an elaborately turbaned gatekeeper with a handlebar mustache, she might have predicted there would be no room for them. Eventually, Gary was able to convince him they required only a bit of floor space for their sleeping bags. The following day, they realized there were plenty of rooms, but the gatekeeper had imagined that an ordinary one would not meet their standards. Except for her nightly hair and clothes washing, Joanne had by then given up all hope of standards. Had Gary to choose a Hindu god, it was clear which one he would settle on.

Picking up their mail the next morning at American Express, Gary learned that Allen and Peter had been in Delhi for four days and that a reunion was possible after all. They raced to the Jain *dharamsala* and, finding them out, left a note and returned to catch up on back issues of *Time* magazine and wait for their room to be ready. By early evening, they were still waiting. Joanne sat down to write a letter to the manager (undelivered), protesting mightily about the delay and his broken promise that a room would be available at two o'clock. "Attention Manager," she wrote.

> We spent the entire morning and the sum of some rupees going to the American Embassy and obtaining the letter you requested. . . . An additional annoyance was the fact that you directed us to the wrong bus to take there and it was necessary for us to take a taxi in order to find our way. We find that the necessity of having a room and a proper place to rest after our long and tiring journey to New Delhi is too pressing, and we are unable to waste any more of our energies waiting for your presence. We are therefore leaving.

Whatever satisfaction an indignant departure might have afforded, as they were also waiting for Allen and Peter, they were not actually able to leave. At ten-thirty, finally rested and shampooed, Joanne opened the door to the more wild and disheveled Allen Ginsberg and Peter Orlovsky.

It was an emotional reunion, made even more so by the fact that both Allen and Peter were high as kites. With the help of Mr. Jain and his jewelry circle, Allen and Peter had managed to score some morphine after less than a week in Delhi, though they had yet to visit an opium den. Nor had they made it to a museum or historic site. And rather than looking up intellectuals or studying their guidebooks, Allen and Peter relied on shopkeepers to serve as their guides to the city. Nonetheless, their unschooled enthusiasm for India was contagious, and the four stayed up so late talking that Allen and Peter were obliged to spend the night.

RISHIKESH WAS THE GATEWAY TO HEAVEN. There the mountains hover above the town like a huddle of gods. For nearly all of recorded history, the area around Hardwar and Rishikesh had sheltered hundreds of rishis—yogis, holy men, and ascetics, all drawn to the place where the Ganges first descended from the heavenly gorge of the Himalayas, cascading down Shiva's crown of hair to make a dramatic entrance to the Gangetic Plain. The two towns were part of a chain of auspicious sites along the foothills of the Himalayas that catered to genteel middle-class Hindu pilgrims on holiday, naked, ash-smeared holy men on perpetual pilgrimage, and orange-robed sannyasi with shaved skulls and alms bowls. More recently, but no less welcome, rootless Westerners seeking enlightenment had made an appearance. Allen could hardly have hit upon a more auspicious place to begin his search for a teacher if he'd planned the trip himself.

After a long bus ride from Delhi to Hardwar and then a shorter one from Hardwar to Rishikesh, the four walked into the main hall of the prominent Yoga-Vedanta Forest Academy, arriving at the end of evening darshan. They joined an audience of American girls wearing saris sitting cross-legged before a visibly infirm, very large, and smiling guru. He was lying out on a couch in a large camel-hair coat surrounded by stacks of cardboard cutouts of himself. It was the eve of Shivaratri, the night of Shiva, and the preparations for the *puja* were everywhere evident. They were given beds for the night but were told their room would be needed the following day to house the expected onslaught of pilgrims. In the audience hall, Gary couldn't help but note that none of the Americans were sitting in the proper meditation posture.

Swami Shivananda, a Tamil, had been a hardworking doctor in Malaysia before becoming a sannyasi, or "world renouncer." After traveling all over India, including stays with Aurobindo and Ramana Maharshi (he danced and sang devotional songs for Maharshi's birthday), he settled in Rishikesh in a small cow shed. For many years, he tended to the illnesses of his fellow sannyasis, traipsing from mountain hut to cave to massage their cramped hermit legs. Orthodox Hindus, perhaps envious of his success in attracting a worldwide following, spread rumors that he was actually a former police official, entirely innocent of Sanskrit, the language of God. In 1936, he founded the Divine Life Society, an eye hospital, and set up the Yoga-Vedanta Forest Academy. He sent one acolyte off to California to establish more Shivananda Vedanta centers, each teaching a simple form of yoga based on Vedic metaphysics. He, in turn, set about answering his followers' heartfelt spiritual inquiries with a series of teachings. He wrote some 386 books "at electric speed," Allen wrote Jack. Jack had written the book on spontaneous prosody.

Perusing his book *Raja Yoga for Americans,* Gary pronounced that "nothing could be sounder, except perhaps Buddhism." In the book, Shivananda quoted Vivekenanda: "One must move from a sporadic experience of mystical experience to a cultivation of it in spiritual life. In India this is known as yoga, union of the individual with the divine." It is possible, of course, to stumble into it, but without the discipline of yoga, it is impure. The Vedantist test of the purity of this *samadhi* is simple, empirical. It must bear fruit for life. Only then is one pronounced enlightened, a sage, a prophet, and a saint. Gary noted that yoga was among Zen's antecedents. Burroughs, however, had denounced California Vedantists "without cavil" as peddling "a pack of horse shit." "A sorry bunch of psychic retreaters from the dubious human journey," he had written with the sour knowing of a former enthusiast. In his declining years, Shivananda greeted the continuing stream of searching questions on the nature of dualism and the self with little more than a benevolent "Om." Learning that Allen had come with three friends, Shivananda smiled and said, "Four is an auspicious number," giving him five rupees and a wink before being carried off by his attendants. Though vigilant for the con, Allen was charmed. He resolved to ask Shivananda where he might find a guru.

The full splendor of the setting became readily apparent in the morning, and after a purchase of Swami Shivananda ayurvedic tooth powder, they moved across the river to another ashram to make way for the incoming hordes. There they were delighted to discover that the resident yoga instructor at Swarg Ashram (Heavenly Abode Rest House) was named Swami Sri Shivalingam. Shiva's devotees know him by any number of names. He is the God With The Moon In His Hair. The Vagrant Mendicant. The Lord Who Is Half Woman. His shrines, however, all shelter a pillar of stone in varying sizes and shapes. This unapologetic phallus is called a lingam and is often paired with an equally evident yoni at its base, neatly capturing the union of the two creative forces of the universe. Swami Sri Shivalingam introduced them to a series of yoga asanas, demonstrating energetic eye rolling as well as elaborate tongue stretches. "None . . . dangerous," Gary noted with approval. Joanne found herself mesmerized by the contortions of Shivalingam's betel-stained, yonilike mouth. Peter, silently appraising his slim and sensuous frame, contemplated abandoning bodybuilding for yoga.

Their rooms were large and clean and empty of furniture. Allen found no difficulty in making himself at home with his air mattress and sheet. From his window he could see the Ganges, gentle, woodsy-looking foothills, and the formidable three-thousand-foot peak that rose authoritatively behind Shivananda's ashram on the other side of the river. After a bracing bath in the Ganges, they discovered three nearly naked men sitting cross-legged on deerskins under a nearby tree. Allen inspected them with frank curiosity, taking in their bloodshot eyes and the stonelike fixity of their posture. Each had a Shiva trident stuck in the ground to mark their sacred space. One had a deformed jaw, and another had a pet cow that promptly pinned Allen to a gate, as if to inspect him.

Could he take a vow of celibacy, Allen wondered, and learn to sit as still as those holy men? Peter was equally impressed by the sight. While Joanne laid out the washing, they walked up several thousand feet to get a closer look at the three-hundred-mile-long Himalayan range and scout out more holy men. In view of Mount Kailash, Gary mentioned that he could sit like that. Peter was incredulous. "Which brought home to me how alien the notion of meditation is to most Westerners," Gary noted.

The timing of their arrival in Rishikesh was excellent. The Shivaratri *puja* marked the opening of the month-long Kumbh Mela at Hardwar, the town they had passed through en route. With Allahabad, Nasik, and Ujjain, the Kumbh Mela at Hardwar was one of four bathing festivals held alternatively every three years in the shadows of the Himalayas, creating a twelve-year pilgrimage cycle. Sadhus making the rounds of these fairs would end their routes at the Jagannath temple in Puri before starting all over again. Leaving Joanne to read Allen's copy of Kipling's *Kim,* Gary, Peter, and Allen went off to attend the opening day ceremony. The festivities were launched with the blowing of conch shells, whereupon an entire army of naked, ash-smeared Nagas ran down a flower-strewn path and splashed into the Ganges.

Some of the Nagas were beautiful young boys with long matted hair, some were balding old men with big bellies, and some were powerful-looking men with hairy bottoms. Once upon a time, those Nagas who worshipped Shiva defeated the Nagas who worshipped Vishnu and that had kept the Vaishnavites from the waters at Hardwar altogether. Unlike more genial traveling mendicants, Nagas found swords and shields quite useful to keep the English at bay and when shaking down villages on their pilgrimage route. They were also sometimes known to be the hired guns of Hindu princes and had established dibs on first entry to the waters through force of arms. Once they were fully immersed, the river was ready to purify the sins of everyone else. Gary made note of their arrogant expressions and the fact that no sooner had they washed the ashes off their bodies than they made off for a temple and powdered themselves all over again. What was the point of *that*?

It was not the spectacle of the Nagas or even the pomp and display of those Mahants mounted on richly caparisoned elephants that held Allen's attention. Instead, he found his eye drawn to the bands of bald and weeping old ladies who followed the Nagas into the water, their orange robes flapping in the high winds and clouds of dust kicked up by the stampede of bare feet. The sight of these widows holding on to one another, singing heartrending songs, brought tears to his eyes with the memory of his dead mother. That night, he asked Swami Shivananda where he would find the teacher. Instead of an answer, the swami patted his chest and told him, "The only guru is your own heart. You will know him when you see him, because you will love him." Until then, he said, whenever Allen had a chance, it was a good idea to chant all the names of Vishnu. After the austerity and paranoia and loveless-ness of Tangier, Allen wrote Jack, somehow this message cheered him. That night, Joanne made note of the peculiar noise Allen and Peter made on their air mattresses every time they shifted. Like tidal waves, she wrote.

They made several more trips up the hill behind Swarg ash-ram, stumbling across tribal barley farms and wild monkeys and a cave community of sadhus. One of the caves, inhabited by a former college professor, was nicely fixed. A section of a nearby creek was partitioned with a special bathing section that Gary greatly admired, comparing its rustic touches with those of a Japanese teahouse. On the hike up, Gary busied himself trying to identify the trees and the Himalayan peaks beyond them. The sight of the white summits of Gangotri, Kedarnath, Badrinath, and Trisul had whetted his appetite to continue their journey on to the hill sta-tion of Almora to see Nanda Devi. Beyond that, he had in mind to travel to the northernmost edge of Kashmir and the Punjab to Pathankot and Dharamsala. He was ready to be on his way.

As for Allen, he would have liked to stay on at Hardwar for the entire month-long festival. He would have liked to hike up into the hills to find once again the beautiful boy with clear skin and long hair they'd met up on that first walk above their Heavenly

Abode. When they found him, he was sitting on a swing hanging from a flowering tree. The three sadhus sitting near the Ganges, the boy said, were just advertisements for the real deals sitting at higher elevations, hidden in the forests and caves. Perhaps this boy, this Indian quintessence of "a super southern californian longhair beat vegetarian hepcat," was the teacher Allen was looking for. Perhaps he could help him find his way up the mountain.

"Just how old are you?" Allen asked him.

"Earthly time is of no importance," he replied, swinging back and forth. Gary sneakily wrote down the impromptu poem that followed.

In our eternal journey
In the path of infinity.
Will shine the mercy of God
Giver of Freedom and Forgiveness

Quite beside himself and mystifying everyone, Allen exclaimed:
"And I will worship him by eating bananas!"

THE MORPHINE DREAM BEGAN at a hilltop cafeteria, much like Foster's in San Francisco, where Allen had once spent lonely hours waiting for assignations with Peter. Allen had taken the morphine in the early evening and, finding he had no appetite for dinner, went to bed early. Peter had also taken an ampoule but on top of that had a black pea of opium at ten. Even then, Joanne observed, censuring his extravagance, he still managed to eat an entire roast chicken.

She and Gary ate dinner alone, talking about the next day's bus journey to Kausani, the closest the Indian government allowed tourists to get to Tibet. Joanne was glad of the respite from Peter's and Allen's table manners. Allen gulped his food. And Peter set upon meals without waiting for anyone else to sit down. She imagined that it was only her black look that made him think twice before helping himself to seconds. Joanne sometimes felt a bit greedy herself, but she remained in command of her appetites. "Only because," she wrote, "I think of manners and control." If Allen and Peter could be roused, from Kausani they would see the famed Himalayan peaks of Trisul, the Nanda Devi, and the Nanda Kot. After eating opium, Peter tended to spend most of the night locked in the bathroom. None of this foretold a bright and early start.

Aluminum tray in hand, Allen went to line up for the vast array of cafeteria food on offer, angling for a spot close to the front. In the dream, he wondered how much it would cost and if he could get away with not paying. Peter had once again disappeared. And where was Gary? He and Joanne left to do some shopping and had never returned. It was worrisome, but hunger refocused him. After an unreasonably long wait, he realized with a start that it was now closing time and he was not getting any closer to the food. Suddenly, he asked himself: Just where had he been the last year? Half-asleep? Still dreaming, he found himself back in New York City.

The fears that accompany traveling, like the fears expressed in dreams, are not easily shaken. There is the fear of missing the boat, the train, the flight. There is the fear of losing your ticket or passport or all your money. There is the fear of becoming separated from your traveling companion. Finally, there is the fear of what will happen at home while you are away. Similarly, the dreams that accompany traveling have an uncanny way of pinpointing your true location. Perhaps, after endless delays and detours, you arrive safely at your destination with your wallet and papers intact, only to find that you have forgotten one crucial item. In a dream, you might find yourself turning around to go back to retrieve it. Then, with sinking heart, you realize you will have to begin your endless journey all over again. This realization is often enough to wake you, saving you the trouble.

In the morphine dream Allen Ginsberg had at the *dak* bungalow in Almora, he unpacked nearly everything he had brought with him to India to discover what he had remembered and what he had forgotten. As the peace and promise of India overtook him, the nightmare of New York and all that he had left behind returned, replaying not only his endless search for Peter that past fall in the Middle East and the anxious effort to connect with Gary and Joanne, but also the unhappy fates of those left behind on the Manhattan pier exactly one year before.

Finding himself back in New York City, Allen discovered once again that he was not yet ready to leave for India. Peter had disappeared with all his money. Gregory, who planned to join them for the trip to India, was once again waiting for him, with mounting hysteria, in Paris. Wandering lost through a vast passenger lounge at the Manhattan docks, Allen came upon a "square" TV family with an insufferably cute little girl dressed like a small furry animal. They were all ready to board the *Liberté* for India. But this was *his* ship, and he was going to miss it. Suddenly, he was back at the flat on East Second Street, being greeted by a crowd of friends. They had been waiting hours to see him off.

Lafcadio, tall and pale faced, was the first to step forward. After their long, fraught years together, in the dream Lafcadio finally recognized Allen and claimed him as both brother and lover. They embraced and wept in each other's arms, Allen covering his face with kisses. Looking into his eyes, he said a prayer. Suddenly, glancing upward, they both saw that the ceiling had opened above their heads. In the free blue sky, there was a Tibetan mandala within the soft funnel of a cloud. This was the sign, the long awaited miracle, Allen felt. Lafcadio felt it, too. The key to Lafcadio's eventual cure lay in India. Perhaps America's salvation could be found there as well.

"FRANKLY, I'm afraid she's going to hell fast. First the health goes, then the mind and the spirit, then the life is shot, how well do I know it." Kate Orlovsky sat at the kitchen table in the former chicken coop in Northport, Long Island, writing a long chatty letter to her sweet Petey-Pete. On July 8, 1961, he had celebrated his twenty-eighth birthday and she sent him her best wishes along with his monthly disability check from the army. He depended on it.

"Of course, she's just another little girl to you," she chided him, referring to Janine Pommy, whom he'd left behind. "I don't know where she is now or how. Can't you do something for her? Don't worry about Laffie or Marie. They're in the family and will be taken care of here, but that's as much as I can handle."

Acknowledging the photos he sent from Tangier, Kate told her son he looked like a weakling compared with those fatted calves Gregory and Allen. Looked just like his father, too, but there the resemblance ended. Petey, you are the passive sort, she said, not unkindly. Fancy having a son traveling halfway around the world, though. What savoir faire! Kate had longed to travel the world herself but got caught up in the marriage merry-go-round instead. Fat lot of good it did her, too. When she was twenty-eight, she had a string of kids and a husband to look after. She should have chucked them all, for the thanks she got. Those years seemed more like a bad dream than real life. But her Petey was a man, and more power to him for that. He had gumption, no doubt about it. She sent her best wishes to his faithful pals Allen and Gregory. As for Petey's news that he was setting off on his own, she thought he would miss Allen and told him so. Allen was like a father to him, and a better one than he had been to Laf at that.

The arrangements he had made for Lafcadio's care had fallen apart soon after their boat left the docks. Kate just called it like she saw it. Janine and Huncke were nowhere to be seen when his sister went by the new place on Sixth Street and discovered Laffie in bed surrounded by strangers. The apartment was papered wall to wall with his crayon drawings. Marie had put him on the train to Northport, but he'd become confused and ended up being delivered home by a squad car. Though he had no identification, the cops were well aware of where he lived.

Since the "so-called going-away party," Kate related, she'd had an earful from those neighbors who'd lain in their beds all night long listening to the "filthy disgusting language" that came from his friends. They were hardworking people, Kate said. "Well, I said it wouldn't happen again, but the eyes of the neighbors have been on me ever since." When Janine Pommy showed up asking if she could stay, after a couple of days, Kate had to send her packing. The girl "lakked experience in life . . .

"I know Janine loves you. What good it will do her, that I couldn't say. . . . Poor little thing. Little butterfly drawn to the lamplight. Singed wings and death in the dew of the dawn."

Kate had once had aspirations to write herself.

Once he recovered from hepatitis and cleared the drugs from his system, Lafcadio began talking a blue streak and shouting at the top of his lungs all hours of the day and night. "Am I dead? Am I alive? Who is Allen?" And at least one hundred times a day, he asked, "Where is Peter?" and, "When is he coming back?" and, "Tell Peter to come back before it is too late." Since drugs were so readily available where he was, Kate asked Peter to please send her some sedatives.

As Lafcadio's talk evolved from the "salad sandwich" sort, his life with Peter and Allen, from San Francisco to Mexico, from the apartment on East Second Street to the new one on East Sixth Street, all came out at high decibels. "The things he says!" Kate remarked, though being mostly deaf, she doubtless heard less than the neighbors. Don't you worry at all, she assured Peter repeatedly, just have a good time on your travels, she said. If thoughts of Lafcadio hadn't much crossed his mind, Kate's letters summoned an image of the brother he'd left behind, "clear as a drink of water."

That past November, when Peter seemed to have simply disappeared in the shifting sands of the Middle East, Kate's long-suffering neighbors called the police. Arriving at the chicken coop, the officers told Kate that they had come to take Lafcadio for an examination. Convinced her youngest was about to be committed, her nerves shot, Kate followed him to the precinct house with a knife under the coat on her arm. "Death allways seems beautifull to me, because the soul is released to free flight, we know not where," she had written. She hoped to spare Lafcadio, as she had been unable to spare his brother Julius, the living death of Central Islip State Hospital. Once the state got its hands on him, the private hospitals wouldn't touch him.

Only the first step into the unknown was scary, Kate had written Peter not long before the police arrived. So on November 3,

1961, with the utmost love in her heart and in full view of the police, she stabbed her youngest son in the chest.

Lafcadio survived and they were both committed.

BUT IT WASN'T LAFCADIO ORLOVSKY, or Janine Pommy, or even Carl Solomon whose fate was sealed by Allen Ginsberg's departure for India. Breaking off from Lafcadio's embrace, Allen turned to Elise Cowen. In his dream, she looked uncharacteristically gay and stylish but was evidently still desolate at the thought of him leaving. "Elise, you need to leave here," he said urgently. "Go where there is hope—if you can get passage later after I'm gone, get a ticket to join me in India. . . . I'll find you a place to live & study & enjoy. . . . I'll agree to let you stay near me at some town or ashram where you'll be in a family." He told her a more spiritual life, with yoga and companionship, was possible and would bring her peace. Rishikesh and Almora were not unlike the Catskills—readily accessible, only more spiritual.

"You will be OK," he said soothingly, before returning distractedly to his search for Peter.

In the months after Allen sailed, Elise Cowen had been sucked further into the drug-riddled night of the Lower East Side. Suddenly homeless or flopping at friends' houses, she carried her poetry notebook and few possessions in paper shopping bags. While interned at Bellevue for hepatitis she'd had a psychotic break, imagining that her consciousness had been taken over by atomic furies. After she nearly fell out a window searching the sky for enemy bombers, her parents moved her to a private hospital. Just after her release, she crashed through her family's living room window and fell seven stories to her death. There was no note.

Allen's dream of a haven for Elise in India came five weeks too late. Her death, when he came to hear of it, would confirm his deepest fear, the one he'd grappled with in the jungles of Peru under the unforgiving eye of the Vomiter. In his effort to relieve the suffering of those he cared for, he feared he would pass along his own nightmare of madness and a lonely, unmarked death instead. Elise had dutifully followed him into this dark.

Allen's cafeteria dream ended when he suddenly realized he still had the key to his apartment mailbox. He'd had it all along. In the box, he discovered a bankroll of money and all his unread mail sorted neatly. At last, too, Peter was found, so intent on retrieving a drug stash from underneath the floorboards, he had completely lost track of the time.

Gary, Joanne, Peter, and Allen made it to Kausani the following afternoon, traveling by a rusty dented bus. The Public Works Department bungalow they'd reserved faced out across another endlessly beautiful valley, the surrounding hillsides covered with blooming rhododendron and deodar pine. When the clouds broke up toward evening, a solid wall of white appeared abruptly before them, revealing the Himalayan horizon within fifty miles of their veranda. This was the Trisul–Nanda Devi–Nanda Kot ridge, stretching from Nepal and Tibet in the east to the Punjab in the west. At dawn, wrapped in shawls and furry Tibetan blankets, Allen, Peter, and Gary rose in darkness to watch the color of the mountains turn from a cold white blue to a furnacelike glow of red.

"Jai Ram!" Gary exclaimed, as the gods at last appeared to him.

THAT SAME MORNING, an Air India flight from Rome touched down in New Delhi exactly on time. On board were Jacqueline Bouvier Kennedy, looking ravishing in an electric pink suit, and her sister, Princess Lee Radziwill.

After World War II, the relationship between the newly independent Indian democracy and the newly empowered America got off to a sticky start. John Foster Dulles, secretary of state under Eisenhower, decided that Nehru's neutrality in the cold war was despicable, and Pakistan quickly became America's favored ally. Like the newly launched Peace Corps program, Jackie's well-timed goodwill trip was typical of the Kennedy administration's charm assault on India. Yet the visit had been postponed twice, and the most recent postponement had been announced just two weeks before, throwing the carefully plotted twenty-two-day itinerary into utter disarray.

The final trip was whittled down to just two weeks, with eleven days in India and three in Pakistan. With the confused air she equated with femininity, Letitia Baldrige, Jackie's social secretary, hinted that illness was the reason for the postponement. If the American ambassador John Kenneth Galbraith suspected, as the Indian government did, that the delay was payback for India's recent appropriation of Goa from the Portuguese, he gallantly held his tongue and accepted the official diagnosis of sinus trouble. Nehru of course forgave her, Galbraith reported; he was halfway in love with her already. Nehru told him he thought of himself as the last Englishman to rule India.

Yet the rest of India also awaited the *Amriki rani* with eagerness. Even the suspicious Krishna Menon was there on the tarmac. ("I have rarely encountered a politician who is more completely exempt from the wish to be loved," Galbraith quipped.) The week following her arrival, there were photographs of Jackie at the Taj Mahal, Jackie sailing down the Ganges in Benares on a launch covered with marigolds, Jackie listening politely to a Buddhist ceremony at Sarnath, Jackie with the two tiger cubs bound for the National Zoo in Washington, D.C. NBC filmed an hour-long spectacular on her tour. In expectation of the First Lady's stopover, the Maharaja of Mysore had instructed his mahouts to train an elephant to garland Jackie with marigolds when she arrived at his palace. The Maharaja of Jaipur planned a similarly elaborate welcome. He and his flamboyant son "Bubbles" were part of the same jet-set circle as Lee Radziwill.

While many of the Rajput princes had been left bereft and bankrupt by the departure of the British, the Maharaja of Jaipur had moved on. He was the first to see the potential of turning palaces into luxury hotels, and Jackie's visit found him in high gear. He had scheduled rounds of polo and cocktail parties as well as a midnight tour of the city palace, the grandest and most noteworthy of his domiciles and recently refurbished. The high-ranking memsahibs of the British Raj had loved the prospect of Oriental spectacle. What other possible reason might the wife of the president of the United States have for visiting Jaipur if not to sample some of this deluxe imperial glamour? There was a bit of a tussle with the central government over the protocols of having her stay as his private guest, but the maharaja still considered himself a power to be reckoned with.

In the shuffling of her itinerary and the forty-seven separate schedule changes that accompanied it, Galbraith was sad to see that Calcutta and the southern parts of India would be jettisoned. He was less unhappy about the loss of Konark temple in Orissa. "Don't you think she's old enough?" JFK had asked, but the Indian government deemed the stone temple carvings far too sexually explicit for a woman unaccompanied by her husband. Mysore and the elephant trick were also scratched. Galbraith was disappointed. Americans rarely ventured off the Gangetic Plain and were thus deprived of the most attractive parts of the subcontinent. Krishna Menon, who considered the United States an even greater enemy than Pakistan, was of the opinion that Galbraith's enthusiasm for India was deeply suspect.

Though her press officer was under orders to develop a bad memory for clothing designers, the subject of Jackie's clothes was nearly always the lead, temporarily relegating the uproar over America's forthcoming nuclear tests to the back pages. Lord Bertrand Russell, in protest at both the Soviet and American abandonment of the Partial Test Ban Treaty, had asked Nehru to send the Indian fleet to the test waters in protest, but Nehru had demurred. In her appearance with the Maharaja of Jaipur, Jackie wore white gloves, a sleeveless and flared satin dress, and her signature bouffant, which made her a full head taller than the maharaja, despite his equally elaborate turban (she noted that one of its peacock feathers was crushed). It was rumored that she had arrived with several trunks' worth of Oleg Cassini gowns, and a minor scandal erupted when the Indian press ran a report that she had spent $200 on Benarsi silks in less than five minutes. Galbraith, taking responsibility for the misunderstanding over the price of the goods, confessed it couldn't have been more than ten seconds. Jackie's last stop was to see the Amber Palace in Jaipur, and the photos of her svelte figure, seated upon elaborately decked-out elephants circling the courtyard with the bare hills in the distance, were stunning.

"These are the pictures that will make the greatest impression in the United States," Galbraith noted resignedly in his diary, "need-less to say, [they] bear the least relation to India as it really is."

LYING ON HIS CHARPOY in the now familiar morphine haze, Ginsberg wondered why he'd come to Jaipur at all. He couldn't even blame Gary, who'd put off the trip to Dharamsala to see the Dalai Lama (and view the Himalayas from yet another angle), in order to visit this historic seat of medieval glory. It had been his idea to write the Maharaja of Bundi from Delhi, requesting the kind of princely hospitality afforded Jackie for America's most famous poet. There'd been no reply, and they ended up traveling instead to Jaipur and staying in a tourist bungalow. After three days traipsing about the Amber Fort, looking at the pink-tinted palaces and the desolate and thorny hills, he'd had enough.

On the stopover in Delhi, Allen found a letter from Gregory waiting for him at the American Express office. In November 1961, Gregory had returned to New York City for his first trip home since he'd left for Europe four years before. Ted Wilentz, the co-proprietor of the 8th Street Bookshop, had written Allen of his unexpected arrival, fresh off the boat, to pick up his mail and royalty checks. Allen's father had reported that Gregory had reclaimed his LPs and whatever papers Allen had packed away in the family attic. In his letter, Gregory wrote that his plan to share an apartment with his own father was a bust. He had promised to get him out of his sordid apartment, and then he couldn't bring himself to go back, finding they had nothing to say to each other. He reported Jack was drinking and out of his mind. As for him-self, Gregory was once again miserable, unable to write and in the grip of "Mr. Death." He had sold all his possessions to pay for the privilege of shooting heroin with Hope's favorite hipster, Stanley Gould.

All fall, Gregory's letters from London had evoked the pain and heavy weight of his financial debt to Allen, plumbing the depths of his sense of obligation and guilt. By the time he'd ar-rived in New York, he was in somewhat lighter spirits, though he sent no check to justify his sense of relief. Perhaps he considered his suffering on Allen's account sufficient repayment, and the question of money didn't arise, except obliquely. "I always laugh when I think of you entering India, I have two imaginary holy men sitting on rock, eyeing you as you leave gangplank, one saying to the other: 'Boy, here comes a live one.'" As for the prospect of joining him there, Gregory was still haunted by his experience of Mexico. He imagined India as unpleasantly hot and brimming with poverty and disease, but with fantastic amber sunsets. He still wanted to come, he claimed, but didn't say when. In closing, he mentioned that he'd heard Hope was back in India, that he had somehow missed her in New York. It seemed this was the real reason for his letter: "Do inquire around for her please, and see her, and tell me all about her, your friend. Love, Gregory."

Allen hadn't been feeling at all well. He'd been flu-ish, and in Jaipur his kidney troubles had flared. Everyone's stomachs were crampy. Just over a week before, he'd seen a man drop dead in a busy marketplace. And that was after the gruesome sight of a coolie's dismembered limbs being collected by a sweeper on the railway tracks. Assuming he lived to see the millennium at age seventy-four, the halfway point of his life was just over a month away, and he felt he had to account for himself. Flat on his back, staring into the dark, and sweating under a thin film of insect re-pellent, he couldn't help but recall his lonely midnight vigil in Denver, hollow-eyed from Benzedrine, waiting for Neal. Or the mosquito-infested nightmare in the Peruvian jungle, where, pinned by the *ayahuasca,* he contemplated the Vomiter's skull with a towel over his face. Peter was sleeping on his side in the next charpoy, still faithful, but he never felt so alone. He had been in India a month, and already he was dispirited. His fingers restlessly thrummed the charpoy as he tried to calm himself.

The most likely daily practice he could take up was sitting and meditating in the lotus posture. Could he summon the required discipline even for that? Every time he sat, he was stricken by a sense of absurdity. Drugs helped his twitching, but he was also racked with impatience, and his fingers ached to answer letters. He wanted enlightenment *now,* was that asking for too much? It was all too easy for him to see himself back in New York City arranging the cheap Tantric figurines he'd bought in Delhi—Tara, Avalokiteswara, Ganesh, Krishna, Shiva, Kali astride Shiva—and typing up his travel notes for posterity while the hair on the top of his head thinned.

On the same day that Gregory wrote his letter, *Time* magazine had run an article on the American poetry scene. According to *Time,* Robert Lowell, Elizabeth Bishop, Adrienne Rich, and Theodore Roethke were good poets, "but to say they are the best of the postwar period is not to say much." Once more, the Beats provided the real copy, with or without a new book to pin it on.

They prefer to wear beards and blue jeans, avoid soap and water, live in dingy tenements or, weather permitting, take to the road as holy hoboes, pilgrims to nowhere. Most of them adore Negroes, junkies, jazzmen and Zen. The more extreme profess to smoke pot, eat peyote, sniff heroin, practice perversion.

Among the Beats, visions induced by drugs were common, but even God was upstaged by sex, and sex was in turn trumped by "excrement." "They sprinkle it like Holy Water; they spread it like the Gospel truth." A photo of Allen, clean-shaven in a suit and tie, earnest in his horn-rims, was captioned "Calculated Squalor." "Howl" was deigned "an interminable sewer of a poem that sucks in all the fraudulence, malignity and unmeaning slime of modern life and spews them with tremendous momentum into the reader's mind." Joanne felt the review was an "unnecessarily vicious" attack on Allen.

Allen Ginsberg lay in a sweat-drenched puddle of suffering. He had so wanted to be a saint, but what was he supposed to suffer for? Of course, there was the rest of India to see, and then on to England, northern Europe, then Russia and China. In another decade or so, he would have circled the globe, his father and the rest of his New Jersey relatives would be dead, and finally, his friendship with the "boys of yore" quite likely burned out. And then what? He beseeched the darkened pages of his journal. Kali! Krishna! Coyote!

Allah! Christ! Jaweh! Ram! Buddha! Brahma! Could *anyone* hear him? Saints and sadhus, *rishis* and all compassionate ones, he begged, "What's to be done with my life which has lost its idea?"

——is Jack drunk? Is Neal still aware of me? Gregory yakking? Bill mad at me? Am I even here to myself? I daren't write it all down, it's too shameful & boring now & I haven't the energy to make a great passional autobiography of it all——for who's all that autobiography for if it doesn't deliver heaven or reasonable equivalent? Young kids after the movies?

He fell into a dream where Bill, sitting at his desk in a French rooming house, appeared to him, Messiah-like. He'd had to banish the most hateful of his two English admirers, Burroughs admitted: "Too much in my hair." Allen wanted to ask about the other one but decided not to, content that Bill was being friendly. Meanwhile, some nerve-racked girl from New York City had become Bill's disciple and was unrolling a mat and plumping a pillow Oriental style in preparation for *darshan*.

DHARAMSALA was an old hill station, set under the crags of the Dhauladhar range, whose upper reaches were known only to mountain goats. On first appearance, the town seemed merely a miscellany of woods, farms, falls, and dwellings haphazardly arranged on the hillside. On closer view, the Trappist monk Thomas Merton decided that Dharamsala was as carefully realized as a thangka painting. As with a thangka, it was necessary to know something of Tibetan cosmology in order to understand what it was you were looking at. To orient yourself in the space of this valley, it helped to visit the *rinpoches* and *tulkus* in the folds of its hills. Seated in shrines and illuminated by butter lamps, each teacher was the center of a circle of thangkas, rugs, and images. And each glowing hut, in turn, was itself arranged around the central presence of the Dalai Lama. When Merton visited several years after Allen Ginsberg, he noted that whatever the fate of Tibet in the aftermath of the Chinese invasion, on this hill the light of dharma would not be readily extinguished.

Like thangkas, which depict the universe of the Buddhas and their many faces and manifestations, mandalas are meditation aids. Each mandala depicts the celestial palace of a particular Buddha and the inner architecture of his mind. The floor plan, presented in a painting or in colored sand, is designed to channel the mind of an initiate first to view and then to enter the mind of the presiding deity into whose practice he is being initiated. Each wing of the palace represents a separate aspect of that Buddha's enlightenment. Though the lama sits on his throne with his pupil before him, the latter imagines that the lama is the deity at the center of the mandala and that he, the disciple, is being initiated within that sacred space.

The key to understanding any single mandala lies with the canon of the earliest scriptures of the Buddhist Tantra. In the ninth century, the Indian Buddhist Padmasambhava had brought them to Tibet, translating them from Sanskrit. Many volumes of Tibetan commentary followed, perfecting and extending the art of meditation. Where the later Mahayana Buddhists generally regard the attainment of enlightenment as a process that takes many lifetimes to complete, the medieval Tantric view offered an express lane to the state of Buddhahood in just one or two. The subtle yogic meditation practices required, however, were undertaken only with the nimble guidance of a teacher who has himself ascended the craggy slopes of these higher spiritual planes. Only a master could elucidate the tricky paths, and only a master could determine that an aspirant was fully prepared for the climb.

It was one thing for a trained *rinpoche* to make such a call when the disciple was Tibetan, but even the Dalai Lama had to contend with a number of blue-haired ladies in pants asking lots of silly questions. He was sensitive to Western misconceptions about Tibetan mysticism and the myths surrounding it. Conversely, with the possible exception of his official interpreter, Sonam Kazi Topgay, most of his advisers were dependent upon *Reader's Digest* and *Time* for information about the world outside the walls of their redoubt. They were incapable of screening visitors. So just as the world was beginning to grapple with a wisdom tradition that had only recently come down off the Tibetan plateau, equally, there had been little in their ancient texts to prepare the entourage of His Holiness for the arrival of four poets from America.

The morning of their audience with the Dalai Lama, Gary Snyder rose alone and climbed to the timberline above the Triund Forest Lodge, where they were staying, eighteen kilometers from Dharamsala. It was his last full day in the Himalayas. The next day they would take a bus to Pathankot, where they would board the morning express train for Bombay, with a side trip to Aurangabad to take in the cave temples and monasteries. From Bombay, he and Joanne would begin the long boat journey back to Japan. Just beyond the timberline, about five kilometers from the forest lodge, Gary came to the wide white expanse of the snowfield that led directly to the summit of Dhaulagiri. He wanted to see how close he could get. In anticipation, he'd bought a steel-tipped cane in the village, the nearest thing to an ice ax he could find.

Gary Snyder had grown up just north of Seattle, surrounded by mountains and rivers. His father's farm was in the shadow of Mount Rainier and the Cascades, and on days when the fog lifted, he could see the Olympic range across Puget Sound. In the forests of his boyhood, he would come across Indians with spears stand-ing motionless on slender planks above the Columbia River, patiently awaiting salmon. When he was twelve, he discovered a Chinese landscape painting in the Seattle Art Museum in which he recognized the tall misted pines, waterfalls, and mountain-scapes of the Pacific Northwest. His curiosity about the tightly braided tradition behind the painting led him to Chinese poetry, Ch'an Buddhism, and the Zen Institute in Kyoto. In Zen he un-dertook a spiritual practice that made no promise of liberation but insisted upon the discipline of daily meditation. In Kyoto he learned: You had to try. And for years he had stood there, spear in hand, staring into the water. Now again he stood, peering at the snowfield and the summit beyond, steel-tipped cane in his grip.

· · ·

LATER IN THE DAY, they would be greeted at the fenced compound of His Holiness by Sonam Kazi, a compact man dressed neatly in Western clothing. The king of Sikkim had made an unannounced visit, Kazi explained, to ask the twenty-seven-year-old Dalai Lama for a blessing on his forthcoming marriage to a Sarah Lawrence girl. They would have to wait. Allen, Peter, Gary, and Joanne passed the time with Sonam Kazi, who, it developed, was also from Sikkim, where his father was a powerful feudal landholder. After leaving St. Stephen's College in Delhi, Kazi had traveled to Lhasa to study with masters of Nyingma sect of Tibetan Buddhism, the most ancient of Tibetan Buddhist orders. Until the Chinese invaded a year after his arrival, Sonam Kazi found Tibet a heaven on earth. He stayed for five years, then left to work as a Tibetan translator for Pandit Nehru.

Among his teachers in Lhasa was a lama named Dudjom Rinpoche, the most revered living repository of the Nyingma tradition. Dudjom had anticipated the arrival of the Chinese, he said, and managed to smuggle his library of sacred texts out of Tibet to the hill station of Kalimpong. Dudjom Rinpoche's own root teacher had prepared him with his prophecy that he would spread Nyingma to every continent. Later, after the Chinese destroyed six of the main Nyingma monasteries, Dudjom Rinpoche's library became the sole relic of Padmasambhava's original translations. By the time the king of Sikkim and his affianced had taken leave of His Holiness, Sonam Kazi had convinced Allen to make a trip to Kalimpong to receive oral transmission from Dudjom Rinpoche himself.

"If you take LSD, can you see what's in that briefcase?" Lounging on his velvet couch like an overgrown schoolboy, His Holiness the Dalai Lama smiled mischievously. Though he listened closely to Peter's and Allen's accounts of experiments with drugs, he didn't really believe that drugs were very useful. In fact, though the psychic states drugs achieved were real enough, drugs themselves were a distraction, doing little to address the central problem of the ego, the source of all spiritual anguish and ignorance.

But Allen persisted. He wanted to know how drug states corresponded to the spiritual states achieved by meditation. He offered to have Timothy Leary send him some psilocybin. His Holiness seemed agreeable, if only because it seemed to mean so much to him and he was sincerely interested in scientific experiments. Then Allen proposed to recite "Howl." Though Sonam Kazi's gifts as an interpreter were unquestioned, he was somehow dissuaded.

Allen could be something of a village explainer, and Gary was eventually obliged to interrupt him midmonologue. "The inside of your mind," he noted in a peremptory manner, "is just as boring as everyone else's," so was it really necessary to go on so? The awkward moment was quickly followed by a mano a mano exchange between Gary and the Dalai Lama. The two compared Tibetan posture and breathing techniques with those of Zen. Gary did a demonstration.

"Couldn't there be another posture of meditation for Westerners?" Joanne piped up. The Dalai Lama looked puzzled and turned to Sonam Kazi. He said something in Tibetan.

"It's not a matter of national custom," the Dalai Lama pronounced. Gary was impressed. An excellent reply, he thought. Allen interrupted.

"How many hours of meditation do you do a day?"

"Me? I never meditate, I don't have to."

If His Holiness was teasing him, Allen missed it. He was thrilled with this answer, Joanne reported. "[Allen] wants to get instantly enlightened and can't stand sitting down," she wrote a friend back home. "He came to India to find a spiritual teacher. But I think he actually believes he knows it all, but just wishes he *Felt* better about it."

EARLIER THAT MORNING, just as Gary reached the timberline, it had begun to snow. Not far out into the snowfield, the wind picked up strength, and even with the steel-tipped cane, it was hard to keep upright. Before long, snow coated one side of his body, and the Dhauladhar range, which had seemed close and clear from the hill where they were staying, disappeared from view. Reluctantly, Gary started back. On the way, he passed a stone platform daubed with faded color. There, hidden beneath two cliffs, a rusty trident marked the lonely nook where a Shiva ascetic had once sat.

Was the abandoned trident a memorial to one man's lifetime of determined austerity? Was it a testament to his having willed himself to the highest station of self-oblivion, unsheltered by a Bo tree's green leaves? Or had he simply given up, left the mountain, and returned to live out a life in the gentler slopes of the valley?

JOANNE STAYED BEHIND to wash her black drip-dry dress before the water cut off at eleven. They had left the cool hills of Dharamsala for the hot plains, and after six days spent exploring the caves of Sanchi, Ajanta, and Ellora, she'd seen enough of Buddhist monasteries and Hindu cave temples. While the caves at Sanchi had produced some handsome rubbings, she found those at Ajanta and Ellora impressive but depressing. The endless rooms cut out of the raw rock of a cliff were populated by hundreds of ponderous Buddhas and crowds of Hindu gods and goddesses. The hectoring tour guide with an affected English accent had been the last straw. Basically, she wrote her friend Nemi, she found Indians "vile and bad tempered beyond Belief."

> Unfortunately they don't understand fuck & get your shiteating asshole hands off my luggage. . . . And when they're not trying to shine your shoes as you walk along or stuff a baby in your face through a train window or trample you to death . . . they are acting unbearable hoipoloi and asking you what part of the "states" you're from, and telling you how screwingly SPIRItual they all are, and how they have two transistor radios in the family.

Nemi, back home in California having an affair with a married veterinarian—"Has his wife had kittens yet? Har Har"—was not to worry. India hadn't changed her, Joanne still hated everybody.

"The thing is, I am sounding rather bitter because its been *years* since I've been able to get any wild martini *attention*." There were no cocktail parties in India, there wasn't even booze. While Allen and Gary argued endlessly about drugs and religious experience, Joanne was dazzled by a vision of herself in smart green toreador pants and Tibetan jewelry, featured as an up-and-coming literary light in *Time* magazine. Recently, however, while washing up at a sink in a ladies' retiring room, an old woman had confronted her with the stationmaster, who had asked her if she was, in fact, a woman. That and the endless parade of Hindu goddesses with full moon breasts were just too much. Joanne wanted fame on her own laundered terms. India demanded accommodations. "I have discovered, by the way, that ironing is not really necessary, you just tell everyone that you just got up from a nap." Before *Time* came knocking, she wanted to try Nemi's recipe for a rose petal beauty regimen.

While Joanne studied her crow's-feet in the guesthouse mirror, Allen was listening to Gary chant "the Sutra of the Perfection of Wisdom of the Diamond that Cuts Through Illusion" into the cool darkness of an ancient Buddhist prayer hall at Ellora. Composed in Sanskrit a millennium before, the Diamond Sutra was a sermon given by the Buddha in a grove of trees not far from the Indian city of Sravasti. The chant had since chimed in monasteries in Tibet and China and was a central tenet of Zen practice. Though Allen thought Gary took himself too seriously, there was something inescapably awe-inspiring hearing the Diamond Sutra chanted in his "tibetan-noh play sepulchral voice" and echoing in the cave at Ellora.

How can one instruct a man who desires to learn the path of a bodhisattva? the monk Subhuti asks in the Diamond Sutra. "A bodhisattva should be detached from all desires," the Buddha replies, whether the desire derives from the senses or from the desire to lead the multitudes to enlightenment. A bodhisattva's love is infinite and cannot be limited by attachment or ambition. "When love is infinite its merits are incalculable." Through Subhuti's questions and the Buddha's replies, the path to detachment is gradually revealed.

But detachment was difficult. The lack of detachment was, for Joanne, a clear failing. But she could not help herself. After six weeks of traveling, Allen amazed and appalled her with his unyielding ego, his red nylon socks, and the curly hair that crawled up his neck. One evening, she had listened to him compare the virtues of two different "Howl" recordings and the difficulty of choosing between them, wondering aloud if the final LP shouldn't have both. She waited for Gary to puncture this fatuousness, but when he didn't even seem to register it, she volunteered that she wouldn't want to hear "Howl" twice. It might have come out rather more brutally than she meant it, as Allen looked as if the earth had given way. This had surprised her. Gary was not so wobbly. This led her to conclude that Allen had a puffed-up ego that was somehow saddled with an equally impressive insecurity. The thought gave her a kick of self-confidence.

Gary's chanting lasted about forty minutes. Afterward, he expounded at length on Zen practice, and Allen was beginning to think he had the hang of it. Gary had given him an example of a real tricky koan involving a man hanging on to a tree branch with his mouth. If a person on the ground asks him, "What is the meaning of those who are coming from the West?" and he doesn't answer, he is evading the question. If he answers, he will fall and lose his life. Once you finished working out the koans, Allen explained to Jack, each one delineating a precise subjective mental state, then you can compare notes with your fellow Zen masters. "Sounds like a simple, persevering, rigid & well worked out scheme," Allen wrote. Obviously, such a practice required time-consuming mental exercises, not to mention learning Japanese and, of course, sitting stone still for hours.

Yet Allen's attention wandered to the neighboring Hindu cave temples. Michelangelo's frescoes paled beside the art he found in multistoried Kailash temple, the single largest monolith in the world. What could compete with dancing Shivas twenty feet tall? Skull-bedecked, tongue-lolling Kalis?

"How can da Vinci beat an elephant on a mouse?"

· · ·

NOT LONG AFTER THEIR MARRIAGE, Joanne had come across a note in Gary's journal that said: "And when you read this Joanne Kyger, as you certainly will . . ." She hadn't hesitated to read further. Now she took advantage of her time alone to read Allen's and Peter's journals. Opening Allen's first, she found a letter from Ferlinghetti in which he inquired about Allen's plan to meet up with Gary. It appeared that Ferlinghetti had been sharing Allen's shifting itinerary with the staff at City Lights all winter. Ted Wilentz had been doing the same with the staff and customers at the 8th Street Bookshop in the Village, and there was now a great deal of anticipation on both coasts about the outcome of Allen and Gary's trip together, as if she weren't along as well. Joanne wrote her friend Nemi that an editor at Grove had wanted to include some of her poems in his forthcoming poetry anthology but had asked *Gary* to send her bio.

At times her life seemed a conspiracy of men talking above her head.

Perhaps her resentment arose because Allen felt so free to bandy about his insecurities. She had been living in Japan for two years trying to sit *zazen,* to live a life of spiritual discipline, and he had only just begun and already it sounded as if he were on the verge of giving up. She was married to a man who not only believed he was a genius, but most likely was. She opened Allen's journal. There was a graphic account of his visit to a Delhi opium den, but she was more interested in his dark night of the soul in Jaipur. She copied Allen's account into her own journal before turning to read Peter's.

"The Indians for their own perverse reasons seem to adore him," she wrote Nemi. With a T-shirt that didn't come close to covering his stomach, and holes in his tennis shoes, Peter was a sight. Yet despite the fact that he spent much of his time in an opium trance behind a curtain of hair, he was the only one who seemed to register her existence and to grant her some measure of clout. "I look at Joann—by silent eye contact of minds we fix past sex intimacy feeling," Peter had written in his journal,

> I then start to think about Gary: is that why he always stays
> close to her—if so then that seems like a compromise on
> his part—the unwritten law between them whereby Joann
> says: Stay around me or I'll sleep with someone else—
> Gary: OK. Will do.

She took all this down in her own journal.

Three days later, they were welcomed to Pupul Jayakar's gra-
cious home in the posh Malabar Hill neighorhood of Bombay.
Though Ginsberg hadn't seen Jayakar since their dinner at the
Chinese restaurant in New York City over two years before, she
had taken them all in. Sinking down deep into her crisp white
sheets, her black dress handed off to a maidservant to wash,
Joanne had a dream in which the Mother of Pondicherry, despite
her claims of immortality, had died. The next day, a cascade of
personal slights descended. A Kansas couple in the khadi shop,
upon learning Joanne lived in Kyoto, asked if she knew Gary Snyder. When she ventured a mild criticism of Gandhi, Maurice Frydman, a friend of Pupul Jayakar's and one of Gandhi's earliest
followers, had told her she was an ant shouting at a mountain.
She'd wanted to tell him that *he* was the damn ant and *she* was the
mountain. When Pupul's daughter brought in the gramophone so
that the men could sit and listen to Indian classical music records,
they waved away her persistent offer of a cold drink. "But what
about me?" Joanne thought, sitting a few feet away, ignored and
thirsty.

It hadn't taken long for the news that the author of "that sen-
sational poem 'Howl,' by which every beatnik swears," was staying at Pupul Jayakar's house. A parade of writers and journalists
arrived to talk to Allen. Ginsberg, with his constant disquisitions
on Beat poetry, had forced her to quit the room when a young
writer showed up to meet him on a quiet Sunday afternoon, waking them all from their naps. Perhaps because the end of the trip
was in sight, Joanne became undone.

"What we are trying to do in America to-day is to create a new
prosody," Allen pontificated. "The roots of this kind of poetry go

back to the Red Indians and to Jazz, which is the one original flower of American civilization. . . .

"Another technical innovation," he continued, "is the cut-up method introduced by William Seward Burroughs. A whole set of lines from one part of the poem is transposed elsewhere in the body of the poem. This is done to counteract any conscious arrangement of the lines. . . ."

"Doesn't this violate the understanding of the poem?" the young man asked worriedly.

"Well, if the poem has anything to say, if it is written from an inner conviction, it has to come off," Allen responded, as if he never questioned his own inner conviction. When the man invited him to read his poems for a small gathering on the terrace of a flat on Warden Road, Allen asked Gary and Peter to join him. Joanne hadn't the nerve to question this lineup.

Instead, she had fixed Allen with a nasty glare and retreated behind the locked door of the bathroom, wondering if he'd even noticed. Washing his filthy hair out of her big pink comb in the sink, she found herself so choked with anger, she could barely speak. She briefly considered flinging herself down on the floor but chose to slip out of the house instead, making her way down the tree-lined streets to the Arabian Sea. There the familiar tang of ocean air calmed her, bringing back college memories of Santa Barbara. She was ready to leave India.

A few days later, she would suffer through Peter intoning his poems in a monotonal frenzy, puffing on a string of bidis, his hair resembling a bird's nest. Allen would read "Kaddish" in his too short shorts and red nylon socks, removing his sneakers before he started. And Gary would round off the evening sitting in his lotus pose on the floor to recite. Looking at her own poems in the manuscript of *The Tapestry and the Web,* Joanne found she had lost the thread of her work, one that would take her down a new corridor. Everything just stopped.

If I should weep
They would never know

and so I walked
silently
shrugging off hands
in treacherous places

           wanting to fall

"The difficulty is Ego," she wrote in her journal. "And if I give up, I'll walk into the ocean and swallow it into myself."

FOR MANY YEARS, the young Asoke Sarkar lacked for nothing. Nagendra Nath and Umashasi strove to fill his every desire. His home, a flat in a massive four-story English residence filled with Chinese, German, Jewish, and Anglo-Indian families, was near the center of Calcutta, not far from the Massage & Bath Clinic Ltd. Illustrious visitors were in constant attendance. One maharaja, at nearly five hundred pounds, was a frequent client and a close family friend. One of his ministers often used to take the young Asoke for drives in his motorcar. Raja Prabhat Barua of Assam was another regular visitor.

Nor had his father, Nagendra Nath, abandoned his spiritual welfare. To the family worship of the Hindu gods Shiva and Kali, Krishna and Rama, he added the Buddha, Jesus, Sri Ramakrishna, the Theosophist Annie Besant, and, inevitably, the mystic Chaitanya. Young Asoke's earliest memories were of the handsome parade of Buddhist and Ramakrishnan sannyasis, Christian ministers, and Theosophists who passed through the family residence. Many of the saints who visited confirmed the promise of the family astrologer. Asoke was destined for great and mystical purposes.

Particularly welcome were the Vaishnavites. It was said that Sri Chaitanya Mahaprabhu had begun his career as an orthodox Brahmin when he met a devotee of Krishna. Thereupon he abandoned the subtleties of Sanskrit grammar and founded a cult of ecstatic Krishna worship. An incarnation of Vishnu, Krishna was the blue-tinged and naughty boy-god, trouncer of the snake king and seducer of dairy maids. The blue cowherd appeared to Chaitanya in a magnificent vision, spinning in the sky with his flute to his lips, his robes whipping as clouds gathered around him. As the winds began to roar with his laughter, the glitter of his eyes played with the lightning. Chaitanya upended all caste distinctions in leading his devotees, men and women, householders and monks, through the streets of his home in Nabadwip in Bengal, singing and dancing and shouting Krishna's name. The songs and poetry written by Chaitanya's followers told and retold the story of Krishna's cunning ploys to win the love of cowgirls of Brindaban. But it was the love of Radha, with her passionate longing for Krishna's return, that brought tears to the devotees' eyes. Such longing was an act of worship; their poetry was the poetry of unrequited, inaccessible love.

Even in the presence of such illustrious company, abundant wisdom, and mystic bliss, the Sarkar home was far from peaceful. Despite her formidable intellect, despite the fact that Nagendra Nath was a loyal husband and a good provider, Umashasi could not rid her mind of the specter of the wealthy Jewess who had preceded her in her husband's affections. She could not believe that her husband did not still nurture a love for Marie in some corner of his heart. The more Nagendra Nath protested, the more suspicious Umashasi became. When Asoke misbehaved, she would say to him:

"You are not my son—you are that Jewish woman's son."

SIPPING PERCOLATED COFFEE at a table with a view of the Gateway of India, Allen tried to ride out his feeling of impatience. Peter's frequent interruptions kept hijacking his conversation with the reporter from *Illustrated Weekly of India*. Allen had wanted to discuss the French lineage of the Beats and elaborate on his reasons for coming to India. The interviewer was clearly impressed by his grasp of Hinduism and had some searching questions. Yet Peter would suddenly make a pronouncement that often seemed to parody the idea Allen had been in the midst of exploring.

In Bombay, Allen and Peter were assumed to be some sort of Western holy men. Peter, encouraged by his Indian admirers, had become quite expansive. He would wander happily around curio shops in nothing more than a torn undershirt and drawstring churidars rolled up to his knees, humming Bach. Peter was generally indifferent to social niceties, and while Allen resisted the temptation to explain Peter's eccentricities, he nonetheless felt unpleasantly on the defensive.

"There is plenty of poetry in a madhouse," Peter assured the young journalist after speaking at length of his work as an attendant. Peter went on to boast of his ability to endure Bombay cinema as if it were an ascetic practice, of his present plan to sleep on the pavement in Calcutta, and of his expectation that he would experience *samadhi* in a cave above Rishikesh. If the reporter questioned him on why he insisted on being called Peter Ganesh Orlovsky, he was crisply interrupted. "Wait a minute; I'm talking in my dream. Don't disturb me." Allen couldn't get a word in.

While Peter nattered on, Allen wrote in his journal a bleak satire of all things Beat, sketching his staging of an International Beat Exhibition tent for the 1964 World's Fair. Step right up and receive *darshan* from Herbert Huncke. Catch Peter Orlovsky's Family Madhouse Act, Kate Orlovsky trainer. Swami Neal Cassady will answer all your spiritualistic questions. Enter Burroughs's funhouse and watch yourself as he cuts you up. See the Wall of the Glorious Martyrs; writings and spectacular paintings of Mystic Madhouse and Suicide Cases, featuring, among others, Elise Cowen. And for the more daring, behind the red curtain watch a private striptease performance by Allen Ginsberg and Peter Orlovsky "You Take down their pants and they do yr. bidding." Though he had visited a Bombay prostitute, Peter's pursuit of morphine and opium had outstripped his pursuit of girls. After Gary and Joanne left, Allen was left alone to fend for himself.

Under a fan on Malabar Hill, Allen had had a dream of the caves at Ellora, where some sort of garden party was taking place. He watched himself arguing with a provincial Indian intellectual about the true significance of the Beat Generation. Behind him, the mouth of a cave gaped, as if in horror. In his dream, the young man didn't seem to think the central character of *The Subterraneans* was sufficiently manly and kept referring to scenes in the novel Allen only barely recalled. The man's questions echoed those of the reporter from *Ilustrated Weekly,* who'd wanted to know if Ginsberg subscribed to Kerouac's "fashionably immoral" attitude to life. Was "singing, swigging wine, [and] splitting" his credo as well? In the dream, Allen, hypnotized by the sharp analysis, watched his literary world and everything he had once believed in crumble in slow motion.

"As for instance," the talkative fellow in the Ellora dream continued, "when confronted with his colored girl's declaration that she has to choose between him and her own life, he doesn't even want her to choose him, as he says he's only playing with her, yet he encourages her to put trust in him which he has no interest in responding to—"

Allen cut him off, "having grasped an idea, any idea, to defend K," and shouted some nonsense about Jack's otherworldliness. Though the argument turned on Jack's sincerity, it was as if the young man had stuck his finger squarely on Allen's own unease. In the backlog of mail that awaited him in Bombay was the news of Elise Cowen's suicide. Had he encouraged her to put her trust in him only to split on her? Had she chosen him over her own life? And, worst of all to contemplate, had he led her to that living room window? It wasn't until he began anxiously practicing yoga asanas—"anything to get out of this situation of self defensive anxiety and bullshit over the 'Beat Generation'"—that he realized the argument at the mouth of the Ellora cave had never really happened. He'd dreamed it. He leapt at the realization, like a man sprung from prison.

What should be on the mind of one who is just beginning the journey to enlightenment? This was the final question of the Diamond Sutra. How should one regard the world of the self? Not waiting for Subhuti to answer, the Buddha himself provided the conclusion to his sermon:

Like a falling star, like a bubble in a stream,
Like a flame in the wind, like frost in the sun,
Like a flash of lightning or a passing dream—
So should you understand the world of the ego.

In a postcard to a friend who had written him of Elise's death, Allen echoed this thought, insisting that no matter how compelling, life and death were as much a dream as dreams themselves. It was a consoling thought, and as he tried to sum up where his head was in his nine-thousand-word letter to Kerouac, he insisted that "the subjective result on me of India has thus been to start dropping all spiritual activity initiated since Blake voice days . . . & stop straining at heaven's door & all that mysticism and drugs & cuts ups & gurus & fears of hells & desire for god."

If you really believed that, Lucien Carr might have parried, why then were you telling the reporter for the *Illustrated Weekly of India* that you were going to start a Ganesha cult once you returned to America?

"IMAGINE THE BEAUTIFUL DRAMA, back alleys up a ladder to a narrow attic, laying on our hip with our head on a brick while the dealer cooked and prepared a classic old smeary black pipe for us." Allen hadn't given up the idea of Gregory joining him in India, and with Gary leaving for Japan the following day, he began a long letter to New York. Smoking opium was three times the pleasure of heroin and eating opium combined, he declared. He was deeply thankful that the gods had reserved this charming discovery for his middle age. Peter had been largely balanced in his indulgence, so it hadn't eaten him up entirely. "It's really bad for you to get involved that way, excessively, as you know. . . . Ends crappily."

All the horror stories about India were no more than old-lady hysteria, he went on, recalling Gregory's freaked-out response to Mexico and his panicky fear of dying in India. India wasn't at all uncomfortable, he insisted, though by the middle of April the hot season was well under way. And if it does get hot, it was an easy matter to hop a train for Kashmir or Nepal to reach the cool mountain air. Nineteenth-century-appointed dining cars served generous cheap meals, Allen wrote, both appealing to Gregory's love of traveling in style and providing him the assurance he wouldn't starve. He described the spacious rooms of India's guesthouses, with "all wood furniture" and "enormous shower bathrooms and ceiling fans and armchairs, spotlessly clean— usually." Even the ritziest restaurants in Bombay were cheaper than Tangier. He gave a rundown of the sights he'd seen from the palaces at Jaipur to the temple ruins in Aurangabad. The Mahabharata and Ramayana, he insisted, more than equaled Homer. And then there was the ease of procuring drugs: morphine in antiseptic ampoules from any corner drugstore, and opium for the asking. As for the sweet, dreamy pleasure of low-down opium dens, they'd found only one in Delhi, but there were sure to be more. There was nothing like it. Peter agreed *emphatically*.

Allen saved the best news for last.

"On top of that Madame Hope Savage is on the scene. Ah, yes, I forgot. All the signs point to your having a fine time in the Orient, Gregory Corso. From Aden to Kashmir she wears shawl and boots. . . . So there's your Hope, still savage."

PART THREE

A Blue Hand

In March 1962, two years after her final letter to Jerry Madden, Hope Savage was back at the American Express office in New Delhi.

"Seems she had been in Aden, Ethiopia, Iran, and then back to India," Gary wrote after they all shared a Chinese meal on a brief Delhi stopover en route to Dharamsala. Unable to secure a travel permit, in April 1960 Hope had abandoned the dream of Bhutan for the free Air India ticket to Yemen. She had settled in its port city of Aden for a year, making what would become her final visit to her family the following June. Upon returning to India that winter, she found her way to a remote and inhospitable valley in the western Himalayas, before moving south to the desert city of Udaipur in February. She had just arrived in Delhi and was wondering where to go next when she found a note from Allen Ginsberg at the American Express office. On Gregory's instructions, he'd been keeping his eyes peeled for her.

Impressed that she had made it alone through the dreadful parts of North Africa, Gary asked what had become of Jean, who had accompanied her to his Mill Valley cabin in 1958. Long gone, she said, and left it at that. Though she still spoke in her familiar bluestreak fashion, Hope would lapse into sudden and awkward silences. Perhaps traveling alone had rendered unguarded conversation difficult. Perhaps she was unused to having to answer for herself. Gary described her as an old acquaintance of Allen's, though he was the only one who'd previously met her. She'd never replied to Allen's first letter, written at Gregory's insistence. Allen's rushed prose was illiterate, she complained to Gregory, but perhaps his overfamiliarity made her skittish. Allen noted that she seemed regularly to shed her traveling companions, as if to prevent any one person from connecting the dots of her existence. Allen, who scrutinized every dot of his own and rarely lost track of an acquaintance, found her unnerving. After Hope saw them to the overnight train to Pathankot, Gary speculated in his journal that she was, perhaps, a little crazy.

Hope next reappeared at the terrace reading in Bombay. At Allen's invitation, she spent the day with them on Juhu Beach, where Joanne took a photograph of her wrapped in a shawl and barefoot. Bit by bit, she related her run-ins with immigration authorities and her difficulties renewing her Indian visa. Indian officials suspected her of being a CIA spy, she told them. At the poetry reading she was agitated, convinced there were people in the audience who thought so, too. For Gary and Joanne, this seemed ridiculously far-fetched. In a shipboard letter revisiting their final days together in Bombay, Joanne suggested to Allen that if he were to pretend he thought she was a spy, Hope was sure to drop him with the same dispatch she had everyone else.

In a curious aside, Gary noted that Hope led their Indian friends to believe she was not American, but Iranian. Was this affectation a measure of her closeness to Iran or the distance she had traveled from America? By the time Hope arrived in Tehran in the spring of 1960, the American policy of containing communism was, at least in Iran, a complete success. In 1953, Dwight Eisenhower had given the go-ahead for the CIA's overthrow of Iran's first democratically elected but Communist-leaning government. Seven years later, the Shah of Iran's face leered from every shop window, even the smallest newspaper vendor. Every published book had his photo on the frontispiece, and every village, no matter how poor, had his statue. The year Hope arrived, thirty army officials had been executed on suspicion of being Communists. Her host in the city had just been released from a year in prison for political activities. Though he said nothing, Hope gathered he'd been tortured. Portraits of Gogol and Victor Hugo hung on the walls of his apartment, enshrined like mythical leaders of an exiled order.

Didn't she look like a spy? Hope asked Jerry that spring, enclosing a number of recent photos. In the photographs she poses against a door, a window, a wall. She is dressed entirely in black, her untamed hair darker and her kohl-lined eyes dramatically offset against her milk white skin. There was something of a Middle East fashion for American girls from good backgrounds, she told him. She felt it wouldn't be too difficult to become a favorite of the recently divorced Shah or, even better, one of the young kings of Jordan or Iraq. Hadn't Hope Cooke made just such a match with the king of Sikkim? Such a connection would make travel in Asia far simpler, she said, as if now that were all that mattered. She was learning Urdu.

How did she explain the patchwork of entry and exit visas, the absence of a husband or visible means of support? Is it ever possible to disown one's country and complicity with its intrigues, without relinquishing the passport that confirms one's identity every time a border is crossed? And the money from home: What kind of parents would let a daughter leave home before she was married? What kind of daughter would leave her family with scarcely a backward glance? Such a woman's loyalties would always be in question, and immigration officials had as much desire to make sense of her as any inquisitive traveling companion.

"Winters in Himalayan Kulu Valley, alone in cabin in village with fire," Allen reported to Gregory. "Made a lot of lonely great scenes." Might she be a lesbian? he asked. He found Hope extremely bright, but "not quite human." Still, he said, she seemed anxious to be polite the few times they had met up. She admired Gary openly. Allen expected to see her again in a few days, adding, "She disappears." He wrested a message from her for Gregory: She hoped he was well.

Signing off, Allen told Gregory to kidnap Jack and bring him to India. According to Gary, the French line Messageries Maritimes, which ran direct from Marseille to Bombay, had a great wine cellar and first-class cuisine. Within two weeks, Allen heard from Ted Wilentz that Gregory was telling everyone he was going to India. Allen wrote again. They were off to Calcutta in a few days but would make the two-thousand-mile journey back to Bombay to meet his boat if he was truly coming. When would that be? In a week? A month? Allen's mood had lifted. Sitting at a café drinking coffee and listening to Peter talk, he forgot to feel annoyed. The sun was setting on the Arabian Sea, and the spectacle relieved him of his perpetual anxieties.

"Everything here paradisal. Hope in Calcutta," he wrote in an update to Gregory just before leaving. "We spent lots of time together here in Bombay, she friendly. Likes Peter. Okay, love, Allen."

THE HINDU PANTHEON is a bewildering clan of gods and goddesses. Ginsberg likened them to Disney characters and incorporated them into his personal iconography. Of all the gods, few were more revered than the demon slayer Durga, and of her many incarnations, none was more terrifying than Kali. In his first concerted effort at writing a poem since leaving New York, Allen chose Kali as his subject. He depicted her as the Statue of Liberty, her neck adorned with the martyred heads of the Rosenbergs, her foot crushing the body of Uncle Sam, while her breasts spurted jazz. Whether or not it was from Kali that Calcutta took its name, it was to this goddess that even the most sedate of Bengali housewives made daily offerings.

Distinct from every other port between Cape Town and Macao once under the heel of England or Europe, this delta city on the Bay of Bengal had evolved a unique civilization, a wellspring of art, religion, philosophy, and science with currents as tricky and muddy as the Ganges itself. From Vedantist and Sufi to Plato and Aristotle, Bengalis proved unusually receptive to different and often contentious philosophies and religious traditions. Yet the polite society of the Calcutta *bhadralok* was known as much for their profligate lifestyle as for their love of learning and the arts. Wearing their hair oiled and sporting Chinese shoes under their immacu-

lately starched dhotis, Bengali babus whiled away their time playing the sitar, flying kites, watching cockfights, and dealing hands
of bridge at gentlemen's clubs. They embraced English literature
and the study of ancient scriptures. Their love of drink and the sen-
timental ballads of nautch girls trumped caste restrictions and
Brahminic prohibitions that held sway elsewhere. The death of
Rabindranath Tagore in 1941 marked the end of this age.

And much else. The following year, a famine left one million
dead in Bengal. In 1946, riots beween Hindus and Muslims in Calcutta added to the carnage of the world war until Gandhi stepped
between them. In the wake of the 1947 partition that followed
the end of English rule, the city was stretched beyond capacity by
millions of Hindus fleeing East Bengal, doubling the population.
Like Nagendra Nath Sarkar, many of those who came retained land
and family ties to what then became East Pakistan. Much as the
English had, Delhi did its best to discourage foreigners from visiting Calcutta, as Bengalis were considered uppity malcontents,
harboring uncertain loyalties to the central government.

Two railway termini connected the city to a vast hinterland of
rich soil and teeming rivers. Reserves of coal, iron ore, and man-
ganese fed the blast furnaces of its industry, the engineering and
locomotive works of Ranchi, Jamshedpur, and Howrah. Yet the
partitions began a slow unraveling. The industrial infrastructure
rusted. Stalinists squared off against Maoists. Nationalists, in turn,
fended off both, leading to a near permanent state of labor unrest.
Only in their mutual distrust of England and America did the various blocs find common cause. Delhi needn't have worried about
tourists: Calcutta's reputation was sufficiently discouraging.

The city itself was a tumultuous clash of animal, human, and
machine. Motor traffic competed with water buffalo and cows
foraging lazily among the two million tons of garbage that ended
up on the streets each day. Waves of jaywalkers and smaller eddies
of hawkers wove in and out of the stream of vehicles, selling rags,
toys, flowers, or ghastly infirmities. All too often, strikes paralyzed the city. In 1962, the thirty-mile stretch of city along the
Hooghly was home to eight million inhabitants, the majority
unskilled young men. They slept huddled together in ramshackle

slums, in factories, godowns, and offices, asleep on docks or construction sites. They sent tiny remittances back to the villages they had come from. Human suffering, of an infinite variety, was everywhere evident.

Yet Calcutta was also in the midst of a sustained cultural explosion. Every branch of the arts was in bloom. In the world of dance, the undisputed prince was Uday Shankar; his dancers introduced Indian classical dance and its music to the world. Allen had watched him perform in New York in 1944. His younger brother Ravi Shankar, a master of the sitar, found his own audience, as did musicians like Ali Akbar Khan and Chatur Lal. They all were as likely to be found in the crowded venues of Calcutta as Paris or Los Angeles. Painting and sculpture were no less astonishing, and Bengali artists like Jamini Roy held the art world in thrall. After Satyajit Ray's *Pather Panchali* trilogy was released in 1955, his subsequent films were received with a hunger bordering on madness. Where Hindi films had happy endings, Bengali films had tragic, brooding ones.

And it seemed that nearly every other Bengali was a poet. Those who weren't had committed Shakespeare's sonnets to heart and would break into a Tagore song at the slightest provocation. Long before he was awarded the Nobel Prize in Literature in 1913, Rabindranath Tagore's prodigious output of poetry, stories, and songs secured him a world reputation. He was a translator, composer, painter, and cosmopolitan. His work celebrated the sunny and spontaneous joys of life, drawing on the folk traditions of rural Bengal. Though Buddhadev Bose bemoaned the political strife and loss of innocence that followed Tagore's death, his own literary salon at 202 Rash Behari Avenue hosted the first and second waves of writers who vied for his mantle.

"Main thing we do in Calcutta is meat Bengale poets by the dozen," Peter Orlovsky wrote Lucien. The pair had arrived in Calcutta just in time for a heat wave and a cholera outbreak, but after picking up Hope Savage at the Y, they set about seeing the city before Allen left to track down Sonam Kazi's Tantric master in Kalimpong. He promised he would send for Peter if things looked auspicious. In Bombay, Peter had learned that his disability check had been suspended and he needed to have his mental instability officially recognized and reinstated. While he awaited his exam results, Peter booked a room at the Hotel Amjadia. But for the fact that it was cheap and within six blocks of the bright lights, cheap restaurants, and opium dens of Chinatown, the hotel had little to recommend it. Peter settled in to answer the backlog of letters.

"We went to the USIS and they give us expert help in contacting old and young," Peter wrote Lucien after Allen left. "In fact the USIS is beginning to feel like an employment agency, they give me names and I go hunt them down." The United States Information Service's list of literary lights included mostly the Calcutta literary establishment. Allen and Peter had encountered a similar crowd in Bombay, among them the fastidious, thin-lipped Nissim Ezekiel, who introduced them at the terrace reading and cited Robert Graves among his literary heroes. Indian writing in English was a hopeless project, Allen felt. Who was their audience?

"The English used in India is too polite and genteel," Allen had told them. "There is no Indian English like there is an American Negro English. . . ." Allen's affinity was for those starving poets who wrote in their mother tongue and readily provided him with a tour of Bombay's seamy underside. Before leaving Calcutta, Allen had yet to find their compadres, but Peter soon did. "Yesterday poet Shankar took me to see theartre group a litle more hip," Peter wrote Lucien. However hip, Peter learned that whether onstage, in films, or in public, kissing was "banded completely." Kissing couples were often imprisoned, he explained. To Allen, Peter confessed that he'd been hankering to make it with Hope. Though he thought he caught a "twinkle eye smile" from her before she left for Dacca, in East Pakistan, to renew her visa, he hadn't been certain enough to risk a kiss.

"Seems the gandhi sperit of going to jail for something ya believe in is absent or forgotten these days . . . but what a lovely thing to go to jail for, because ya kissed a girl. . . ."

. . .

"BEHOLD, THIS IS THE UNIVERSE," Krishna announced, casting aside his disguise so that the young Prince Arjuna could admire his cosmic dimensions. Before Arjuna's eyes arose the Vision of the Universal Form, the one hundred thousand faces that hide the unknowable mystery of God. "This is my glory," the Blue God preened, "unveiled to mortal sight." Arjuna's vision in chapter XI of the Bhagavad Gita, Allen decided, rereading the passages in Darjeeling, was a literal and exact "objective symbolic correlative" to the pinwheeling wheels within wheels and prickling sensations that he had experienced under LSD and *ayahuasca*. Robert Oppenheimer had quoted from the same chapter to describe what he had seen at Trinity, the day the first atomic bomb exploded.

Suppose a thousand suns should rise together into the sky: such is the glory of the Shape of the Inifinite God.

While Pupul Jayakar, Buddhadev Bose, and the Dalai Lama might not fully appreciate the mushroom cloud of Timothy Leary's explosive little pill, elsewhere in the world, psilocybin was being taken seriously. Before he left Calcutta, Allen received a letter and gift package from Leary. "We have grown into a classic mystic cult," Leary wrote breezily from Copenhagen, outlining his plan for a chain of ashrams and cheerfully describing the witch hunt under way at Harvard. He prophesied the next millennium cycle would most likely begin in North America. It was a good thing Allen was in India, out of reach of the newspapers, drug enforcement agents, and local outrage. He had a backup plan for an ashram in India, too, in case events took a different turn. Leary's idea was that enlightenment was no longer the sole province of saints and poets. Set alongside this robust "potentiality of human consciousness," the pills were merely the skeleton key to save the world from destruction. The package nonetheless included a generous supply of "the fragile vehicle of my devotion."

Despite Allen's own belief that these drugs bestowed divine sight, whether of Tibetan monster gods or Arjuna's vision of the

Universal Form, he couldn't contemplate Leary's unexpected gift of LSD without shuddering. Now those who had once demanded he renounce his visions as madness were seeing what he had seen. He saw his dread of further visionary encounters as his failure, evidence that he was once again clinging to ego and the fear of death. "To be afraid to enter is a terrible fate," he wrote in his journal. Where was the teacher who would acknowledge the gift of drugs? Where was the teacher who could teach him how to get beyond his fears?

On June 3, 1962, his thirty-sixth birthday, Allen Ginsberg traveled to the old hill station of Kalimpong. He first met an English lama of the Yellow Hat (Gelukpa) sect, who, apart from being a rich source of gossip about the other sects, offered him a young Tibetan, insisting sex with young boys was just a little sin. "Apparently lots of boy love in the yellow hat monastery," Allen explained to Peter, waiting for news in Calcutta. Dismissive of both Sonam Kazi and his guru, Dudjom Rinpoche, the Englishman told Allen he should have signed on with the Dalai Lama's guru back in Dharamsala. He offered to write a letter, but Allen declined both the boy and the letter. He was intent on the fast track of the Tantrically inclined Red Hats. He felt they might have the wisdom technology to make use of the pills he carried, like radiant isotopes, in his backpack.

"What is the mind? *Where* is the mind?" Dudjom Rinpoche, titular head of the Red Hat (Nyingma) sect, tried to reel Allen back to more basic questions. Is the mind somewhere in the body? Or is the mind merely the rise of one thought after another, like waves traveling across a great ocean? Visions were no different from mundane thoughts, or dreams, or the fever of love. They led equally to hopelessness. Dudjom counseled neither submission to nor renunciation of his visions, but detachment. "Watch the wheels within wheels, but don't get attached to anything you see," he told Allen. "Let it pass into you, but be inactive and not grasping nor rejecting. If you see anything horrible, don't cling to it; if you see anything beautiful, don't cling to it." Only when the mind is quiet, when the mind finds its natural state of stillness, he said, can you discover a temporary radiance.

Sonam Kazi had suggested that Allen pursue *wang,* a Tibetan initiation rite in which the initiate is empowered to engage in Tantric practices that lead to the attainment of Buddhahood. The practices are meditative, initially involving mantras and visualizing oneself in the form of the deity into which one has been initiated. "You get this wang," Allen explained to Peter, "plus a mantra and a text to follow and meditate like on LSD." As there were propitiatory rituals that needed to be done first, Dudjom Rinpoche invited Allen to return in September. Even before Allen left Kalimpong, it seemed unlikely he would. While the initial impact of the *wang* was doubtless "a real splash," Allen felt that the rest of Tibetan Buddhism appeared to be, like its Zen cousin, "a long journey." He wanted something shorter.

Allen understood the privilege of the historical moment he found himself in. Whatever their sect, the exiled lamas were now eager to transmit a wisdom tradition that had previously been inaccessible and secret. Still, he was unable to let go of the conviction that his visions represented a deeper reality, not an illusory one. He still felt he had been specially chosen and that his Harlem vision had conferred upon him special powers. Or perhaps it was Rinpoche's asthmatic wheeze that put him off, or the ladylike bun at the back of his head. To cap it off, Dudjom Rinpoche wasn't willing to try Dr. Leary's pills.

The head of the Kagyu sect was more responsive. The Karmapa at the Rumtek monastery outside Gangtok, the capital of Sikkim, was prepared to take Allen on the day he arrived. The Kagyus were a Black Hat sect who traced their lineage back to Marpa and his disciple Milarepa, an eleventh-century poet. Marpa went to India twice to receive initiation into the teachings that he then translated and passed along to his disciples, establishing the Kagyu lineage. A lama in Kalimpong had told Allen of a Kagyu meditation practice whereby you imagine you are screwing the image on your thangka. Even better, the Karmapa at Rumtek was ready to try Leary's pills and said he needed only a week to teach Allen something. There would also be a small fee. Unfortunately, somewhere between Sealdah station in Calcutta and Siliguri, Allen had lost both his passport and a good chunk of money. And as there were tensions with China on the northeast border, he could manage to get only a three-day pass. Plus, he couldn't help it: The Karmapa reminded him of a B-movie character actor. It was hard for Allen to take this jolly, baby-faced man seriously, much less love him.

Allen returned to his flophouse in Gangtok disconsolate, walking the ten miles back from the monastery in rubber flip-flops that made loud slaps on the pavements of the quiet, sleeping capital. What did he fear most? he asked himself. Was it the dread at coming face-to-face again with the serpent monster the Vomiter, "the ogre that goes with the rose"? Was it madness? The loss of the possibility of love? He was beginning to feel that his love for Peter had been just a temporary reprieve, a masking opiate "to cover the real pain . . . the task of preparing to die." As with drugs, one needed stronger and stronger doses, but his love for Peter had instead grown weaker and weaker. As the prospect of finding a teacher who could love him diminished, the prospect of a lonely death loomed. His mother had died that way, abandoned to her madness. With insufficient mourners for a minyan, she had not even received the prayer for the dead. Would this be his fate?

Allen turned once more to the Bhagavad Gita, revisiting not merely Arjuna's awe at the glorious sight of Krishna's hundred thousand faces, but his terror:

> Terrible with fangs, O mighty master,
> All the worlds are fearstruck, even as I am
> Now with frightful tusks your mouths are gnashing
> Flaring like the fires of Doomsday morning. . . .

In the flaming maw of the "Great Gnashyfang," Arjuna witnessed the incineration of the universe and the god's feast upon legions of the heroic dead. It was as if, Allen felt, Arjuna saw the war toward which Krishna spurred him already lost, the battle-fields soaked with the blood of his kin. If Allen took Leary's pills, he would die. If he didn't, he'd die anyway, felled by "the hosts of Rheumatism & Cancer." When the prince beseeched Krishna to return to his human form, the Great Gnashyfang insisted that it was a blessing to see him this way. "He says he's a friend," Allen wrote in summary in his journal, "and he says, None shall Escape me." Under the searing flash of a thousand suns in the Nevada desert, Oppenheimer fixed on the same image of implacable destruction.

"I am become death, shatterer of worlds."

After descending once more to the sultry plains of Siliguri, Allen returned by train to Calcutta, deflated and depressed. He had now scaled back his expectations of heaven. He no longer hoped for a place of permanent ecstasy, but simply a state of mind beyond "shit and desire." That was enough. A place where there was nothing and no one to fear.

"When will I be ready to die?" he beseeched himself. "And when will I ever turn my attention . . . to the streets and figures of daily India?"

BENGALI INTELLECTUALS with more time than money can be found at all hours of the day arguing literature and politics in the College Street Coffee House, adjacent to Calcutta University. Fueled largely by state-subsidized milky tea (to keep them quiescent), similar *addas* can be found under way at any corner tea stall. But College Street, packed to the gutters with book stalls, is *adda* central. There, derelict old houses are filled with so many books and publishing concerns that one has to stand in a sweaty line on the pavement and wait to be served. While the College Street Coffee House was already legendary, in the 1950s and early 1960s those holding court there represented a new generation. Amid the cafeteria clatter and clink of spoons on china and stainless-steel tea services, the high-ceilinged room maintained separate tables for different genres. There was a table for those who wrote children's stories, another for those who wrote for films, and yet another for story writers and novelists. The most notorious table, however, was the one set aside solely for a close circle of young poets. There were instances of writers abandoning their genres and taking up verse so they might sit among the personalities holding forth at the poet's table.

Among these poets was a young man named Sunil Gangopadhyay. Gangopadhyay (or, anglicized, Ganguly) was the founding editor of the literary magazine where most of their poems could be found. Heavyset, open, and forthright, the son of a poor schoolteacher, Sunil came of age in a tiny apartment with his parents and younger siblings. His vigor seemed to spring from the village of his East Bengal childhood rather than the decaying city he lived in. Not long after he first arrived in Calcutta, he heard rumors of a neighborhood boy who was known as a poet. Everyone spoke of this boy with a respect bordering on awe, as if the ability to make rhymes and write in meter had marked him for a secret purpose. I could do *that,* Sunil said to himself, thinking of the pretty girl next door, whose recitations always left him tongue-tied. He composed a poem in the form of a letter to her and submitted it to a magazine he knew her parents subscribed to, unaware that *Desh* was the most prominent publication in Bengal. Not long after, the girl arrived at his door.

"Look," she said, holding out the new issue to him. "Someone with your name has written a poem."

After Sunil finished college, his ailing father insisted it was time he found a job. He would have liked to attend university, less to get an MA than for the chance to meet a girl, but he set about looking for a post without complaint. He soon learned that for every job there were ten thousand applicants, and of these only two hundred made it as far as the interview. Quite often, the interviewer would know full well the job was already spoken for. Yet Sunil was not discouraged. After an interview for the post of a forest ranger, he easily saw himself deep in the forest with gum boots on his feet and a rifle over his shoulder. When he came in first on the written exam for a railway clerk's position, he was jubilant. On the oral exam, he did so well with the first four members of the board that he imagined working at a tiny rail station with an expansive view of the mountains. The last questioner, however, did nothing but stare at a button on his shirt. Suddenly, the man grabbed a thread that was sticking out and the button popped off.

"Mr. Gangopadhyay! Is it right to wear such a *loose button?*" he demanded. "It must be that you lack concentration!" His name was struck from the list, and thereafter he could never pass a railway clerk without inspecting his buttons. They were invariably missing.

A story made the rounds of the coffeehouse that perfectly captured the quandary of young men like Sunil. After the death of the orangutan in the Calcutta Zoo, the story went, the zookeeper decided it would take too long for a new one to be sent from abroad. A postgraduate in Sanskrit grammar answered the ad he placed in the *Statesman,* and the zookeeper showed him how to wear the hide of the dead monkey. The youth soon learned how to jump around to keep the spectators happy. The higher he jumped, the faster the coins came. One day, in his enthusiasm, he jumped right into the tiger cage. The tiger crept up to him, and though nearly dead with fright, he heard a voice whisper, "*Dada!* Don't be scared, I'm an MA in Bengali literature."

On Monday evenings, Sunil made his way to the College Street Coffee House, where he would meet up with his friends, some with government jobs, some squeaking by giving tuitions, one or two with real jobs in industry or academics, but all intent on poetry as their sole source of real sustenance. It was out of these conversations that Sunil first conceived of a literary magazine only for young poets like themselves. The first issue of *Krittibas* had appeared while he was still in college, and subsequent ones arrived haphazardly. If Sunil had two tuitions, he would give only one to his father and the other he would keep for the magazine.

There was Utpal Kumar Basu, a shy, bashful presence at the table, a young geology instructor who weighed his comments carefully before sharing them. Only then was the sharpness of his mind and the breadth of his reading evident. Both his parents had died untimely deaths, leaving their only child to live alone in the ancestral home in north Calcutta. Tarapada Roy was as explosive as Utpal was retiring. Stories, jokes, and poems burst from him in rat-a-tat fashion, stopping only for him to take a drag on a cigarette or a gulp of tea. The son and grandson of Dacca lawyers displaced by partition, he worked as a clerk in a government office, one of thousands sitting on high stools laboriously translating thick ledgers of government documents from English into Bengali. Tarapada claimed his only patrimony was his voice. It had the range of a pipe organ in a vast cathedral, filling every space, hitting every note between absurdity and pathos. After disquisitions on the mysteries of a single Bengali word, or a fervid recital of a poem by Jibananda Das, any one of the *Krittibas* poets might suddenly start up from the table and shout, "Let's go to Howrah station!" It was a happy fact that there were many opportunities for dereliction of duty in government jobs and a measure of how far gone the city was that even after a week's absence, their empty desks were barely noted.

Shakti Chattopadhyay, the youngest, burned brightest. Sunil had first noticed Shakti sitting with his friends from Presidency College at a nearby table. Although he was far from handsome, his goatee and ever-present bidi nonetheless marked him as a *boulevardier*. "Bidis are like lovers who are difficult to please," Sunil heard him say with an air of experience, "they must be kissed constantly." It didn't take Shakti long to switch tables. Upon his arrival, he boasted he was the noblest born of all of them, lived in the biggest house, and had taken a first in all his exams. Sunil, impressed at the clarity and confidence of his literary opinions, still wondered, "Why should a love for Kafka require a disdain for Chekhov?" Why refuse to read Amiyo Chakrobarty's poetry just because you were infatuated with Jibananda Das? But it was Shakti's much vaunted experience with women, his knowledge of female anatomy, that Sunil most envied. Sunil's understanding was limited to the clay Saraswati whose lissome figure graced the city during *pujas*.

Rabindranath Tagore was like the tree around which the life of an entire village gathers. His portrait hung in every middle-class Bengali home. In the 1930s, when Tagore was still alive, a group of writers tried to break away. They read Freud, quoted T. S. Eliot, and became Marxists, but their style remained derivative. In contrast, the bookshelves of the *Krittibas* poets held the Penguin classics of Modern French poetry as well as the works of the great Bengali writers. Buddhadev Bose had translated Rimbaud, Verlaine, and Rilke into Bengali, and this work had electrified them just as Burroughs's library of French surrealists once had sparked Ginsberg and Kerouac. They scorned the official Marxist tropes of the literary establishment; they had their own means of épater le bourgeois. They decided they would dispense entirely with the Tagore lexicon, the campy "vegetarian" vocabulary of the *bhadralok*. They would declaim using the demotic language of the street, market, and factory.

This language had never been heard in Bengali literature. With it they hoped to break down meter, rhyme, and, while they were at it, conventional morality. Yet they could not write what they had not lived. Despite their meager resources and family duties, they studied the lives of artists like Vincent van Gogh and Gauguin for guidance and did their best to imitate them. They slept with the Anglo-Indian prostitutes on Free School Street. After collecting the money from *Krittibas* sales, they got plastered on rice wine at Khalasitola, long past the hour the trams shut down. Then they would shamble home to their worried mothers, solitary figures walking beneath streetlamps that cast a calming blue gray light over the one hundred thousand souls asleep on the pavements of the briefly still city.

With the exception of Tarapada, who grew up in a village for East Bengal refugees, only Sunil knew the Bengal countryside. The village he'd come from was so remote, it was accessible only by boat. He knew the miles and miles of jute fields and the delta's vast tangle of tributaries. And it was not until he arrived in Calcutta that he saw his first tram car. While Shakti received pocket money into his twenties, from the age of ten Sunil had helped his father support uncles who'd arrived from the village with nothing. He edited *Krittibas* with an independent hand, publishing and sometimes rejecting his friends' work. After his father's death, he worked even harder, read and published more than the others. Yet his name and that of the more footloose Shakti were perpetually linked. There was a time when Sunil and Shakti would begin the afternoon together and engage in a conversation that lasted past midnight.

But where his own crowded flat in Baghbazar was always open, Sunil had never once crossed Shakti's threshold. He stood outside and called to Shakti from the street. Only after he learned that Shakti's father was dead and he was living as a poor relation in his uncle's house did Sunil realize that everything Shakti had ever crowed about at the poet's table was a lie, save for his claim he was a poet. So a few hours into his country liquor, when Shakti veered from the books he was reading to insulting other writers, it was Sunil who rebuked him. When Shakti shouted and jumped about like an obnoxious child, announcing to the world, "I am Shakti Chattopadhyay, I am a poet," it was he who slapped his face. It was Sunil whom Shakti feared.

Despite the way Sunil carried himself, and the closeness he felt to his friends, like Shakti, he harbored a secret. His pride would never have allowed anyone, but most of all Shakti, to come close to guessing what it was. This was his secret. Alongside the others, he felt the weight of his own inexperience of the world. Next to their city sophistication, he was still a child of the village.

"When I saw that tram, I couldn't figure out how it moved. There was no water."

IT WAS A RELIEF to travel outside his own head, and when he returned to Calcutta, Allen discovered that the world at large seemed to have nearly as much going on. He had always nurtured a love for newspapers, immersing himself in every conflict, relishing every outrage, large and small. He spent the rest of June reading two weeks' worth of the London *Times* at the British Council Library and back issues of *Time* and *Newsweek*. He arranged for the Calcutta *Statesman* to be delivered to the Amjadia. Locally, the cholera outbreak had now reached epidemic levels, and there were rumors of the arrival of the monsoon, but the larger headlines seesawed between the U.S. nuclear tests over various Pacific atolls and Russian nuclear bombs going off in the Arctic. Closer to home, Chinese border incursions near Ladakh were extensively covered and commented upon. In a seven-page letter to his father, Allen bemoaned the fallout from two decades' worth of Dulles's containment policy. Where Allen obsessed over America's hypocrisy and self-delusion, Louis Ginsberg tended to view his adopted country more benignly. The outrages committed by the United States, Allen insisted, as much as those committed by the Stalin-Khrushchev regimes, sustained a "2 way psychosis." Progress, he said, depended upon a "complete re-thinking and re-realization of what's happened from Hiroshima day onward."

As for his own progress in rethinking and rerealization, Allen had not entirely abandoned his search for instruction in Hindu philosophy. At the Ramakrishna mission, access to the meditation room required three keys and six subjanitors to enter a dank, carpeted room with a broken air conditioner, confirming "local pious opinion" that the Ramakrishna scene was dead, having devolved into a worldwide social services organization. The real deal, Allen reported to a Vedantist acquaintance in San Francisco, according to the "old fashioned hindus" and "westernized Indians who drink martinis and attend Krishnamurti Lectures," was Ramana Maharshi. Still, he had yet to find a teacher he "really dug."

More than the poetry of Ramana Maharshi or a heart-to-heart with a Tibetan lama with blackened teeth in Kalimpong, it was the city and denizens of Calcutta that increasingly found Ginsberg's sustained attention. Shouting above the disputatious noise of the College Street Coffee House, Allen asked where he might find the *Krittibas* poets he'd heard so much about. While Peter became a habitué of a nearby opium den, it was at the coffeehouse that Allen discovered a nearly familial feeling for the Bengalis. For one thing, he had grown up listening to his parents (his mother a Communist, his father a Socialist) have the same political arguments as the *Krittibas* clan. For another, they were as mouthy and outrageous a tribe as he had found at Columbia.

As for Sunil and his friends, they had read Buddhadev Bose's sympathetic account of Allen in *Desh*. The Beats, they imagined, were like the Bauls, those troubadours of the Bengal countryside who rebelled against the conventions that marked class and religious differences. According to Bose, the Beats embraced the world of sense experience. Like sadhus, they searched for an extraterrestrial world under the influence of substances not unlike ganja and bhang. Finally, they understood "Beat" to mean an artist who refused to acknowledge any social obligations, who was not beholden to anyone for a living. For Shakti, then sporting a beard, such a lifestyle and philosophy held enormous appeal. His entire existence was taken up with writing poetry; and he felt that poetic license justified every possible delinquency. For Sunil, the sole support of his now fatherless family, such an existence filled him with wonder.

Allen Ginsberg was therefore a subject of great curiosity, with his beard, nervous tics, and orations on the mind-expanding properties of LSD. They were astonished to see Allen squat to pee in the street. Sunil wondered why he dressed like a poor person. Why did he stay in a third-rate Mussalman hotel, in a damp room with dirty walls, windows that would not shut, and two small beds full of bedbugs? The bathroom was indescribably dirty. It was beyond his imagination that white Americans could tolerate such hardship. Was this some kind of *sadhana*? Or was Ginsberg, as the writers at a neighboring table insisted, a CIA agent? And Orlovsky, was he Russian or American?

Most disconcerting of all, Allen Ginsberg seemed to overlook all they'd been schooled to find backward—their poverty above all, but also the decay of their city from its storied history as the seat of the raj. Park Street was still known as Sahib Para, and from a distance Sunil had often watched foreigners patronizing the fancy shops on Chowringhee. Though the British ruled for nearly two hundred years, even educated Bengalis rarely came face-to-face with a sahib. Never having spoken to a white person, Sunil was impressed by how patiently Allen repeated himself when they couldn't understand his accent. When they struggled to make sense of the long loping lines in "Howl," Allen explained them. They couldn't but be charmed by his interest in their poetry and his tenderness with every rickshaw wallah who crossed his path. Eventually, they realized that when Ginsberg introduced Peter Orlovsky as "my dear wife," he was aiming to unsettle just those pointy heads of the literary establishment they had set themselves against. When Peter's VA check was delayed, they even lent them money. Finally, despite themselves, they began to indulge Allen's

interest in Hindu philosophy, a subject they, as militant rational-
ists, had no earthly use for.

Sunil could see Allen was amused that he still lived with his
mother, that she still cooked for him and washed his clothes.
When Allen and Peter visited, the neighborhood ladies gathered
behind the door, covering their faces with their sari ends and gig-
gling at the sight of two foreigners eating fish with their fingers.
Sunil's uncle arrived to practice his English, and when he began to
recite a Shakespeare sonnet, Allen stopped him: "Can you recite a
Bengali poem by heart?" He couldn't. Allen was still mystified by
the fact that none of the Indian poets he knew wrote about their
gods, caught up as they were with the gods of modernism. He introduced them to a few more: W. C. Williams, e. e. cummings,
Vladmir Mayakovsky, and Gregory Corso.

So when the Calcutta Marxists began criticizing Allen for pol-
luting the cultural scene and corrupting the youth of Bengal, the
Krittibas poets decided they were happy to be polluted. Allen relished the irony and despaired at the absurdity.

IN THE DREAM, Allen retrieved the two bottles from his knapsack. One was his mescaline supply, and the other was filled with
minute candy-coated psilocybin pills. Each of the latter was five
times more powerful than the ones he'd taken with Leary at Harvard. He put aside the mescaline and took out four of the mushroom pills, hesitated, then put the fourth one back. Three was
still fifteen times the strength of his previous dose, he told himself. Peter declined to take any. It was too sudden. After swallow-
ing them, Allen waited awhile but didn't feel anything. If anything,
his perception seemed dulled.

Upon awakening, he attributed the dream to a conversation
with Jyoti Datta the day before. Buddhadev Bose's son-in-law was
the one member of the *Krittibas* circle both married and gainfully
employed. Jyoti worked at the Calcutta *Statesman,* still run from
London and overseen by standoffish and haughty English editors.
As a student, Jyoti had been a Communist and fiery anti-imperialist,
but he had since become an equally impassioned skeptic, flying the

flags of European civilization and the Enlightenment. Plato was far more important a thinker than Shivananda, he chided Allen. India had seen enough of spirituality, of Tantra and gurus, he said, warning him he was heading down a blind alley.

It shocked Allen to hear Jyoti disavow the inheritance of his own civilization. Yet in the wake of this bracingly skeptical conversation, it occurred to Allen that mind expansion through drugs had become something of a blind alley of its own. Public pronouncements aside, the *idea* of widening his consciousness, of going beyond mere conceptual modes of thought, had overtaken his actual *experience* of these mental states. Gary had argued that while drugs might be illuminating, visionary, and beneficial in terms of grasping the modalities of consciousness, they were never enlightening. Satori could not be achieved with them, and although he had yet to try psilocybin, Gary hadn't found that mescaline threw the least glimmer of light on koan study. Whatever the case, the fact that he no longer relished the prospect of taking the pills, Allen saw, had left him stranded, not only spiritually but creatively.

Once again he considered writing Burroughs, but he already knew what he would say. There was no such a thing as "poetic" subject matter. He was too chained to memory, imagery, and the "humanistic storytelling" that Bill had abandoned. While his consciousness might have gone beyond such things, his writing hadn't. Even if he wasn't spooked by the prospect of taking the pills, it remained to be seen what kind of writing would come out of it. He really didn't know what he was doing as a poet anymore. How long had he had these Leary pills now? A month? What exactly had he been waiting for, anyway? It was a relief to actually do something about them, with such apparent coolness and resolve. Even if it was just a dream.

Jyoti's father-in-law had become increasingly alarmed by Allen. Admittedly, each time Buddhadev Bose encountered him he was newly convinced there was something "pure" about him. He was ready to overlook Allen's enthusiasm for ganja and opium, his disorderly dress, his seeming pro-Soviet sympathies, and his attraction to fake god-men. But Buddhadev drew the line at his relationship with Peter Orlovsky. During a formal dinner party,

Peter had read from a soon-to-be-published transcript of a Tangier lovemaking session. He said he had typed it up on Allen's back in the middle of fellatio. The hostess fainted, and the party ended in confusion. Even worse, Peter had asked to use his daughter's shower, only to emerge from it stark naked, terrorizing the family maidservant.

One pundit, writing in *Swadhinata,* was even more severe. He had been keeping an eye on the pair from where he sat at the coffeehouse, noting how Peter retrieved an extra chair by . . . putting it *on his head!* Ginsberg and Orlovsky, "top notch among the Beatniks," insulted the good manners of the people of Calcutta. Their embrace of instinct, at the expense of "civilization and rationality," had led them to appear on "the streets in a semi-naked condition at times, to interrupt women speakers at literary meetings with unmannerly shouts, and to write vulgar poetry." They had even been seen at night with an unmarried Bengali girl. "They are looking out for 'ganja' since their arrival . . . that is supposed to lead one to 'nirvana,' although they have a costlier drug with them—a Mexican pill made from dried mushrooms. They say: usually you see what your mind tells you to see, but if you take these pills you will see their real nature."

Sunil and Shakti, veterans of similar skirmishes, were eager to try the pills. Allen had advised them to have a friend watch over them in case they got scared. They went to Tarapada's house in Kalighat with four doses. Preparing for the worst, they wore their best clothes. As there was madness in Tarapada's family, he agreed to attend to them. Sunil lay on the floor, happily absorbing the colors that seemed to swirl around him in huge puddles. The electrical lines running across the walls took on the appearance of snakes before actually becoming snakes. Whatever he thought of materialized, as if there were no line at all between the practical and imaginary world.

Shakti began thinking of death, only to have death become real to him. He panicked.

"Tarapada, am I going to die?" he shouted.

"No, Shakti, you are not going to die."

"Feel my feet, are they not feeling cold?"

"No, they are not cold."

"I *am* dying," he insisted, then commanding: "Write down my last words!"

Tarapada threw away the last two pills. Sunil was disappointed. He hadn't been scared at all. Yet the next time Allen saw Jyoti, to their mutual bewilderment, Allen gave *him* the bottle.

AFTER HUNKERING DOWN during the nasty summer months, Allen was chagrined to find that when the clouds rolled in and the rains came down, the monsoons also opened the gates to a plague of illnesses. He was beset by dysentery, kidney stones, chest infections, and worms. Between his bouts of illness and letter writing, Allen would take half a grain of morphine with atropine, sleep away the midday heat, and wake up feeling fit for another evening with Sunil, Shakti, Jyoti, or Utpal. Tarapada had been rechristened Torpedo. Both Allen and Peter began wearing hand-loom kurta pajamas with a red towel on one shoulder and a sling bag on the other. In Calcutta, the jhola bag and kolhapuri sandals were the badge of the intellectual. Suddenly, beatnik parties were the new rage.

With the departure of Hope for Dacca, Peter had set his romantic sights on Manjula Mitra, a slim, sharp-featured student of Buddhadev Bose in the comparative literature program at Jadavpur University. Conveniently, she lived alone in a furnished room with a private entrance in Jodhpur Park, and he began spending evenings there. To the *Krittibas* poets, she gave the impression that she had come from nowhere and, through her own determination, was trying to secure her future. Too proud to rely on feminine wiles to ingratiate herself with Bose, whom she admired greatly, she wore simple white saris and worked hard at her studies. She was determined to live abroad, and for that she was entirely dependent upon Bose's favor. She introduced Peter to the sarod, while he showed her how to play the guitar. Allen found her boring. If it occurred to him that Peter was disappearing more and more into his own world, he made no note of it.

Lying abed nursing his illnesses alone in the Amjadia, Allen was equally unaware of the dimensions of the festival taking shape outside his Muslim neighborhood. By early September, the city was already heaving with pilgrims and holy men who'd arrived in anticipation of Durga *puja*. One evening, listening to rickshaw handbells below his balcony tinkle hopefully, Allen looked up to discover a stranger in the room. A long-haired man in a saffron robe had walked in unannounced, madly waving a letter to Bertrand Russell. He wanted Allen's help in crafting an appeal, convinced that Hinduism held the key to world peace.

Inevitably, the man reminded Allen Ginsberg of his mother.

MUCH LIKE HIS FATHER, Nagendra Nath, Asoke Sarkar was destined to be torn between the aspiration to a saintly life and the hungers of an earthly one. The radiant orange robes of saints and sannyasis had followed the young Asoke when his family moved from Calcutta to Behala, but the procession soon tapered off when word got out that the Sarkar patronage had been severely curtailed owing to Nagendra Nath's business reverses. Until then, the boy had been raised to become a Buddhist priest or Hindu pandit. Suddenly, Asoke was hearing talk from his father that he should study harder. Umashasi now wanted her son to attend Eton and Cambridge so that he might become a solicitor at the Calcutta high court. Asoke mourned the sudden loss of his heroic sadhus and the company of the well-heeled clientele of the Massage & Bath Clinic Ltd. He blamed his father for their absence and abruptly left home to become a magician. He was fourteen.

Four years later, he went into film acting before marrying a widow with two daughters. He had two children with her. When he was twenty-two he contracted tuberculosis, and Nagendra Nath took in his wayward son, nursing him back to good health. After his recovery, Asoke returned to scrambling to support his wife and brood, writing screenplays or running the Rupali Cinema tea shop. He thought nothing of dropping in on the governor of West Bengal, talking his way past the security desk at Raj Bhavan. He made a practice of befriending what foreigners did come to the city, regularly touching base with the various consuls and cultural affairs officers to learn of the new arrivals. His English was perfect.

The catholicity of Asoke's professional life was mirrored in his spiritual one. When he fell for another girl in Calcutta, he married her, too, using Sufi rites and appropriating the Sufi surname "Fakir" to rationalize the acquisition of a second wife. Where a sannyasi or sadhu denoted a Hindu ascetic mendicant, a Sufi fakir was a Muslim mendicant. In Arabic, *faqir* meant "poor" and described the man (or woman) who realizes that all wealth belongs to God alone. Like sannyasis, fakirs were nomadic, following the same pilgrimage routes as their Hindu brethren all over Bengal. Formerly, both were treated as an infestation by the British and with reverence by the peasants and nawabs and zamindars from whom they extorted charity. It was Asoke Fakir who walked into the top-floor room at the Amjadia and thereby became Allen Ginsberg's guide to all things holy and Bengali.

Asoke first brought Allen to Ganja Park in South Calcutta, near Rashbehari Avenue, his mystic equivalent of Allen's Harlem tenement. There Asoke pointed out where he had been lying dazed with hunger on a bench, his head turtled into his chest, when, opening his eyes, he suddenly recognized Kali's feet passing so close to his head that he might have touched them. This vision led him to take up the life of an itinerant and minister to the poor. He founded a Vedanta center at 184 Sarat Bose Road with a mission to work toward "the Reformation of Humanity." Nonviolence was the "seed mantra" for those who wanted to create a world of love.

Asoke then brought him to the temple at the foot of the Howrah bridge. There he introduced him to the sadhu who lived in a burlap tent near the muddy steps. The sadhu tended the shrine favored by the truckers who passed through the city. As a tram thundered across the bridge above them, Asoke translated the sadhu's reflections. Indicating the steel roar of the bridge above him, but in a motion that seemed to Allen to suggest the entire universe, the sadhu shouted, "It's a great machinery." From there Asoke led Allen north along Mahatma Gandhi Road, through a side street to Burrabazar up Chitpur Road, talking nonstop about sadhus and Sufism and Baul singers, his many physical sufferings, and the all-powerful significance of their shared birthdates. "The difference is 1926 and 1925," Asoke wrote upon his return home, "but ONE YEAR has beaten the next by miles of insults, pains, shocks, pleasure and passion."

With the black puddles of mud spackling his calves as he navigated the broken pavement, Allen dutifully followed Asoke Fakir's saffron robe all the way to the burning ghats at Nimtola.

"HARI BOL," THE MEN CRIED. "Har Har Mahadeva!" they shouted, invoking Shiva before cupping the glowing chimney of smoke to their lips and blasting. At the cremation ghat, death wears a human face. Corpses lay garlanded in flowers, waiting their turn in the fire pit. A small child, coated with ghee and wrapped neatly in muslin. A prosperous-looking man in a dhoti resting peacefully on wood blocks under a blanket of wood chips. On his first visit with his notebook, Allen's eyes skirted the pyres to find the sadhus squatting in circles around tiny piles of flowers, singing and chanting. In the temple next door, a half-naked young man sat next to an older orange-robed saint with a mane of white hair. A eunuch stood up and, to the beat of a blind drummer, slithered sensuously in a burlesque dance for money and offerings.

Meditating on the cremation fire dissolves ego, ignorance, anger, and lust. Attachments burn away with flesh. Grief itself becomes a *sadhana*. Asoke told Allen that there were spiritual practices, called *smasana sadhanas,* tailored for cremation grounds. That there were places in the countryside where Tantric sadhus sat on skulls to meditate, slept alongside corpses, where they slept *with* corpses, in order to overcome the fear of death. Allen walked from pyre to pyre, inspecting the cross-legged and meditating sadhus who waved him off with an air of contempt. He retreated with a *namaste* of respect and made excited and fearful plans to return. He planned, eventually, to spend an entire night there.

Thereafter, a typical evening would begin at Chang Wa or Nanking in Chinatown to eat fried noodles, drink, smoke cigarettes, and talk, and then the lot of them would pile into a taxi to go to Nimtola. Sunil noted that on those evenings when Asoke accompanied them, he would announce that he was ending a lengthy fast, leaving it up to Allen to pick up the bill. At Nimtola they would go first to the temple and shove a five-rupee note under the toe of a sadhu, who after a glare in their direction would send an acolyte off for some ganja from the nearby paan shop and prepare the pipe. After taking a coal from one of the funeral pyres, the sadhu would take the first hit, and then the poets would compete silently to see who could inhale without coughing. Ginsberg was the acknowledged champion. Fully stoned, they would sit and watch the stream of corpses arrive on charpoys bedecked with flowers, the pyres roaring around them. Tuesday night was Kali night. People would come to sing choral hymns to the mother goddess, passing the pipe.

As the poets were almost all Hindu Brahmins, it was hard to conceive a larger insult to caste prohibitions than to be sitting in the ash and billowing smoke of the charnel fires smoking ganja without a relative to mourn. Only Tantrics, who believed in neither caste nor purity, behaved with such impunity. Yet they all treated Nimtola, a new thrill, as a lark. Sunil, who had seen his father's body to Nimtola the year before, joked it was an ideal place to find job leads. When a middle-aged corpse arrived, they might take advantage of the lengthy cremation with an eye to learning the late householder's place of employment.

The sadhus were not eager talkers, so Allen began coming on his own just to sit and smoke and listen to the chants and music. After repeated visits, he forced himself to witness the exact process by which flesh was transformed into bone and ash, moving from pyre to pyre with his journal to describe the sight, sound, and smell of a cremation with nearly hallucinatory intensity. He would make a point of being there on Tuesdays, shyly hanging on the periphery. But it was that first night, the evening of September 5, 1962, that caught him completely by surprise.

Afterward he walked home alone to the Amjadia, passing the sleepers on curbs and on the tables of shuttered restaurants. He lay on his bed, a glass of milk in his warm hands, and fixed his eyes

on the crude wooden shutters of his room. Could he not, by will
alone, get the shutters to open once again on the voice of heaven?

> When I was young you came with the
> voice of the tender rock
> Transformed the Sun.
> Exact pictures no longer describe.
> My poetry no longer describe. The
> Contact. Dear Blake, come back.

The shutters did not open. Allen had not quite realized it yet,
but he had found his *sadhana,* if not quite the teacher he'd expected. That night he dreamed again of Bill, returning home to
find him in his room at the Amjadia, cool and distant as ever.

"It isn't enough for yr heart to break, because everybody's
heart is broken now."

"IF I THOUGHT his figures & reasoning were really correct, I
would be inclined to do something," Allen wrote his father. Allen
had appended a note to the bottom of Asoke's letter to Bertrand
Russell, one of the founders of the Campaign for Nuclear Disar-
mament. He had doubts about joining any organization, his note
said, as that would inevitably implicate him in just the sorts of
power plays that now held the world hostage. Wouldn't it be better to use psychology or drugs to heal the cold war psychosis?
Allen threw in Blake as well, as if poetry constituted a possible
fifth column. Though Russell acknowledged the unearthly power
of Blake's poems, he didn't share Allen's faith that poetry would
make a difference. The odds of a nuclear conflagration amounted
to a near mathematical certainty, he stated grimly. It was now
"Act or Perish."

"I'm not sure he's exaggerating or not," Allen wrote again to
his father three weeks later. "Yet on thinking it does seem to make
sense, that with all the hysteria & hairtrigger network. . . ." He'd
pretty much ignored the apocalypse scenario as an actual possibility. Intuitively, however, he had thought something was up. Death's-

heads had begun popping up in his dreams, along with odd encounters with JFK and Khrushchev. If, as the Hindus believed,
time came in rounds of four cycles, or yugas, such a development
would likely occur now, during Kali Yuga, the fourth and final
one. Kali Yuga was known as the Age of Destruction. Then again,
wasn't Russell's alarmist talk projecting the same Henry Luce
hallucination? "What you think?" he asked his father. Allen wrote
similar letters to Gary, Lucien, and Jack to muster their opinion.
Gary replied that if the world crisis was still going on when he'd
finished what he had to do, he was prepared to get into trouble.
Another question arose: Was the human race worth saving?

"To be or not to be" was still the question, Allen sighed.

At the outset of the Cuban missile crisis less than a month
later, he backtracked in a panic to the specter of Burroughs cutting up newspaper clippings and typescripts in Tangier. Was the
world's political leadership truly being directed from an outer space
satellite manned by alien insects? He tried cut-ups for the first
time, halfheartedly mixing snippets of JFK's statements with those
of the TASS news agency. The results were inconclusive, proving
only the emptiness of the language of both sides. Thus, the timing
of his and Peter's trip to Tarapith couldn't have been better. The
monsoons had moved on, and according to Asoke, Tarapith was
the place to find those Tantric adepts and fakirs who worshipped
both Tara, the blue goddess of the burning ground, and Kali, "the
missus of destruction." That had to be worth something. Gregory
doubted it. Allen didn't know one "damn thing about the missus
of destruction." Asoke and Shakti accompanied them.

Two hundred miles north of Calcutta, Tarapith was a quiet
river town set amid the paddy fields of Birbhum district of Bengal. At the end of their third day there, Allen, Peter, Asoke, and
Shakti sat on the porch of the temple priest's thatched hut, completely stoned. Fireflies blinked in the woods, where the sound of
scattered voices singing, "Hari Bol, Hare Hare Krishna!" could be
heard from the lean-tos, hutments, grass shacks, and tombs that
peppered the place. While Asoke rambled on, Shakti ridiculed his
holy man blather, accusing him of being as ignorant as a goat. Asoke
ignored him. *Pranayama* breathing, Allen had learned, required a

slow inhale for four counts, holding breath for sixteen, and exhaling over eight. He'd begun spending five minutes every morning and evening doing several rounds of it. Peter practiced it, too, at least when he was smoking ganja. Allen scribbled by lamplight, describing the sadhu scene as reminiscent of Mill Valley, the sadhus themselves "gentle homeless on-the-road teaheads" before whom even respectable, weekender-type pilgrims paid their respects. He was still trying to absorb his first experience of a blood sacrifice.

"You must write when you're dead," Asoke said, watching him scribble. "Give consciousness to the mind which will write— One mind in the burning ghat, one walking in death & one watching and writing." Allen wrote that down.

"As I'm *not* dead, I can smoke again," Shakti added, lighting another pipe. An hour before, walking back at dusk from a country fair, Shakti watched, terrified, as his body became denuded of color. He began to shout, gripped by the delusion he was being burned to a crisp. He had since calmed down. By inhaling even more deeply, Shakti imagined he was goading death into making another move. How was it, he asked, that death came all at once, instead of by degrees?

"Yeah," Peter squeaked, struck by the thought.

Sitting beside him in a red kurta, Allen wondered if killing mosquitoes was against dharma. As if from a great distance, he saw one on his pajamaed knee and then wrote down in detail what he remembered of the sacrifice of the small furry lamb the night before. It was a goat.

"When again & again the world will be covered with vice & sin, I will come to bring peace to the people in vice and sin—I shall come to *Establish Religion* . . . ," Asoke thundered incoherently before hitting a prophetic note: "Shakti, get up—you will go high, but you will not die." Allen watched an insect climb the red mud wall behind Asoke's head.

A story is told that long, long ago, in the first of the four yugas, a meditating sage began to curse the Tara mantra he'd been given because it had failed to secure him the powers he'd hoped for. Tara promptly cursed him back, driving him off. The sage returned home crestfallen, and his father suggested he go north to Tibet to ask the advice of the Buddha. The Buddha told him to return to India and worship Tara making use of Tantric practices. At first the sage resisted, relenting only when the Buddha insisted there was no other way. He went to Tarapith, and it was there, on a seat of five human skulls, that the sage repeated his Tara mantra three hundred thousand times. Tara, mollified, materialized to grant him one wish.

When Tara arrived in Bengal from Tibet, she took on a number of Kaliesque qualities. She haunted the cremation grounds and was generally found astride a corpse, brandishing various sharp weapons in her four hands. Like Kali, she wore a necklace of severed heads, welcomed blood sacrifice, and had a blue complexion. Not far from her temple at Tarapith, along the banks of the river, is the vast burning ground. Those who cannot afford cremation are buried in shallow graves until the animals or the rains disinter them. It is here, among the smoking, half-burned, half-buried corpses, that Tara is said to keep company with jackals. This is the blue goddess who draws Tantric sadhus and fakirs to Tarapith.

Among them was the lunatic Bengali saint Bamakhepa. The day before, Allen, Asoke, Peter, and Shakti had all attended a special *puja* for him. After failing his studies, Asoke told Allen, Bamakhepa left home, sent to work first as a temple cook, then as a cowherd. But at every task save devotion, he was hopeless. He took to drinking rice wine from empty skulls and sleeping in the cremation ashes, abandoning caste entirely. On his lone visit to Kalighat in Calcutta, he was discovered by Ramakrishna and pronounced a saint. Asoke, having changed into a purple lungi and torn white shirt for the *puja,* told Allen how Bamakhepa had accidentally set fire to his house, made an image of Kali in cow dung, and banged tin pans all day. After many years, Asoke said, Tara finally appeared to Bamakhepa in a blue light, standing on a corpse with an erect snake arising from the matted hair of her head. Thereafter, they would play hide-and-seek on the burning grounds, with Bamakhepa running and cutting his feet on the bones, falling and weeping so that Tara would comfort him.

And why wouldn't a death-haunted, motherless, wandering Jew like Allen Ginsberg also be drawn to Tarapith and the story of Tara and Bamakhepa? In late October 1962, the world waited in the shadow of another holocaust, one in which the earth itself threatened to become a vast cremation ground. Tara brings liberation by terror. The "old woman of skulls" of "Kaddish" had long before held her youngest son similarly rapt and terrified. As a child, Allen had contemplated his mother's naked body, fat from Metrazol and crisscrossed by jagged scars, with love and revulsion. The wires inside her head, Naomi insisted, transmitted radio signals from Hitler; she had found his mustache in the sink. At twelve, Allen had asked her doctors to give her the blood transfusion she begged for. In his twenties, he had signed the papers opening her skull to the third eye of the lobotomists' pick. "Kaddish," his death prayer for her, bared his intimate knowledge of the missus of destruction.

> Oh glorious muse that bore me from the womb, gave suck first
>   mystic
> Life & taught me talk and music, from whose pained head I
>   first took
> Vision—
> Tortured and beaten in the skull—What mad hallucinations
>   of the
> damned that drive me out of my own skull to seek Eternity till I find
> For Thee, O Poetry—and for all humankind call on the Origin.

In the darker inner sanctum of the temple at Tarapith, behind a hollow metal image of Tara, there is a stone wrapped in a red sari. Those pilgrims who wish to see it are admitted in small groups. This is Tara's true form, they are told. It is said that when Tara appeared to the sage to grant him his wish, he asked that she show herself as the Buddha had described her to him. Immediately, Tara laid down her weapons and gently took Shiva to her breast, like a mother who can deny her child nothing. And then she turned to stone.

Two days after the 1956 telegram announcing her lonely death at Pilgrim State, Allen received Naomi's final blessing. "Get married Allen," his mother wrote, "don't take drugs—the key is in the bars, in the sunlight in the window." To honor an old woman tending Bamakhepa's shrine, singing to him like Tara Ma herself, Allen gave her tea, rupees, and a piece of sugar candy before departing, walking back through the paddy fields to catch the night train to Suri.

THEY WERE KNOWN as holy fools. Until Tagore discovered the gentle haunting beauty of their songs, they were regarded as vagrants who wandered the Bengal countryside, their only home the open road. Translated, their name—Baul—means "possessed." They sing accompanied by a one-stringed ektara and drum, purposefully flouting every term in the social contract to assert their independence. One will wear the cast-off lungi of a Muslim, a kurta from a Hindu, and a ragged patchwork coat called a *pied gauri* to show his scorn of worldly things. Under the influence of Sufis, Tantrics, Buddhists, and the Vaishnavite's devotion to Krishna, a Baul believes the five senses will lead one astray like a drunken ferryman and will pride himself on being aloof to sorrow, joy, and regret. From Tarapith, Asoke brought Allen, Peter, and Shakti to Suri, where he knew of a large clan of Bauls. There Allen found the aged Nabini Das Baul on his deathbed, half-paralyzed and unable to wander farther. Upon being introduced, the old man said of Allen and Peter, "They are born Bauls, they will spread the Baul message, and true peace, friendship and dharma will arrive." Sitting by the old man's bedside, Allen took down Asoke's translation of the old man's quavery song.

> O blue dressed woman why don't
>   You put on your blue dress again
> Put vermillion on yr forehead
>   & come before me as a lover,
> & wind & bind & plait my hairs . . .
> I came to play the flute in Brindaban
> Now I give the flute to you,
>   young girl— . . .

Why don't you take my flute
  & let it sing on yr lips
  Radha Radha Radha

A Baul is only helpless, it is said, before the sound of Krishna's flute.

THE DAY AFTER ALLEN had left Calcutta for Tarapith, Ambassador Galbraith met with Nehru. The prime minister had just sent a letter congratulating JFK and Khrushchev on the peaceful resolution of the Cuban missile crisis seven days after it had begun. The Indian government had withheld its ritual criticism of American actions when it became clear that the Soviet Union would not be siding with India in its border dispute with China.

The preceding week, while the world was riveted to the spectacle of the two superpowers threatening everyone with Armageddon, fighting had broken out in two separate places along the Himalayan border. In the arid altitudes of Ladakh at the northernmost tip of the subcontinent, the Indian army had held the line. Thousands of miles to the east, in the territory known as the North-East Frontier Agency (NEFA) near Bhutan, the Indian army collapsed and suffered serious casualties. In the aftermath of the rout, the general in charge was rumored to have had a heart attack. Galbraith arrived at the Nehru meeting knowing full well that fellow nonaligned nations had, like Russia, balked at going up against China and that India stood alone. With unsettling swiftness, the first of the American C-130s arrived in Calcutta four days later, stocked with infantry weapons and light artillery.

It was a nearly tectonic realignment. "The most treasured of preconceptions have been shattered," Galbraith wrote to JFK. Krishna Menon, intent on the wickedness of the United States and Pakistan, had not taken the threat of Chinese invasion seriously; the Indian troops were poorly equipped for battle at high altitudes. The Calcutta Maoists were convinced Nehru had taunted the People's Liberation Army with Indian troop posturing. The territories in question were in the high Himalayas, impassable in winter and, but for the gods and the most hardy tribals, mostly uninhabitable. Few could say for certain where the borders were. Still, the underlying fear was that India might become the next Tibet. In Delhi, people began digging trenches. In Calcutta's Chinatown, Nanking and Chung Wah restaurants were attacked by mobs. That it was America that rushed in with planes was, for the Calcutta Stalinists, further disgrace.

"Now nothing is so important to [Nehru], more personally than politically, than to maintain the semblance of this independence," Galbraith wrote JFK. "His age no longer allows of readjustment." Eventually a border settlement would be reached, Menon would be sidelined, and, six months after the assassination of the American president in November 1963, Jawaharlal Nehru would die, never having fully recovered from the shock of the war. Yet, however swiftly it ended, the questions raised by the provenance of the conflict would never be settled.

Returning to Calcutta calmed by the pastoral stillness, Allen told Sunil he supported the idea of India defending itself if attacked, but privately he found the idea of Indian warmaking as absurd as the tinny World War I–era military bands being trotted out in moth-eaten uniforms. Given the difficulty of mailing a single letter at the Indian post office, he observed, it was hard to imagine the government tackling anything more complicated. Sunil, too, hated the shouting in the streets, the lies of the politicians, and the proliferation of third-rate verse celebrating India's greatness. *Desh* told him he must now write in a more patriotic vein. When Sunil said he was prepared to believe India had been invaded, the Stalinists and the Maoists accused him of being a government lapdog.

Shakti was even more unsettled. He had joined up with another poet named Malay Roy Choudhury to publish inflammatory manifestos and broadsides. They called themselves the Hungry Generation. He started writing poems in English. Sunil was crestfallen; he believed Shakti had the makings of a great Bengali poet. Only after Shakti had returned to Bengali did Sunil confess to Allen that he had blamed him for this injury, however inadvertently committed.

Allen was now convinced that all such conflicts were the result of government-organized hysteria and media manipulation. What was really needed was a change in the global emotional climate. Asoke Fakir was now taking him to Nabadwip, the birthplace of Chaitanya Mahaprabhu. With Brindaban, where Krishna was said to have dallied with the cowgirls, Nabadwip had become a hotbed of the Krishna love cult. A big sadhu convention was in the works, Allen told Ted Wilentz, and he was looking forward to the mass experience of universal bliss.

LIKE THE REST OF THE NATION, the old man spinning his *charkha* on the Benares porch had been traumatized by the twin events of the sudden war and the brink of nuclear annihilation. He had come to a decision. He would lead a four-thousand-mile peace march from Delhi to Peking, in the spirit of Gandhiji's salt march. Under the banner of the World Peace Brigade, he would send out flyers from his ashram in Benares inviting peace organizations from all over the world to India. Some of his friends tried to dissuade him. He was nearly seventy; what need did he have to get mixed up in politics again? Even Krishnamurti tried to talk to him. But he was adamant. India would be forced once again to take Gandhi's measure. Even Russia and America, at each other's throats, might reconsider the parlous path they had taken. In Bombay the year before, Krishnaji had asked him:

"If you knew that you were about to die, what would you do? Can you live one hour completely—live one day—one hour—as if you were going to die the next?"

Shankar Rao Deo, former general secretary of the Indian National Congress, prominent in the struggle for Indian independence, decided that he could.

"ENCLOSED PICTURE OF HOPE high on bhang. Dancing India style," Allen wrote Gregory in mid-October. Made from crushed hemp leaves mixed with almond milk, bhang is considered the sacred potion of Shiva. Under its influence time is dissolved and perceptions intensify until the most complex arrangements of Indian classical music unravel, the parts played by each instrument prised apart and experienced singly and simultaneously. Yogis use bhang as a meditation aid. Its visions are said to re-create the sensations immediately following death, when the body has passed over but consciousness of life still lingers. Hope had taken to bhang with enthusiasm, Allen wrote.

Upon her return from Dacca, Hope spent her days in the Asiatic Society Library on Park Street, one of the largest and oldest depositories of Indian history, language, and culture. In the evenings, she could be found with a Brooklyn girl she had met on her travels. "First time I've seen her sociable to a companion like girls should be," Allen observed, adopting a fatherly tone. She had also fallen in with a number of boisterous young Muslim businessmen, racing around the city in motorcars. Nearly every time Sunil saw her, she was with a new boyfriend, often with a veil that partially obscured her face and gave her an air of mystery. She rarely said a word. Sunil, shy and self-conscious about his weight, was impressed by Allen's casual manner toward her. Dancing lessons had been added to her study of Urdu, Allen reported to Gregory. "All very ladylike," Allen remarked, before asking, "You still getting married?"

At first, Gregory had justified his perpetually delayed departure for India by distinguishing his poetic themes from Allen's. He worried that Allen was mixing up all the myths. He was sticking with God. And, of course, Zeus and his minions. "First you say we take India gods [too] seriously," Allen pointed out, "and then you say we treat India like a coffee house." He threw up his hands. "How should I know what I'm doing in India anyway? All I know is that it's a ball, and I feel great." In May, writing from New York, Gregory promised he would make a final decision on the boat to Tangier. In the meantime, he sent his love to Hope, his "ideal revolutionary." On board two weeks later, he wrote that he was now determined, at long last, to come. However, if he took the month-long boat passage from Marseille to Bombay, he didn't think his money would hold out. If he took an airplane, he warned, he might arrive completely broke. But he was definitely coming.

Upon his arrival in Tangier, he found a letter from Allen. Gregory's affectionate greeting to Hope had not achieved the desired effect. Hope thought he was a romantic idealist, Allen now informed him, one who had little grasp of either India or herself. Allen quoted her: "He's trying to flatter me, but he doesn't know what I want to hear. So he's trying this approach." Corso, stung, replied he was only trying to be nice. "She still be my angel in this here love girl soul life and what can I say who hath not seen or heard from her in such a long time." His plans shifted, and he decided to go to Florence until after the monsoons. Allen continued to instruct him on what India books to read, what he would need for his visa, and what shots were required, but he also said nothing to allay Gregory's financial anxieties. Corso's next letter, written in August, included a check, courtesy of a new girlfriend. He had fallen in love with a Cleveland schoolteacher and was going to marry her. "I love her, love her more than anything, more than Hope ever." Two months later she was pregnant, and they planned to return to New York. "It's what I want," Gregory wrote definitively, "a life that shall bear life, produce in a funny kind of way." He signed off, "Give Hope my ever undying love."

Either the life with wife and child will clarify him, Gregory wrote the very next day, "or I can run to India and embrace thee and Hope and sing and bang my head against the Indian temples for joy and forgetfulness." What should he do? In November, Gregory wrote again from Paris. The pregnancy had turned out to be illusory.

"I wish I could zoom to India and see you and Hope."

"THE LAST TIME I SAW HOPE she had changed her name to Delores," Gregory began one account many years later. She and Jean had greeted him at the door of a Paris hotel room. They wore long black overcoats and beautifully polished black boots. "How like Russian revolutionaries they looked!" Under their Cossack shirt gowns cinched at the waist by big black belts, each carried a gun. Hope reached for hers and tossed it carelessly on the bed. When Gregory picked it up to look at it more closely, she snatched it back.

"Nobody touches my gun," she said.

"This is a story about a girl," he continued, as if to begin again. "An american girl born in the south of aristocractic heritage, her frail delicate mother was a Bostonian and her Mayor father from a long line. . . ." He went on for a few more lines before stopping. He would never finish.

What happened between Gregory Corso and Hope Savage in February 1957 upon his first arrival in Europe? After Hope left Paris on her travels with Jean, Corso fell apart. He tried heroin for the first time. He bought himself a gun. He wrote bad checks and made drunken scenes in Paris cafés and Spanish bars, living off one girl after another until Allen arrived in Amsterdam to save him from the thugs he'd swindled. "Went thru one year of complete hell for such a soul as I who has known hell to be heaven," Corso wrote Peter, as if the nightmare were over.

Instead, the memory of Hope's last "no return address" letter had lodged like a tiny bone in his throat. For years, he struggled to name the nature of his loss and the course of his regret. In unfinished manuscripts hawked to collectors, he promised to tell only the nonfiction "Truth" about their legendary romance, without resort to "fiction exaggerations." How it began, how it developed, and how it ended. If Allen could make a myth out of a pack of college boys, he could do the same for his Hope. "A fine small jewel of a book," he promised, soliciting Gary's recollections of her in India. Visiting Joanne Kyger in Northern California, he ripped the picture of Hope at Juhu Beach out of her India album. Actual facts might have gone missing, along with authenticating letters and diaries, but he was certain Truth was still accessible. There was a hurried, guilty air about this project, as if he knew he was committing a travesty far worse than any other. "I need not . . . tell the whole truth, some remembrances are no body's business," he wrote, as if addressing Hope herself and allaying her fears that he would be anything but discreet.

In Gregory Corso, the romantic and the nihilist sparred perpetually. Beauty, he granted, had once served him well. His eye for beauty was keen because he needed beauty to obscure the doleful memories of his childhood: the old man in a cloud of feathers who plucked chickens on Delancey, the sight of a man peeing into another man's mouth on Ward D. All this dispersed in the light of beauty, a light Hope Savage embodied. His history with "Truth" was more troubled. Truth hadn't done him any favors. He made a virtual profession of mocking the so-called Truths of others. The "Beats" were fair game. But only Truth would do for Hope. Truth and Kindness.

Though she was his first great love, he said, trying again for Truth, they were never lovers. He revised himself. Sex meant nothing to her; she felt it made men into animals. Terrified of pregnancy, she made him wear two condoms. She was indifferent when he slept with other girls. Though she paid the rent on Macdougal for the year they lived there, they actually had separate rooms until Gregory insisted on breaking through a wall to join them together. After giving him the beautiful poet's cloak, she made him promise to stay out of her room, however insistently he pleaded. "I have known Almighty Kindness Herself! I have sat beside Her pure white feet, gaining Her confidence!" However it pained him to admit it, he was not her lover.

Yet Hope did love him. She loved to read to him, to buy him books and music. For both Shelley reigned supreme, and they pored over the details of his life like starstruck devotees. They would have long talks about their dreams. They spent afternoons making portraits of each other and their Siamese cats, Daphne and Oedipus. Then again the picture changed. While they were living on Macdougal Street, he became convinced she was turning tricks. He ended up following her to the post office. This was how he learned she received money from home and that her real name was Hope Savage. And she wouldn't ever read his poetry, he said; she didn't care for it. Some days she seemed to care only for Swinburne and Christopher Smart and Walter Savage Landor. It was difficult for him to listen to her recite other men's work, even long dead poets. Her plan to commit suicide frightened him. She introduced him to the work of the great German romantic Heinrich von Kleist. Von Kleist had found himself captive to the gifts of a Hedda Gabler–type woman and agreed to die with her, shooting her first and then himself. Was this what Hope expected of him?

At night, he would wake to the sound of her weeping. She would pace her room and speak to him only from behind a locked door. *"What is wrong?"* he would demand. He could not abide her tears. Her tears made him wild. All he could do was listen as she tried to explain. She claimed that her parents had sent her to a psychiatrist for shock treatment. This had stolen something from her, leaving her unfinished at the age of sixteen, her life beginning and ending in 1953.

"I don't know what they took away," she told him, "and therefore I feel I could never do anything perfect or complete." That was how, he claimed, she explained what was wrong and why she could not write poetry. He listened, he lost his temper. He lashed out at her parents, at her. He hit her once. He tried to force sex on her but relented in the face of her fierce resistance. She was only spirit, he wrote resignedly, devotedly. And then she left him to go to Paris, where she rescued another, less worthy man.

> But when the conquered spirit breaks free
> And indicates a new light
> Who'll take care of the cats?

The problem with Truth, Gregory reflected, is that once you say something is true, you cannot move forward: The way is blocked. If you merely say, "This is true," where do you go from there? It wasn't clear to whom Gregory Corso addressed this question, only that he was sincerely at a loss. So it had helped him to regard Truth as kin to confession. The fathers at the home for delinquents where he had spent part of his childhood had seen to it that Gregory absorbed his due of Catholicism. "The priest cut open my stomach, put his hands in me and cried:——Where's your soul?" he wrote.

Confession, he knew, required a complete airing and necessarily began with the profession that what was to follow was the Truth and Nothing But. Only then was it possible to go "beyond

Truth." Once a person's sins were forgiven, he imagined, nothing but Truth would be left. Perversely, however, his desire to confess had led to lies. He hadn't ever masturbated in church. He hadn't masturbated in front of Jesus on the cross. The largest lies, he discovered, were those confessions that seemed by their very nature monstrous; those were the ones they all had readily accepted as Truth. And still they forgave him. Allen forgave him, she forgave him. Perhaps he had left out the petty, ignominious sins, for their love of the extravagant false ones.

Thereafter, he believed that no matter how cruel the world had been to him, he deserved it. Because he had done bad things, and he hadn't confessed completely. She, however, was an innocent girl of sixteen when injustice found her. She had wanted to read Nietzsche and had been offered Albert Schweitzer. She wore a cape and black boots and was treated like an outlaw. She had defied the sheriff when they tried to shoot squirrels on her father's property. She had run away. These were not crimes, but evidence of her saintliness. Yet because her father was the mayor, because her behavior was frowned upon by ignorant, small-minded people, she was punished. It was also true that when he listed those at whose hands she had been ill-treated, he neglected to include himself.

> *I ran to Kindness, broke into Her chamber,*
> *And profaned!*
> *With an unnamable knife I gave Her a thousands wounds,*
> *And inflicted them with filth!*
> *I carried Her away, on my back, like a ghoul!*
> *Down the cobble-stoned night!*
> *Dogs howled! Cats fled! All windows closed!*
> *I carried Her ten flights of stairs!*
> *Dropped Her on the floor of my small room,*
> *And kneeling beside Her, I wept. I wept.*

ALL THE PITS WERE AFLAME, and the thick, oily smoke with the scary smell rolled over them, whirling madly up the lamp poles, haloing the lights, and spreading out over the Hooghly like a shape-shifting serpent monster. In homage to the mother goddess, one sadhu put a third eye over Allen's horn-rims from a paste of ash and vermilion. Allen found again the handsome sadhu with the radiant oiled body who had welcomed him the night he spent there two weeks before. This time Hope, Asoke, and Sunil had accompanied him for one last Tuesday evening at Nimtola. It was Allen's practice to approach each sadhu and inquire about his divine experiences. With Sunil translating, Allen went through his usual questions. What was the meaning of karma? What was meant by maya?

In the past, it had seemed to Sunil that sadhus never gave a straight answer. They would tell Allen to practice *pranayama* breathing or insist that there was no one definition, you had to understand it from your experience. But this evening, the sadhu resisted. How could Allen begin to understand the answers to these questions?

"You are an *angrez*," Sunil translated, "how much do you know about our culture? Unless and until you understand that, how can I answer you?"

Allen turned to Sunil. "Tell him that I am an infant, tell him I would like to begin at the very beginning. . . ."

Sunil had once tried to learn French so that he might read French poetry for himself, but Bengali was so much a part of him that other languages, even Hindi, did not come to him easily. No sooner had he begun to translate than, to his astonishment, Hope, tossing back the veil covering her face, interrupted him in perfect Hindi.

"Not 'I *was* an infant,' but 'I *am* an infant.'"

Allen collected the name and address of the sadhu's guru in Benares. He left the can of syrupy rosogolla as a gift before backing away, his hands pressed together in good-bye.

"I KNOW HER TO BE A GREAT LADY, fine brow, noble mind." Allen put the remark in quotes in his journal just as the *Doon Express* pulled out of Howrah station. Had these been the words of

Sterlyn B. Steele, cultural affairs officer at the USIS and generous dispenser of Cutty Sark? Had he offered this flattery to soften his insistence that there was nothing he could do, and of course he didn't believe a word of what people were saying?

On December 10, the day before Allen and Peter left for Benares, Hope Savage received an expulsion notice from the Indian authorities. Accused of "immorality," she had ten days to leave the country. When she made inquiries, it was suggested that she had been sleeping with Allen. "Of all people," Allen said to Jyoti. "Such crap." That night Allen was also detained, hauled off to the police station to answer questions. What was he doing sitting under the Howrah bridge with a large group of foreigners and disreputable poets if his intention was not, as he now insisted, to blow it up?

While there may have been a few U.S. consular officials relieved to have Ginsberg, his "wife," Orlovsky, and his girlfriend Miss Hope Savage finally leaving the city, Sterling Steele wasn't one of them, though he had more reason than most. Ginsberg had shown up at a USIS party at his home commemorating the fiftieth anniversary of *Poetry* with a crowd of young poets who proceeded to empty every whiskey bottle in the place and break some china in the process. One of them appeared the following day to apologize to his wife. Steele's superiors had doubtless fielded numerous inquiries from Indian intelligence about Ginsberg and his friends, but what did they expect? They were poets. How many American writers even bothered to come to India, much less Calcutta?

Allen had spent the day prior to his detainment nursing his angry kidneys and helping Hope write her letters of appeal. That evening, he and Peter had gone to the coffeehouse on College Street to see Sunil and the gang one more time. Shakti was there, holding forth before a group of Fulbright fellows and already quite drunk on rice wine. From Sunil Allen heard the news that a border settlement had been reached. Two weeks earlier, Chinese had pulled their troops from NEFA and called for a cease-fire, opening the way for diplomacy. Tired of speculating on the perpetually mysterious motivations of the Chinese, they all left with Allen so that he might sit one more time under the Howrah bridge. When someone pulled out a map to try to see if the temple was identified on it, two black-coated policemen with red hats appeared from nowhere and asked them what they were doing.

"We are trying to see where we should put our bomb," Peter volunteered in an insanely misjudged attempt at humor. Despite his holy fool affect, Peter often entertained some very dark thoughts.

Whistles were blown, more police arrived, and everyone was taken in to be questioned. Sunil was convinced he would lose his government jobs; having two of them was highly illegal. Luckily, one of the Fulbright fellows was able to convince a senior police official that it was a simple misunderstanding. When his friends asked him just how he'd managed that, he reluctantly produced a letter from his pocket. It read, in part, "I have known —— and his family since he was a child living in my same hometown in Texas. Please show him the same consideration you might give me." The letter was on White House stationery and signed "Vice President Lyndon Baines Johnson."

The day of Allen's departure, Hope made the rounds of offices to collect documents that would enable her to remain in Calcutta while waiting to hear from Delhi about her appeal of the expulsion order. Allen promised to come back to try to settle the matter if she needed him to. "Hope's integrity lost," Allen wrote on the train as it rattled out of the city, comparing the injustice of her plight with that of a heroine of a nineteenth-century classical romance, "the picaresque of the Pure Girl." Would Shelley have married her? Should he?

Neal Cassady had once tried to explain to a disbelieving and distraught Allen why Jack was getting married. Like his own marriages, Neal said, Jack's decision was the result of a combination of things: "a willful blindness, a perverted sense of wanting to help the girl and just plain what the hell." Peter felt the same about helping Manjula get out of Calcutta. He had also proposed marriage, but she was holding out for a foreign fellowship. Gregory, reliving his visit to Hope's parents in 1956, had a different view of marriage, but no less impulsive. "Should I get married, should I be good? / Astound the girl next door with my velvet suit and faustus hood?" For Corso, marriage would save *him*. The alternative was turning old alone in a furnished room with "pee stains on my underwear." Allen understood at least part of what Neal meant. He, too, wanted to protect Hope from getting caught in the gears of a paranoid state bureaucracy. For once, however, Allen wasn't worried about growing old alone and unloved. Allen thought his marrying Hope would "keep her free." It was as if the idea of Hope out there, forever wandering, elusive, and answering to no one, was now vital to him, too. As if her freedom were for both of them.

"My god!" Neal had exclaimed after his nuanced analysis of his own and Jack Kerouac's relationships with women. "I sound like the ladies home journal."

HENRY AND ELIZABETH SAVAGE lived for many years after Hope left, sending their letters and checks to a succession of American Express offices. After her 1961 visit, they never saw her again. Her brothers and sisters would grow up, find lovers she would never meet, have children whose names she would never know. Did they ever speak of her? Who wrote her of the deaths of her parents? Of her sister? Was she told of the death of her older brother's son? Or had she traveled so far away that such information could have no meaning? What love and longing they had for her, whatever mystery she presented to them, they kept to themselves.

And what of Thoreau's ideal of a free and true life, cut off from the claims of kinship and community? Though Hope's siblings found more certain futures up north, her parents eventually returned to Camden. Each spring for the rest of his life, the smells and pleasures Henry Savage had known since boyhood confirmed his intimate sense of home. He recognized Kershaw County's claims upon him with his numerous civic obligations and conservation efforts. After his death, his law partners would describe him as a devoted family man and true southern gentleman. "He was never boastful or harsh . . . and although he might not agree with you, he would never criticize or belittle anyone." His obituary in the local paper credited him with finding peaceful solutions to racial differences but did not mention his northern exile.

If these were Henry Savage's habits, if these were the claims he honored, can it justly be said that he did not live both a free life and a true one?

LIKE VENICE IN THE OFF-SEASON, Benares in winter has a magisterial indifference to those who come to walk the ghats and contemplate eternity. Yet in Venice the weight of one's irrelevance is lightened by this pitiless thought: The city is clearly mortal. In Benares there is no such consolation. The sight of the faithful reenacting ancient rituals in the midst of its undying grandeur can keep a person awake at night, haunted by the rickshaw wallah's sleepy conversations in the street below. The widow with her brass can, making her mincing, bowlegged way down to the Ganges, was there long before Allen Ginsberg took care to describe her, and she and her like will be there long after. It is not merely that this is the most ancient continuously lived-in city in the world. It is that Benares is forever and we are not. That is the song of Benares in winter.

The river plays the major chord of this lament, and in December 1962, the river was everywhere. It was in the air, mixed with the smoke of the dung fires, funeral pyres, fried noodle stalls, and bidis. It was in the shapeless black woolen sweater that Ginsberg wore to keep warm. It was in the thin red towels that would never dry out, and, most stubbornly, the river was in his lungs, which no cough, no matter how long or how deeply he hacked, would ever clear out. At night he coughed. In the morning, amid the sounds of the city bestirring itself, he coughed. Every pharmacist shrugged: He was a foreigner and unused to the climate, there was nothing to be done. But it was not only Allen Ginsberg who coughed, who fought off the river fog that settles like a cat on one's chest. The arrival of the yellow fog in the early morning was greeted by a cacophony of coughs. In winter, even the maharaja in his palace upriver coughed.

Allen spent the first few days in Benares staring into the funeral pyres at Manikarnika Ghat. After Nimtola, he found the scene tame. In front of him lay the Ganges, and behind him were the palaces and ashrams and *dharamsalas* and temples, stacked along the riverfront as it bent away from the train bridge to the south. The ghats lay at the feet of these palaces, Escher-like stone stairs of varying widths and depths. Some were steep and some were shallow enough for even the most ancient and buckled of widows to make their way from the lanes to the river's edge to bathe and receive ma Ganga's blessings.

Early one evening not long after they settled in, Allen stood on the balcony that overlooked the vegetable market at the intersection leading to Dasaswamedh Ghat. His journal lay open in front of him. Peter had gone out for tandoori chicken. The desk officer at the foreigner registration bureau had asked Allen why he stayed so long in India. And now, wrapped in a blanket to ward off the chill, he looked down at the evening crowds, the burping cows, and saw them as if for the first time. What he saw were moving corpses, dead things covered in clothes, bodies destined only for the pyres. With all the gongs being rung, all the cigarettes being sold, rickshaws flagged, meals cooked, clothes washed, tickets bought, it was hard to see what it all added up to beyond the tired thought that everyone, every living thing, was doomed.

One of the first things Allen did upon settling in a new city was to arrange to receive his mail at the nearest post office. In his own letters he argued politics with his father, sketched his itineraries, and conducted the business of having books sent, taxes paid, and proofs corrected. In letters, too, he would give rushed, condensed summaries of his travels, as if he didn't entirely trust language to carry the weight of what he had seen but couldn't bear being alone with it, either. A description from a letter to Lucien would end up repeated in another to Gary or Jack.

Unlike his letters, Allen's journal writing was a kind of solitary meditation. There, too, his observations tripped over one another, half-undressed, too much in a hurry to do more than sketch the tableaux of Dasaswamedh market or Manikarnika

Ghat. Yet, as he stood there on his balcony, light-headed with hunger and impatient for Peter to return with his chicken, suddenly the greedy litany he'd collected seemed "sleazy." He couldn't bring himself to reread any of his journal, much less mine it for poetry. In the shadows of the arcade overhang below him, the dying called out weakly. These frail shades had not yet made their way into his journal or his letters, but they hadn't escaped his eye. Having observed the dead so closely, having cataloged the raw incineration of flesh, would he now, from his perch, document these death throes as well?

Not long before leaving Calcutta, Allen had accepted an invitation to teach a three-week course in Vancouver the following summer. In exchange, he would receive a plane ticket home. Like a man who, without fully awakening, sees that he is dreaming, he suddenly realized that the time he had left in India was no longer open-ended. Had he found what he had come for? He had smoked in an opium den a few times, he had shot up morphine even more than that, but he'd abandoned his psilocybin. And what of finding a teacher whom he could love? What of getting closer to God? What of touching poverty? With the knowledge that he was running short of time came a sense of heightened urgency. He hoped that Benares would provide answers to these questions. But there was yet another lingering uncertainty. How was this all to end? Upon his awakening, would the long, winding sentence of India finish with a period, an exclamation, or a question mark?

In the midst of his reflections, Allen's eye was caught by a devotee profusely garlanded with flowers sprinting around the corner of the street below. He was carrying a brass tray of offerings and making a beeline for the ghats. Approached by the beggar camped next to the tobacconist's, the man grabbed a handful of sweets and filled the open palm before continuing merrily on his way. Allen turned to Peter, who had just returned with two dead birds to eat, snuck in under the nose of the landlord, a Brahmin pandit.

"They're all mad," he said, finishing his thoughts, at least for the day.

HE DIDN'T HAVE A WATCH but felt it must be near midnight. Not long after settling in Benares, Allen and Peter went off to spend Christmas at the Taj Mahal and, on their way back, New Year's Eve at Brindaban. What was the gang up to for New Year's? Allen wondered, scribbling in his journal by candlelight and contemplating their fates from his seat on the bank of the Yamuna River. Neal was out of jail, working in a garage. Jack was doubtless at Lucien's New Year's Eve party, and Gregory, though still nursing his old heartsickness over Hope, sounded cheerful in Paris. His father would be lifting a glass of champagne to Times Square on TV, up to his hubcaps in snow. And, after a year's long silence, finally a letter from Bill, content in Paris, forswearing drugs and writing maniacally. Nearby, a Shiva temple marked the starting point of the circular pilgrimage of the twelve forests of Brindaban. This was the spot where pilgrims are warned that the path ahead was a razor's edge and, though a million may complete the journey, few attain the goal.

Bankey Behari, a former lawyer from Allahabad, had given Allen and Peter the key to the empty garden house on the river. An intimate of Gandhi, Tagore, Krishnamurti, Maharshi, and Sri Aurobindo, Bankey Behari had spent his youth living with Sufi mystics before moving to the Himalayas to study the lives of the Vedantists. Like Allen, Bankey Behari had tried to learn from the path of those who had realized God in their lives. He translated poetry by Sufis, mystics, and saints. After taking a vow of silence, he spent eight years studying every faith, from Christianity to Vaishnavism, in an effort to choose his own. The poetry of the sixteenth-century saint Mira Bai eventually led him to Brindaban, the setting of Krishna's love scenes with Radha and the cowgirls. In these groves every tree, every stone, and every cow is witness to his trysts. For thirty years, reading and rereading Mira Bai's love poems, Behari had lived in hope of seeing the face of the blue god.

Mira Bai, a princess of Mewar, had been promised to the Maharaja of Chitor, and when she turned eight, she went to live in his

palace. Though her husband worshipped Durga, the annual *lilas*
reenacting the life of Krishna had bewitched Mira Bai, and at her
wedding, she gripped a tiny figurine of him. One day, Mira Bai was
standing on the palace balcony when she looked up to see Krishna
watching her from a short distance, his eyes shooting desire. He
called her name softly before taking up his flute.

Her ecstasy, Bankey Behari wrote, would be followed by an
endless lament. Poetry poured from her. Krishna's earrings reflected the light on his bright cheeks, "as if a fish were playing in
the blue deep." In the palace, Mira Bai began to live the life of a
hermit. Out of his mind with jealousy, her husband poisoned her.
He gave her a bed of nails and garlanded her with a cobra, only to
see her embrace her martyrdom with even more fervent worship
of her absent lord. "She carried the cross so that she might wear
the crown," Bankey Behari wrote with ecumenical élan.

In Mira Bai's poems, Bankey Behari found the inner map of
Brindaban that he was to follow. Faith was the first station, as it is
faith that provides the strength to overcome the obstacles that
prevent the pilgrim from entering the sacred groves. Mira Bai finally found her way to Brindaban. Then the pilgrim must visit
with the local saints, questioning them, taking *darshan,* dwelling
in their holiness. The resident saint refused to see Mira Bai because, as a sannyasi, he was forbidden to look upon the face of a
woman.

"In Brindaban, who except Krishna is a man?" she demanded.
Even Shiva must take the form of a cowgirl and surrender his ascetic ways in Brindaban. The saint fell at her feet, and Mira Bai was
pronounced an incarnation of Radha.

Worship leads to the next leg of the journey, the removal of
hindrances between devotee and god: In Brindaban, the compet-
ing claims of family and society fall away. The householder must
leave his home and his possessions, carrying only his love. Out of
this obsession is born the final stage of pilgrimage: the devotion that
will win Krishna's heart. In Bankey Behari's description of the
journey through the twelve forests, there is no austerity, no self-
denial. The end is not *samadhi* or satori, enlightenment or wisdom. The goal is not even the satisfaction of desire. Instead, the

traveler to Brindaban steps knowingly into a divine play, the endlessly circling *lila* of love and universal bliss.

The sounds of a radio carried across the water. Allen's mind
sailed through the last twelve months like a sailor revisiting port
stays on a long ocean journey. He measured the year in the full-
ness of his beard and the balding of his pate. Would Krishna come
and offer him his beautiful blue hand, he wondered, and change
his mind from mindful logic to mindless bliss?

Just as he had taken Mira Bai as his teacher, Bankey Behari told
Allen to stop looking for a living human guru or a god to worship.
In an unexpected Hindu twist, a lady saint in Brindaban concurred,
telling Allen to take William Blake as his saint and the focus of his
devotion. Let Blake be the star around which his world would
turn. Bankey Behari had spent thirty years waiting for Krishna to
appear to him, only to realize himself that it was not Krishna he
sought, but the love he inspired.

"Best oriental wisdom I heard yet," Allen wrote Lucien on his
return to Benares. "So I got, more or less, what I came here to
find out."

"WHAT DOES WRITERS' WORKSHOP mean in America?"
Sunil wrote from Calcutta to ask. Paul Engle, director of the Iowa
Writers' Workshop, had arrived in Calcutta and was talking
about trying to find the money to bring one of the *Krittibas* poets
to America. Engle struck Sunil as more of a professor than a poet,
but he entertained them lavishly with "costly alcohol." Shakti, it
was rumored, had already been promised the scholarship. Where
Shakti's Bengali verse was effortless, another *Krittibas* poet had informed Allen, Sunil's was more self-consciously literary. And
Shakti's Hungry Generation bulletins were causing a stir at the College Street Coffee House. Had Allen received them? Their goal
was "to undo the done-for world and start afresh from chaos." At
Allen's suggestion, Shakti had sent one to the *Evergreen Review*, and
they had published it.

Shakti was meant to have translated "Kaddish" for the new issue of *Krittibas*, but everyone agreed his version was awful. He was

too much his own poet, it was explained to Allen, to take up another's diction. Sunil had ended up doing it. Another *Krittibas*
poet, smarting from Sunil's rejection of his own poem, had translated a poem by Gregory Corso. He told Allen that Sunil's translation of *"Kaddish"* was passable if only because he made a genuine
effort. What did he think of it? he asked, forgetting that Allen did
not read Bengali.

Asoke's litany of woe had followed Allen to Benares. His second wife had left him, he said, because he was a useless husband
unable to feed his family. He'd fainted on Dharamtolla Street
from hunger and was nursed back to health by his first wife. Then
his second wife took ill with septic fever, and he was forced to
care for her. Sunil had given him a poem to translate, but he said
he could pay only after a year. Hope had made a few corrections.
Sterlyn Steele, the USIS cultural affairs officer, had been im-
mensely impressed with his translation of a Gary Snyder poem
and had promised him more work. In the meanwhile, he had
grown thin from hunger, and his breath now came in gasps. "How
can I earn money for me and family when I see my friends are dying, throwing themselves under the train wheels, drinking poison, hanging or drowning themselves, for food, for shelter, for
job and for a little sympathy and love that isn't anywhere."

Sunil, too, missed Allen. After a period of sobriety, he had returned to heavy drinking and carousing. Nimtola wasn't nearly
the same without him there, he wrote gloomily. He and Torpedo
even found themselves following a naked sadhu and trying to get
him to talk to them. Of his entire circle of friends, he felt he had
to be the most wretched, weighed down by his family responsibilities and lacking any faith in the value of his poetry. Shakti was
writing brilliant Bengali poems, he said. Utpal and Jyoti were also
writing poems, while the others only made plans to write.

The new *Krittibas* issue had already attracted some police ha-
rassment, but no actual obscenity charges had been filed. Buddhadev, however, had warned Jyoti about hanging out with them
all. Though Sunil wasn't involved with the Hungry Generation
business, Utpal and a few others had now joined Shakti's name on
the broadsides. The prime mover, however, was a Patna bank clerk

named Malay Roy Choudhury, whose intense grievances against the establishment were only partially masked by his grandiose estimation of his own genius. Through the winter, the tone of the Hungry bulletins had become increasingly provocative, and though their aim was to "Quit Colonial Aesthetics," poetry had quickly taken a backseat to cant. Plans were afoot to send two hundred paper masks depicting demons, beasts, and Hindu gods bearing the message "Take Off Your Mask" to leading Calcutta citizens, from the police commissioner on down.

In his letters to Allen, Sunil didn't mention that Shakti had been upset about his decision to use Allen's photo of a Calcutta beggar on the cover. Despite having published a selection from Allen's journals in his Hungry Generation bulletin, Shakti tried to argue that Allen was an outsider. He didn't belong in *Krittibas,* he said. Sunil ignored him.

"WHY DOES THIS GIRL come to Benares from Calcutta?" Sub-Inspector Kripal Singh of the special police wanted to know. "No young girl comes to Benares traveling alone without father and mother." For two months after they returned from Brindaban, Allen and Peter had been plagued by visits from an intelligence officer assigned to keep an eye on foreigners. The trouble had begun after Allen had insulted the chair of the English Department at Benares Hindu University but had really gained steam with the simultaneous arrival of a photographer from *Esquire* and Peter's girlfriend, Manjula Mitra. En route to Poona where she hoped to apply for a scholarship, Manjula made the mistake of spending the first night of her visit in Allen and Peter's room on Dasaswamedh Ghat.

The absurdity of Sub-Inspector Singh's line of questioning, however, was matched by Allen's inescapable sense of déjà vu. Hope's problems with her visa had originated in official concerns about immorality. Manjula and Peter were followed to the train station and questioned, with more investigators waiting for her when she arrived in Bombay and Poona. When police inspectors showed up at her home in Calcutta, she worried that word of the relationship with Peter would get back to Buddhadev, with disastrous consequences for her degree, her reputation, and her ability to get a passport and secure a fellowship abroad. At the coffeehouse, there were already rumors that she was pregnant.

"The circle we have got here is rather a small and limited one," she explained to Allen, upbraiding him for gossiping about her with one of the *Krittibas* poets and pleading for advice about admission to American universities. "I am ready to do anything." Manjula saw Hope nearly every day to commiserate and kept Allen apprised of Hope's efforts to appeal her expulsion order.

Meanwhile, Sub-Inspector Singh had taken to dropping by at all hours of the day and night with new questions and insinuations. "You visited only the lower-level sadhus, lower-class types, no high-class ones. . . ." He asked for a demonstration of the asanas they had learned. As for the sadhu whom Allen sat with at Manikarnika who'd taken a vow of silence, he asked: "What can be learned from one who doesn't speak?" And again there was the question Allen had been struggling himself to answer.

"Why do you stay here in India so long? People come, see and they go. What do you DO here? There must be some reason for you to stay so long." Glancing at a copy of *Howl,* the inspector asked if Allen didn't have a more recent publication, intimating he wasn't working very hard. Their application for a visa extension was denied. Finally, Singh told them that if they didn't leave in two or three days, they would be put in jail for five months and pay a heavy fine. "Your convenience is not the same as government convenience."

"If we get arrested," Peter retorted, "thousands of journalists will come and visit us in Benares in our jailcell. There'll be stories in the paper about what is happening."

"Let them."

They'd sent pricey telegrams to Nehru and Galbraith but ended up having to travel to Delhi to sort things out. Allen arrived at Pupul Jayakar's Delhi flat shoeless and shattered, his hair matted with ashes. He wasn't ready to leave India, he told her; he needed more time. Jayakar put in a call to the home secretary. Like Singh, he wanted to know what they were up to in Benares.

"They smoke ganja and drink bhang and wear saffron robes," she told him.

Allen's and Peter's visas were renewed for another six months. "India will become the holy place of pilgrimage for the young!" Allen crowed, triumphant that his mission in India had been recognized at the highest level. "They will come like birds migrating to a promised land." Intent on making the best of the ten weeks he had left, he and Peter hurriedly left Delhi to catch up with Shankar Rao Deo's Friendship March.

Having abandoned his Benares porch but not his *charkha,* Shankar Rao had left Delhi for Peking on March 1. Allen had never participated in a political demonstration before, and though Pupul Jayakar was an old friend of Shankar Rao's, even she was skeptical about the outcome. The old man had left Delhi with only eleven people pledging to make the entire journey. After a week, the marchers had covered only seventy miles, drawing little in the way of mass support. After getting off the bus at Khurja, Allen and Peter found Shankar Rao giving a speech over a windy mike in a dusty village soccer field. Several old Gandhians with busily spinning *charkhas* sat behind a line of local politicians in Congress hats. The national papers lampooned the entire undertaking, attacking Nehru and Gandhi with equal scorn, as if the marchers' stubborn faith in nonviolence too easily reminded them of the nonaligned dream from which the entire nation had only just awakened. The attacks of Radio Peking were just as virulent, and the likelihood that they would be able to cross the border seemed slim. "If God wills," Shankar Rao said when anyone asked.

After all the loudspeakers spewing jingoistic propaganda in Delhi, these quixotic, saintly people, talking with "person-to-person calm," charmed Allen. Both he and Peter spent the night and the following day marching with them before returning to Benares. When the marchers arrived in Benares the following week, Allen again sat with them, touching their tired feet in a sign of respect. "I only wish people in US would recognize need for a similar anti Dulles-Luce popular revolt," he wrote his father. Unlike the Soviet Union, which had had a readily identifiable monster in Stalin, America had only "Babbitt monsters" disguising the cold murderousness at the heart of U.S. policy, under a bland suburban cleverness.

"Nobody yet recognizes how really perverse America became, and how much there is to revolt against."

ALLEN FIRST HEARD it from his room: A high-pitched wail in the middle of a hot night in early April. A man was crouched in a fetal position against a urine-stained wall below their balcony, too weak even to beg. A mute. Allen had seen others like him, their large eyes peering out from the shadows beneath the market arcade. "That Buchenwald look," he wrote when he finally acknowledged them. Days later, he'd find their lifeless shapes on the street. One man lay dying near the funeral pyres for weeks. Allen watched his knees become knobs, his legs reduce to bone and skin, but he could not overcome his fears. The morning after he first heard the wails Allen gave the mute some milk, but the nighttime keening continued.

In Calcutta, Peter had worked alongside the nuns at Mother Teresa's ashram for the dying. In Benares, he took on the care of several lepers. They lived in an alley near a small shrine, in easy reach of the pilgrims who passed them en route to their ritual baths in the Ganges. Though he was proud of his medical experience and his ability to stomach the most awful sights, Peter found that his attention was easily deflected. At Dasaswamedh Ghat, he discovered a leper woman wearing a burlap sack tied with a string, crusted with dirt. When he helped her change into a newly bought sari, he discovered deep, maggot-infested wounds on her buttock and hip. "I was so supprised I dident know what to do for a second—then I hide tailed it to a doctor." He disinfected her wounds, looking into her eyes as he fed her. Upon their return from Delhi some weeks later, he stumbled upon her body and veered away in surprise. "I dident think she would go so soon. What fooled me was her calm eyes, living so peasefulley above her hip woe—" As with his brother Lafcadio, the fate of the leper lady would haunt him. It took very little to convince Peter of his own selfish stupidity and laziness. Until Allen discovered the mute, he'd stopped trying to prove he was otherwise.

They carried the man to the river to wash the filth from his body and treat his open sores with sulfur ointment. Peter poured hydrogen peroxide in his ears to kill the maggots. Simple starvation, the doctor they brought to look at him pronounced. They replaced his rags with fresh pajamas and found him a place to lie under a peepul tree in leper alley, just off Dasaswamedh market. There was a young boy there who looked after the lepers in exchange for a portion of their begging earnings. As lepers were not allowed down to the river, he would bring them water. Allen hired him to keep the mute clean and bring him food.

Though he photographed beggars shamelessly, often posing Peter alongside, Allen had written little of the dying destitute of India. After the mute awakened him, he began to write of their conditions with more confidence. He distinguished those neighborhood fixtures who were strong enough to beg, like the madwoman who lived by the Kali temple, from those others who were in their "classic shit rag death throes." Allen calculated that the mute had no more than ten or twenty hours of life left in him when they found him. He and Peter began to fatten up a few others who seemed on the brink of death, only to see dysentery shrink them down again. Peter tried and failed to get the sanitation department to put in a water pump. As the weeks wore on, however, Allen began to resent the thought that whether any of them lived or died depended on the pittance he provided. In letters, he treated the matter as a nuisance, trivialized it as a "soap opera," and tarted up the gruesome details, as if to elude his own unease. He harassed officials at the Beggar's Home to take in the worst cases, to relieve him of the responsibility.

A sadhu, watching him bathe the mute, told him he was committing a sin by intervening. He'd thought about that, too. What was the use of helping the man get better when he would only have to go through the horror again after he left? Justifying himself to Gregory, Allen quoted the Gita: "Do not look to the fruit of your actions." Mostly, he wanted to be spared "the thought

of the skeleton lying under the tree in street" so that he might
continue to seek his heaven. Instead, Benares seemed intent on
showing him there was no heaven, no place at all beyond shit and
desire.

> . . . *whispering*
> *to friends last words from bedcovers*
> *or alone by streetcorner wall,*
> *The same nowhere to go.*

There was one more holy man in Benares to see.

When Devraha Baba came down from his Himalayan cave for
his annual visit to Benares, Allen convinced Peter to join him for
darshan. Peter's patience with sitting around stoned sadhus chanting *bhajans* at the burning ghat had fallen off precipitously. In contrast with the gentle souls at Manikarnika, however, Devraha Baba
was a fierce Shiva-worshipping ascetic with a big head of matted
hair. A deerskin rug, a wooden pot, a jute mat, and wooden sandals were his only possessions. He sat on a platform in the water
on the far side of the river, where he threw fruit at those devotees
brave enough to wade out to see him. Access wasn't guaranteed;
when Indira Gandhi came, he showed her the bottoms of his feet
in contempt.

Though Allen was granted a hearing, in the middle of his account of the Blake vision, Devraha Baba's gaze wandered impatiently to where Peter was smoking a cigarette farther down the
beach. He told Allen to have Peter come sit, but Peter waved
him off, picking up a clay pot to balance on his head. Thereupon
Devraha Baba dismissed Allen peremptorily, telling him to come
back again when Peter could listen. Allen was so startled, he remain rooted to his spot.

Not long before, Allen had had a dream in which he saw himself standing by the side of the road waiting for a bus. Beside him,
there was another person lugging a huge suitcase. As Allen saw
the bus coming from far away, he began to cross to the other side
of the road where the bus stop was. When he turned around, he

saw that his companion was taking much longer to cross the road. Out of politeness, he tried to stay by his side, only to look up in time to see the bus roar by. Expecting his companion to be dismayed, he was shocked to hear him say it didn't matter about the bus, he wasn't going to take the trip anyway.

Whether it was his morphine and opium habits, his perpetual longing for a girlfriend, or his care for the lepers, Peter had always traveled in a different India from Allen's. With Manjula's encouragement he had taken up the sarod, having given her his guitar. For a while he stopped shooting morphine, and after she left Benares, Peter found a fatherly guru to give him sarod and singing lessons. The flat began to fill up with young Indian tabla players who would hang around drinking tea. They taught Peter the Hindi words for cock and pussy and were so mesmerized by his *Playboys* that they had little time for Allen. Peter, too, had become sullen and distant, as if he were nursing a grievance. When Manjula's letters arrived in Benares, conveying her increasingly desperate circumstances as a result of the surveillance, Allen dutifully wrote his lawyer brother to ask if Manjula could be his secretary or if marriage to Peter would guarantee her a visa. The impasse over Manjula's fate had somehow become Allen's fault, or at least representative of the larger standoff between them. Perhaps Allen's care of the mute was his way of finding his way back to Peter.

Faced now with Devraha Baba's irritation, Allen recognized that what was troubling him was closer to hand than his Blake vision and the puzzling nature of karma. To his surprise, he found himself admitting that he and Peter had fought. He had accused Peter of having a morphine habit, which suppressed his desires. Peter had accused him of selling out; in accepting the invitation to Vancouver, he had broken his vow of never reading poetry for money. Peter had shaved his head, as if he'd already moved on, like an Indian son after the death of his father. Though they had been together for many years, Allen confessed to Devraha Baba that he was returning home alone.

On his tiny platform suspended over the rushing waters of the Ganges, Devraha Baba looked at Allen. He tilted his head from side to side gently and sucked his teeth.

"Oh!" he exclaimed. And with a tenderness that struck deep at Allen's heart, he said softly: "How wounded, how wounded."

THE MUTE UNDER THE PEEPUL TREE found his voice while Allen was away. Peter had looked after him when Allen left on a circuit of Buddhist pilgrimage sites in the middle of April. At Bodh Gaya he sat under the Bo tree, emptying his head. He dutifully sang the Blake poem, "Ah! sun-flower . . . where the traveller's journey . . ." as he climbed the stone steps to the spot on Vulture Peak where the Buddha had lived in a cave. He visited the ruins of the ancient Buddhist university at Nalanda, the cradle of Mahayana Buddhist philosophy for six centuries. And before returning to Benares, he stayed a night at the Patna home of Malay Roy Choudhury, the firebrand of the Hungry Generation. Though Peter hardly spoke to him on his return, the dying mute was no longer dying or a mute.

In a high, squeaky voice and in English, the man told Allen his name was Kankal: Hindi for "skeleton." During partition his tongue had been cut out by Muslims, his body crippled by stabbings. Six months before, he had been accused of being a thief and, unable to defend himself, had left home in despair, wanting to die. On a piece of paper, Kankal now wrote, "I want to go to my house where my family . . . I want my bed and clothes." A letter was written to an address in Hardwar, and to Allen's amazement, a reply arrived soon after. His mother had been inconsolable since her son's disappearance. His younger brother was taking a train to come claim him. After some bureaucratic wrangling, Allen got him admitted to a hospital, along with a woman who appeared to be in the final stages of malnutrition. "Everybody afraid to bother for fear of getting inextricabl[y] involved in insoluable problem," Allen wrote to Paul Bowles, adding that he had seen four people die below his balcony. He was no longer afraid himself.

On May 18, 1963, Kankal's brother arrived to take him home. As if to puncture the simple miraculousness of this development, that same day Peter moved to a flat near his teacher in Bangali Tola. After watching Peter disappear down the street in his pink lungi, Allen went down to the river to wash his hands and throw cooling water on his head, giving a farewell salute to the glowing pyres of Manikarnika in the distant darkness. After fifteen months in India, the next day he would take a train to Calcutta, and a week later he would fly to Bangkok. From Bangkok, he would travel to Hanoi, where the American war in Vietnam was heating up. He planned to spent a month with Gary and Joanne in Kyoto before arriving in Vancouver for the poetry conference in late summer.

He returned to the swept and nearly empty room. There was the Hindi alphabet sheet tacked on the wall by what had been the kitchen, the copy of Blake beside his sheet, blanket, and air mattress pillow. His ashtray and rubber flip-flops. The four walls radiated loneliness. "Now all personal relations cold exhausted," he wrote in his journal gloomily. Two water buffalo snorted at each other on the street below. Like Kankal, he too was going home.

"I WANT YOU BACK," Gregory wrote, as if to contest Allen's belief that no one awaited his return. "India you had, good, but don't die there, don't [grow] old there." Writing once again from New York City, Gregory had himself convinced the Second Coming was nearly at hand in America. He sketched a vast cosmology. Christopher Columbus was directed in his dreams by angels to find America, right? His name meant "Christ bearer," did it not? It naturally followed that America's destiny was to vanquish death. And he, fallen angel Gregory Nunzio Corso, now felt he had death "by the balls" at the very least. He would tell Allen the rest of it when he returned. With the death of William Carlos Williams, Allen needed to take heed of his home ground, he lectured. Jack needed him, too. "I tell you he needs help, a real good awakening or he is forever lost." Bill was doing all right. Gregory had finally got him to confess to his belief in the essential dignity of man. He might be a "very important functionary in the nether world," but Gregory insisted that Bill was definitely *not* the "central boobugaboo." *Allen was*. "I'm asking you to come back Allen. Yes, because here is your home and your source and here you can write your big mango-eyed epic."

Allen had to bring Hope back with him. This was key. Gregory had started paying close attention to his dreams, and recently, he'd had a dream in which she was once again kind and loving. It was a *wonderful* dream. He wanted Allen to speak to her on his behalf, to be John Alden to his Miles Standish. He wanted him to tell her that he was her real live poet, not a dead one. He wanted Allen to convey that he, Gregory Nunzio Corso, couldn't bear to marry anyone else and that he would go to his death loving her. "Must I threaten you with my demise, you and Hope? I believe a meeting will be a revelation for us all, and of course assy silly goodly Peter, too."

Allen promised to type out the relevant sections of his letter and pass them along to Hope when he saw her. With the help of Pupul Jayakar and the vice chancellor of Rabindra Bharati University, Hope had managed to secure a twelve-month visa to continue her dance and Urdu studies. As Allen would be flying out of Calcutta at the end of May, he would give her the letter then. Still, he felt it would be better if Gregory made his appeal in person, "see the situation and meet her yourself." He expected to be back in New York in the fall, after Vancouver and a stay in San Francisco to help Neal Cassady with his memoirs.

"For God's sake," Allen told Gregory, "sit still till I get there. I be there, I guess September? With white silk suit? What'll I do with my long hair and beard."

"FROM A CERTAIN POINT onward there is no turning back," Kafka once wrote. "That is the point that must be reached." How far do you have to travel and how long do you have to be away before you reach this point? When do you become a foreigner in your own country? A stranger to your family? Once you have reached this point, even a postcard at the holidays might require too much of you. And after that, do you finally lose sight of where your story once began? And if you do, do the memories just fade away, or are they forcibly expelled, like undesirable aliens in an insecure country? Is this the last border crossed?

By midsummer, Manjula Mitra would reach this point and leave India without looking back. During his stopover in Calcutta, Allen showed her the letter in which his brother Eugene outlined the various ways Manjula might secure a U.S. visa. While Manjula wanted a letter promising employment, Eugene was clear on not needing a secretary. Unless a scholarship came through, that left only marriage to Peter. Allen was noncommittal on the subject. After she mentioned she could always resolve the matter with sleeping pills, he related the "case history" of Elise's suicide with an aloofness she found chilling. No doubt Peter would forget her just as easily. If she realized that Peter's offer to marry her had as much to do with guilt as chivalry or love, her own feelings were equally jumbled. Though they exchanged many letters in an effort to find a name for what they had shared, by the time her exams were over, Manjula had secured a fellowship to study abroad. No one knows what became of her.

In Allen Ginsberg's vast archive at Stanford University, cataloged under "Miscellaneous, 1963," you can find Peter's blond ponytail, cut off in Benares and stuffed in a City Lights envelope like a Beat reliquary. Among his thousands of correspondents, there is not one letter from Hope Savage. There is a letter in Ginsberg's archive, however, from a young southerner traveling abroad for the first time. Dated May 2, 1963, and addressed to Gregory Corso, the letter was written in a café on St.-Germain in Paris, perhaps not far from the spot where Gregory ran into Allen and Peter en route to India two years before. It was springtime in Paris, the sun was shining, and a funeral was under way in the cathedral across the street. "Dear Gregory," he began.

> . . . I've just read your last book. I doubt you particularly care about my praise but I give it anyway, free, like a smile sort of. So. It's a beautiful book. But I guess the real reason for this letter are the poems to Hope. I have never known her very well, partly because she left home when I was

young and partly because we are . . . too much alike to be able to do more than love each other in secret. I suppose you know her far better than I ever will. So "Sura" a fair haired poem for anyone, was for me something super-beautiful and kind of heart-breaking—and I'm grateful to you for it. . . .

Forgive me if I sound a trifle mad, but when you end up alone in a strange beautiful city things like these poems fall like kisses out of your past and all ascendancy comes tumbling down and you're left drinking a café, watching a funeral, writing a letter, and tears in your eyes.

I guess you wonder will I speak of Hope, but I know nothing but that she is in the Orient and well (from a card to my parents at Xmas) and a few months ago she ran into Gary Snyder and Allen Ginsberg who would know more of her than I. I have never written to or received a letter from my sister.

Well, just wanted to say I think your book is fucking grand and was written for me alone and am grateful,

Sam Savage.

Gregory received the note on the day of his wedding to the schoolteacher from Cleveland. He enclosed it with a letter to Allen in Benares, asking him for his blessings on both his marriage and his pending fatherhood. Peter forwarded both to Calcutta, where Allen had just conveyed to Hope Gregory's insistence that he could never marry anyone but her. So the last time Allen saw Hope Savage, it was to give her the news of Gregory's marriage. Did he also show her her young brother's sweet letter? To whom does it matter now?

On his final night in Calcutta, Allen met Sunil and Shakti and Utpal at the College Street Coffee House. Relating Gregory's new householder status, he caught himself thinking that now he'd have at least a couch to sleep on in New York when he returned. He immediately regretted the thought, imagining himself the hairy old uncle who gives candy to children and dies alone. Later that night at Utpal's house, he closed his India journal with a question:

Another day and I leave India,
And I never crosslegged pierced Heaven
With a thought or found bearded Guru
in Brindaban or levitated in Bodh-Gaya . . .
am I a "Beatnick" Is that all the
years have to offer?

ALLEN GINSBERG IMAGINED that he was returning home with nothing to offer those who so eagerly awaited his news. This time it was not fear that defeated him, but exhaustion. The result was the same: When he had reached the point of no turning back, he turned for home instead.

Yet the day he left Gary and Joanne's cottage in Kyoto bound for Vancouver, two months after leaving Calcutta, he heard the voices of India's holy men as if for the first time. Krishnaji's last words before his vow of silence: "Silence would be good for America." Shivananda's directive to look within: "Your own heart is your guru." The Dalai Lama's lighthearted and skeptical probe: "If you take LSD, can you see what's in that suitcase?" Dudjom Rinpoche's sage guidance: "If you see anything horrible, don't cling to it; if you see anything beautiful, don't cling to it." And the sensible suggestion made by the lady saint at Brindaban: "Take Blake for your guru." Overcome with "the sweetness of all those Gurus sinking in to me & then Joanne & Gary both so nice to me," as he wrote to Jack some months later, he had a thought that flooded him with joy. Like the most powerful revelations, it was really a rather simple thought, but sitting in his train seat on the Kyoto–Tokyo express, he wept when it came to him.

He, Irwin Allen Ginsberg, had no powers beyond those granted to the living over the dead. And like every other passenger on this journey, he was alive—

a universe of skin and breath
& changing thought and
burning hand & softened heart in the old bed of
my skin.

What held Allen Ginsberg and would hold him for the rest of his life was the sweetness and sympathy he found in the company of India's sadhus, charlatans, poets, and saints. They sang to him, and they held his hand. They reached out to his lover and touched his feet; they sucked their teeth in sympathy when Ginsberg confessed his fears of demons, childlessness, old age, abandonment, and death. "How wounded, how wounded," Devraha Baba had crooned. The blue hand he grasped was not necessarily that of the pied piper Krishna, the ashen Shiva, or the mad and motherly Kali and Tara. The blue hand was something far more ineffable, delicate, and tender. In his train seat, Allen realized that he would not, after all, return to America with nothing. He would bring India with him.

Every year, Jerry Madden tells his writing students at Louisiana State University the story of Hope Savage. And when Gregory was dying, he tried once more to find Hope, but her sister told him she didn't want to be found. For Hope Savage did reach the point of no turning back. Perhaps this was always her destination. The final erasure of home came when she realized that the questions she had so dreaded being asked, she would never hear again. By then, there was no longer anyone left living to lay claim to her, no one who would presume to ask where she had been and if she would ever return.

I never found her.

Jessore Road

THE LOW RUMBLE OF THEIR TAXI is swallowed up by the air blast of a diesel truck trying to pass. There is a zoo of horns. Some sound like plaintive geese honks, some like chick cheeps, others like asthmatic mules. There are the whirring pull bells of bicycles and the hollow Santa ring of rickshaw bells. The cassette tape also records the intermittent sound of children's voices, but they sink beneath the cacophony. At intervals Allen Ginsberg's voice describes the scene, providing details the tape alone cannot record. Suddenly the rumble stops. His narration pauses. There is the sound of a car door opening and closing. The bikes sound farther away. The water has reached the road.

"We will go as far as we can," someone says.

ON SEPTEMBER 9, 1971, Allen Ginsberg and Sunil Gangopadhyay traveled out Jessore Road from Calcutta to visit refugee camps near the Bangladesh border. It had been almost a year since Ravi Shankar and Ali Akbar Khan had asked George Harrison to organize a few friends for a benefit concert on behalf of the victims of the cyclone that had hit East Pakistan on November 13, 1970. A storm surge had swept an estimated half million people from their beds into the Bay of Bengal. In the aftermath of the deluge, West Pakistan, one thousand miles across the subcontinent, had done little to ease the suffering. In less than six months, a bloody war for independence had broken out. Five months after the new nation of Bangladesh was declared, the war still raged, the waters rose, and refugees poured once again into West Bengal. Refugee camps were overwhelmed. Families who had walked for weeks to get to the border died waiting for food, latrines, medical supplies, and money.

The Living Theatre was inaugurating a new company in Calcutta and had decided to mark the occasion with another benefit for the refugees, featuring the Bauls of Bengal. Since Allen Ginsberg had introduced the Bauls to America via Bob Dylan's manager, Albert Grossman, a man named Robert Fraser sent him a prepaid round-trip ticket on TWA. "You know Robert Fraser don't you?" Burroughs had written. "Friend of the Stones, Living Theatre and just about everybody now living in India with a temple dancer." Burroughs had been asked to go, but ten days before Allen was due to depart, he hadn't got a ticket. "I hear that Keith is definitely going, but not sure about Mick," Burroughs said. Jan Wenner, impressed by the success of the Concert for Bangla Desh, was also weighing going. Allen asked Fraser what he should do when he got there. Whatever he wanted, Fraser replied.

In the end, Burroughs didn't see the point in laying out that much cash for a week in Calcutta, plus he was too busy with the film of *The Naked Lunch*. Jack had died of drink two years before. Gregory had just been kicked out of the Chelsea Hotel. Peter was busy harvesting cucumbers on Allen's farm in Cherry Valley. The previous winter, they socked away 188 bottles of pickles. So it was just Allen, lugging his notebooks and the fancy tape recorder Dylan had given him. He wanted to buy a new harmonium, get some khadi shirts made, buy a lungi for Peter, and try to find a Shiva trident in Benares. He also wanted to collect more devotional songs; he'd been singing the same *kirtans* and *bhajans,* chanting the same Hare Krishna, at readings, be-ins, and protest sit-ins at the Pentagon for some time. He drove all his friends crazy with his chants. During the Chicago riots in 1968 where he had chanted "Om" for seven hours to calm everyone down, an Indian gentleman had passed him a note telling him his pronunciation was all wrong. So he was going to work on that, too. Of course, he would visit Nimtola burning ghat, Tarapith, and Suri, as if India now held the key to his past as it once had unlocked his future.

As the plane descended toward the paddy fields surrounding Dum Dum Airport, Allen invoked the memory of Peter. He saw him still young, emerging from his bath, wet blond hair falling to his shoulders, dripping in the Calcutta heat of the Amjadia rooftop. The fumes of nostalgia floored him once again.

"How many lifetimes ago?" he asked himself.

AT THE ENTRANCE to the Ramakrishna mission office just ten kilometers from the West Bengal border town of Bangaon, Allen is greeted by a bureaucrat who assures him that the crisis is under control. The cassette recorder is left on.

"These people are not scared of flood, because Bangladesh is full of water."

"I would like to see where food is distributed," Allen says.

"Why are you standing? Just take a seat, please."

"I would like to see where food is distributed."

"Food is given? Food is generally given to the destitute just on Thursday. That picture will not be available today."

"I see."

"Only on Thursday. Once in a week. The ration is being distributed once in a week and that is on Thursday. That is why you are not in a position to take a picture."

"That's all right, I'll see what there is."

"What more can we help?"

"I don't want to take up your valuable time."

"There is another committee, locally managed, also distributing rices who are arriving recently, supposed to arrive today. They are appearing before the medical board."

"We saw that."

"You have seen that? They are issuing sleeps and on the basis of that sleep, that local committee is distributing rices, et cetera. You have also see that? Nothing more is available then."

"How many camps are there along the road?"

"Lots of camps will be available. Lots of camps."

"What is happening in the camps?"

"All the camps are flood affected."

"And the people?"

"No! Relief is being made, they are being helped. We also used to go there to give them relief."

"Thank you for your time, good luck. *Nomoskar.*"

"*Nomoskar.*"

The bureaucrat leans aside, asks Sunil where the man is from in Bengali.

"America," Sunil replies.

Thik. Thikachhe.

ALLEN GINSBERG started it all while he was living in Calcutta, Paul Engle reported to the chair of the English Department at the University of Iowa. "He succeeded in doing the heretofore utterly impossible—bringing dirt *to* India."

In July 1963, the Asia Foundation sent Paul Engle a check for $1,700 to cover a year's fellowship for an up-and-coming Bengali writer. He'd chosen the leader of the young poets in Calcutta, Engle explained excitedly. "He belongs to a group called the Hangry Generation because they are hungry as well as angry." Malay Roy Choudhury had been playing with the name of his troupe; "the Hungryalists" had grown to around forty writers, and they had worked up quite a head of steam. A recent manifesto on religion began: "1. God is Shit." "Like, crazy, man," Engle wrote.

Contrary to Engle's understanding, the poet he had chosen, Sunil Gangopadhyay, had had nothing to do with either the Hungry or the Hangry Generation. Convinced that he'd been cheated of the fellowship, Shakti Chattopadhyay did not come to the airport to see Sunil off. But in mid-September 1963, just as Sunil was preparing to leave, Peter came through Calcutta to bid everyone farewell. Though Allen wanted to send him money for an airplane ticket, Peter had decided to return to New York the long way. His plan was to travel alone, overland, through Pakistan, Afghanistan, the Middle East, and Europe. "This was unimaginable to me," Sunil wrote Allen, distraught. The night Peter left, Sunil wept, perhaps as much for himself and his own looming journey. "I never felt so inclined for any man in my life," Sunil confessed to Allen. "I will never know why he did not accept the plane fare from you." As his own plane flew west, he looked down, as if he might see Peter making his lonely way across the desert plains of Rajasthan.

With Sunil gone, Malay and Shakti stepped into the breach. Hungry Generation manifestos of increasing fury and gratuitous crudeness eventually secured them the notoriety they sought. When Malay sent the Calcutta establishment engraved, obscenity-laced invitations to a topless bathing suit contest, however, Shakti turned on him. Newspaper editorials quoted from the manifestos to prove the Hungryalists were bent on nothing less than the destruction of the state. Civic authorities called in the police. Twenty-six were detained and questioned, and five were arrested, charged with conspiracy and obscenity, before being released on bail. "Our frustration is not just personal," Utpal tried to explain to a *Time* reporter following the case, "it comes from the strains, the poverty, the squalor of our society." Though he had not been charged, when the *Time* article was published, Utpal was forced to resign his teaching position. "I am nearly ruined," he wrote Allen.

Shakti was among those who had turned themselves into "darlings of the press," Utpal said, forsaking his *grand passion* for "a willingness-to-oblige." Sunil, hearing of the uproar in Iowa, condemned the government's persecution of the poets as a dodge to divert attention from the city's real problems. In the end, charges against all but Malay were dropped. Most of the others were forced to sign statements promising to never again write obscenities. With Allen's help, Utpal went into exile in England. Malay, believing himself a truly great poet, felt abandoned and betrayed. After writing letters denouncing all of them, he demanded Allen secure him an academic appointment in America.

"I think I am the only person here who will be able to explain what is INDIA. . . ."

· · · ·

THE TAXI'S MOTOR STARTS UP again, changing pitch with the wind, like the sound of flames. Bicycles hug them on the road, ringing their bells, squeezing horns.

"Is everyone here aware of Maha Maya?" Allen asks Sunil, hoping perhaps that the idea that all suffering is an illusion might provide some consolation.

"Yes," Sunil replies. "People in this part of the world are very fate conscious."

"Yes," Allen says. "It has to happen."

"Well, the rain has to happen. Everybody understands that."

"Shall we get out and walk around?"

"Better not try."

"Is there another road?"

When the driver stops to have a long discussion in Bengali with a rickshaw driver, a young boy sticks his head through the taxi window to observe them more closely. Again the car door opens and closes. The road is now impassable. They have to abandon the car and take a rickshaw.

"I'll help you carry it."

"I'll carry it."

"Leave your shoes here."

"We can walk across there."

"It is ten to eleven, we have to be back at five so should turn around at two."

Setting out on the rickshaw, Allen starts the tape up again so that he might record what he sees. As with his journals, whether he is looking at himself in a restroom mirror, gazing out an apartment rear window, or describing a scene of unimaginable misery, the images come quick and fast. Allen Ginsberg doesn't ask himself who will ever listen to this cassette or similar recordings he will make in the coming days. Similarly, the journal he keeps will be typed up and filed away. Though he will later write a poem titled "Jessore Road," he seems unaware of the insufficiency of the words he speaks into the mike: "There is an iron bridge over the river, crossing the bridge now, tile roofs, sunk down, reflected in water, barred windows, bamboos of one roof, floating on the surface of the water." These descriptions quickly sink beneath the splashing sound of rickshaw wheels going round and round in water. Yet through the din, his eye remains detached and open.

Sunil translates what a man walking alongside them says, and Allen repeats the words into the tape recorder.

"Everything is flooded and the government doesn't do anything, one shopkeeper walking along with us explains."

In India, where realized men and women are cherished as gods, it is sometimes said that one of the ways in which the gods among us can be recognized is by their unblinking eyes. It is through these eyes that the human world is known to them.

IT WASN'T UNTIL ALLEN made him rice and dal that Sunil realized lentils and dal were the same thing. For ten months in Iowa, he had missed the taste of home, only to discover it had been there all along. In the summer of 1964, Sunil stayed with Allen in New York City before returning to Calcutta. A few days into his visit, Allen, who liked to walk around naked, proposed they sleep together. "Why not, let's try," Sunil said. When he learned he was to be the one on the bottom, he balked.

Sunil met the whole gang. William Burroughs imagined Calcutta was covered in grass because of all the cows. He knew *nothing* about India. When Jack dropped by, Gregory began berating him. Jack owed him royalties from *The Subterraneans;* he'd been grossly exploited. Though Allen made Gregory promise not to borrow money from Sunil, "a poor Indian poet," as soon as his back was turned, Gregory hit Sunil up for $50 so that he could treat a girl to dinner. Sunil was so swept away by his plea, he gave him the money without thinking. Jack, after asking him about his LSD experience, told him that if you took four hits of acid, you could remember your way back to your mother's womb. Novel writing was a snap, he said. He gave him some advice.

"Take a date of your life, 3rd of March 1962—think about it and start writing from there."

Sunil's first novel, *Atma Prakash,* was written in confessional style. Later he would write a trilogy of historical novels on the Bengal renaissance, as well as children's books, travelogues, and memoirs. Two of his stories were made into films by Satyajit Ray. Like Tagore, he traveled all over the world representing Bengali culture. Still, he thought of himself as primarily a poet.

"If you want to be a poet," Allen told him, "don't get a job. Be a poet for twenty-four hours."

TWO DAYS AFTER HE ARRIVED, Allen left his hotel to stroll down to the theater where he was to meet up with Sunil and Shakti. On the corner of Chowringhee and Park was the YWCA where, Allen recalled, "Gregory's old 'Revolution Is the Solution'–uttering girlfriend" had received her love-struck and virginal young businessmen suitors. He couldn't remember her name. At the theater, Shakti, already tipsy, was fatter cheeked but unchanged. Sunil, still chubby, seemed no older. They went off to visit Jyoti. On staff at the Bengali daily, Sunil now had a car and driver at his disposal.

Jyoti Datta had also been to America, but in a fit of guilt and homesickness he left a lectureship at the University of Chicago to return to India to live a life of "pure, holy, Gandhian poverty." He moved with his wife to a small hut on an island in the vast mangrove swamp just south of Calcutta. Barefoot, vegetarian, eschewing tobacco, alcohol, and motor vehicles, he devoted himself to poetry, writing a weekly column for the *Statesman.* Sunil had taken him to task for remaining aloof from the civil war raging around him, but he felt there was no point in joining the chorus condemning West Pakistan's war in East Pakistan. There was no doubt who was wrong, but he insisted on keeping his pen unfettered for poetry. On the roof of his hut, Allen crooned the Padmasambhava mantra and gave Jyoti his blessing. Earlier that year, Allen believed he had at last found a teacher in a Tibetan Buddhist named Trungpa Rinpoche. He planned to visit a few Hindu saints in Benares nonetheless.

From Jyoti's they went to Sunil's for rice and dal, tea and reminiscences. Remember the transvestite's bar they'd brought him to? The conversation took its inevitable melancholic turn: the corruption, the strikes, the abject state of their beloved city. After the India-China war, Chinatown had been evicted to the outskirts of the city, aside the rank tanneries. Only Nanking was left. It was impossible to go there now, they said. The area was overrun with *goondas* and Maoist rebels called Naxalites. For the past six years, Calcutta had been prey to a violent insurgency; the Bengali middle class was the Naxalites' chosen target. Eighty people had been murdered in one neighborhood alone! The government had recently begun an equally vicious crackdown. Filled with rum, Shakti became obstreperous, as if to distract Allen from the shame of it all.

At midnight, Allen and Shakti shared Sunil's car back to the city.

"I loved you very much," Shakti said, kissing Allen's hand drunkenly and touching his feet when the driver reached his house. "Second rate, your chanting. Come see my wife and baby family."

THE LOKA DHARMA MAHASHRAM consisted of a small brick house in the village of Champahati, fifteen miles south of the city. In April 1967, Albert Grossman traveled to Calcutta to look for Asoke Fakir, who, he hoped, might help him sign these Baul singers Allen Ginsberg kept on about. When Grossman's tourist guide finally found the house, Asoke wasn't home. Upon Asoke's return that evening, his wife described the man who'd left the note. Suddenly the face of his dead father appeared in his mind's eye.

Nagendra Nath had missed his father's death at his childhood estate in Khulna. To his lasting misery, he had returned too late, and his younger brother had lit Mathura Nath Sarkar's funeral pyre. On his own deathbed, Nagendra Nath was determined to reconcile with his prodigal son. But when the time came, no one could find Asoke. Nagendra Nath's body was brought to Kalighat to be cremated, and Asoke was just three blocks away, knowing nothing. In his stead, his nine-year-old son lit the pyre. Five years later, the boy would do the same for his grandmother Umashasi.

Now, with the arrival of this Albert Grossman, sent by Allen to find him, Asoke was haunted by his father's face. Inexplicably, he was seized with the idea that he had been an American in a previous life and Albert Grossman had come to bring him home. He had felt much the same when Timothy Leary had come to Calcutta. Tim described himself as like Shiva, the god who creates chaos and destruction so that a new generation might grow from the ruins of the old. He and Tim had discussed founding an ashram in America based on a fusion of their ideas of spiritual coexistence with Leary's on LSD. Tim's last letter, however, had indicated that he was embarking on a year-long solitary meditation in a thatched hut somewhere. Now, here was Grossman. He couldn't sleep.

The next morning found him knocking furiously on Grossman's hotel room door, and before Albert's wife could hang the DO NOT DISTURB sign under his nose, Asoke blurted out:

"Your coming is God-sent."

After hearing the Baul songs of Purna and Laxman Das, both sons of the dying Baul who'd sung for Allen in 1962, Grossman put Asoke in charge of putting together a group to come to the United States. In no time at all, Asoke had become a Baul guru himself, "empowered to initiate." He had new stationery printed.

Asoke's arrival in San Francisco was delayed, as he had booked his ticket through Tokyo for a few days' sightseeing. This meant that he missed the initial performance at the Fillmore, where the LDM (Loka Dharma Mahashram) Spiritual Band opened for the Byrds. When he finally arrived, Purna Das was furious to discover that Asoke had brought his wife while his own wife had remained behind. He wasn't even a real Baul! In the end, Asoke did not join them for either their nine-month tour of the States or their recording sessions in the Catskills. Instead, Asoke, his wife, and his young daughter settled into Timothy Leary's house in Berkeley, and he began making a serious study of the "Hippie World." Soon Asoke became known as Timothy Leary's guru.

AN OFFICIOUS VOICE with a clipped English accent interrupts Allen's voice-over, as if suddenly bored with his recitation or worried that in his official capacity as government escort, he should try to distract him. Though Bengalis have never been known for their martial temperament, he begins to recount instances of Bengali bravery in the 1965 war with Pakistan over Kashmir. Bengali soldiers were also supporting the insurgency in the civil war raging across the muddy border. Allen does his best to ignore the interruption.

"Old lady bent to the ground with her stick, doubled over . . ."

"For self-respect, we must demonstrate that we can fight . . ."

"Like everyone else," Allen replies, unable to help himself.

"Better than anyone else," the man replies instantly, proudly.

"What a karma. I'm warning you, that is a terrible karma, you won't want it. That's what the Jews in Israel say."

"I see now what they feel."

"But they're wrong!" Allen raises his voice, annoyed. "They are wrong. What about *that*?"

A political argument starts. The escort insists that Nixon wants a naval base in Bangladesh, that it is, strategically, a vital area. The CIA supports Pakistan against India. The Chinese do, too. Ginsberg finds this ridiculous. How could China make a deal with an agent of U.S. imperialism? Allen continues his voice-over, determined not to be distracted.

"Straw shops by the roadside waiting for food all day. Smells of shit and flood and bidis. Heavy rain, cholera epidemic. A man standing on the side of the road with a many-pronged spear. Tensions between poor residents and refugees. 'You are behaving like a lord,' the refugees complain to the poor villagers. 'The refugees are shitting on our lawns,' the residents complain."

EVERY YEAR ON HIS BIRTHDAY, Allen Ginsberg received a call or a letter from Asoke Fakir. In the late 1960s, because of an FBI report detailing his association with Leary and Ginsberg, Asoke, along with a second troupe of Bengali performers, was refused entry into Canada and nearly deported. Abandoning the troupe, Asoke and his family changed their clothes and were allowed entry into Vancouver. For years he kept a low profile, eventually changing his name back to Sarkar. He worked as a super in his building complex. His wife found work as a cocktail waitress, leaving him to marry another man in 1973 and later taking his daughter from him. They were bitter, lonely years.

Allen was Asoke's only link to his past. As he grew older, he began telling Allen the fable of his life. He wrote of his childhood in Calcutta and Behala, of his father, Nagendra Nath, and his mother, Umashasi. He wrote also of exile. For a while he was Ramdas the Magician, pulling playing cards from naked women in a nightclub. The life of holy poverty he'd once led, when he used to sleep under trees, get high at the burning ghat, and live in slums, seemed like a lost world.

Every time Allen saw Asoke, he told him to write. Asoke had written some poems when his wife left him, but after a heart attack in 1979, he began writing in earnest. In 1982, Allen came to Vancouver to celebrate their birthdays. Having finally gained landed status, Asoke was now less guarded about his past. By the end of that decade, he was doing well, kept busy as a journalist, a radio talk show host, and a writer of TV serials. He followed the "four regulatory principles," performing twice daily *pujas* to Lord Krishna and chanting sixteen rounds of the Maha mantra every day. He turned sixty-five in 1990. "Yes," he told Allen, "I like to say I am sixty-five."

That year, he wrote Allen a longer letter than usual. He said he had now passed into the third stage of Vedic life, the stage of Vanaprastha. In this stage, a man abandons thoughts of sex and focuses himself on the dharma. He'd been alone already for eighteen years. There was a part of him, he confessed, that longed for a companion. He was getting old, he wanted someone to look after him, someone with whom he could sing *bhajans* to Krishna. Allen had done so much to further Krishna consciousness in the West. He'd helped Bhaktivedanta, founder of the International

Society of Krishna Consciousness, establish a center on the Lower East Side. He had brought the idea of universal bliss to America, tempering her murderous, bloodthirsty desires.

Asoke came to the point of the letter. Did Allen know he had been married three times? That he had five sons and two daughters? That he was estranged from all his wives and had little contact with any of his children? He thought it better that his children think he was a womanizer, he told Allen, than for them to know the truth. Did Allen know why he had forsaken his families? Did he never wonder why he rarely spoke of his wives and children?

Why? Because he had wanted to be a saint. He wanted to live a pure and sexless life. He could count on the fingers of one hand how many times he had relations with them, though he was perfectly virile and enjoyed sex very much. And though he loved his children, they were proof that he had had sexual relations. "What have I done to these wonderful women who wanted to be my wives? What have I done to these wonderful children by causing such pain and grief at their tender years. . . ." He begged for Krishna's mercy.

"You are the only person I thought I will not be ashamed to tell my tale."

"DO YOU WANT TO SURVIVE ARMAGEDDON?" Sunil asks Allen on Jessore Road.

"No. Sure. I'll take it either way. Gary Snyder is preparing to survive. Without saws or machine tools he built himself a Japanese-style temple."

"Underground?"

A nearby goat bleats insistently. They receive news that one refugee camp, inundated with water, has washed out. What happened to the people? Allen asks. He receives a vague answer.

"Smells like cow plops here. Air filled with cooksmoke, gray clouds," Allen continues doggedly. On both sides of the road now thousands of people are standing and sitting in water. The ill and the starving are being carried to tents covered with blue plastic. Trucks filled with Sikh soldiers and rice appear sporadically.

Allen's rickshaw is suddenly surrounded by a group of refugees. The camps are all underwater, they are told. Despite the trucks heading inland, there is not enough food. The road has washed away; it can no longer support the trucks. Bags of rice are falling into the water.

There is a pause in the conversation.

Someone asks for a cigarette.

They turn back.

NOTES

ARCHIVE ABBREVIATION KEY

Beinecke: Beinecke Rare Book and Manuscript Library, Yale University.

Berg: The Henry W. and Albert A. Berg Collection of English and American Literature; the Research Libraries of the New York Public Library; Astor, Lenox, and Tilden Foundations.

Columbia: The Allen Ginsberg Papers and the Barry Miles Papers at the Rare Book and Manuscript Library, Columbia University.

Davis: The Gary Snyder Collection D-050 at Special Collections, University of California Library, Davis.

Ginsberg Trust: Allen Ginsberg's letters to Gregory Corso exist only in transcription on file at Ginsberg's former residence and office. There are also photocopies of the letters and photos Corso sent to Hope Savage for safekeeping in Camden.

Iowa: The Papers of Paul Engle, the University of Iowa Libraries, Iowa City, Iowa

Stanford: The Allen Ginsberg Papers at the Department of Special Collections, Green Library, Stanford University Libraries, Stanford University.

Texas: The Peter Orlovsky Papers and the Gregory Corso Papers at the Harry Ransom Humanities Research Center, the University of Texas at Austin.

Virginia: The Papers of Allen Ginsberg, MSS 7883, 7883-a, Clifton Waller Barrett Library of American Literature, Special Collections, University of Virginia Library.

I am grateful to the curators at the above institutions for permission to cite their collections.

PART I: THE COLUMBUS OF ETERNITY

IT WAS WELL AFTER MIDNIGHT: **As a young man . . . leavetaking.** Barry Miles, *Ginsberg: A Biography* (New York: Simon & Schuster: 1989), p. 43. I have drawn on all three major biographies of Allen Ginsberg to write this book, but as they often include the same information, I have not cited them individually, except where I have found that information does not appear elsewhere; this does not lessen my indebtedness to all of them. I am particularly grateful to Bill Morgan, not only for his book, the most recent of the biographies, *I Celebrate Myself: The Life of Allen Ginsberg* (New York: Viking, 2006), but also for his bibliographic works on Ginsberg, his edition of Gregory Corso's letters, and his organization of Ginsberg's archive, which is now housed at Stanford. Michael Schumacher's biography *Dharma Lion: A Critical Biography of Allen Ginsberg* (New York: St. Martin's Press, 1995) also helped me understand the evolution of Allen Ginsberg the poet; **"She, Allen, is our Rimbaud and more today."** Bill Morgan (ed.), *Accidental Autobiography: The Letters of Gregory Corso* (New York: New Directions, 2003), p. 6; **Ginsberg sat cross-legged . . . The Journey to the End of Night**. Allen Ginsberg, *Indian Journals* (New York: Grove Press, 1970), pp. 118–120. Naturally, the *Indian Journals* are an important source for this book, both the 1970 published version and the unexpurgated and unedited journals themselves, as Allen Ginsberg drew on several notebooks and at least one letter to create what became the final version of *Indian Journals*. I have, however, cited this work only where I have quoted directly from it. All interviews are with the author.

SOME TIME LATER, WITH BRAKES HISSING: **"Burdwan??"** *Indian Journals,* pp. 117–121.

ON JUNE 3, 1925: **With the Mughal invasion of the subcontinent . . . to make love to.** Ashoke Sarkar to Allen Ginsberg, February 24, 1977, Stanford; **Even Muslim Sufi saints, the fakirs . . . Tantric yoga.** Richard M. Eaton, *The Rise of Islam and the Bengal Frontier 1204–1760* (New Delhi: Oxford University Press, 1993), pp. 78–79; **Mathura Nath Sarkar was the first . . . radiant white skin.** Ashoke Sarkar to Allen Ginsberg, February 16, 1977, Stanford; **He called his son Nagendra Nath . . . was Asoke's father** Ashoke Sarkar to Allen Ginsberg, February 24, 1977, Stanford. Ashoke Sarkar not only used widely different spellings of his name, but also went by Asoke Fakir (which was how Ginsberg first knew him) for a time before changing it back in the 1970s. Elsewhere I have chosen to impose consistency on the spellings of Bengali names; in his case I have used the spellings he used in sourcing the letters because it seemed truer to his changeable nature and true, too, to the land he emerged from: Bengal, East Bengal, East Pakistan, Bangla Desh, Bangladesh.

IN THE SUMMER OF 1948: **Heartbroken for the first . . . ancient voice again.** Interview with Tom Clark, "The Art of Poetry," *Paris Review,* Spring 1966, in David Carter (ed.), *Allen Ginsberg: Spontaneous Mind: Selected Interviews 1958–1996* (New York: HarperCollins, 2001), pp. 35–44; **Their visit ended . . . of analysis.** Allen Ginsberg to Jack Kerouac, n.d. [early November 1948], Columbia; **"Columbus of Eternity."** Unpublished spiral "Lion's Bond" notebook, Israel, November 1961, Stanford; **Allen made it a practice to keep . . . something over.** Lucien Carr, "The Clubhouse Fool," ca. 1949, unpublished ms., Stanford. This is a piece of fiction in which the main character is clearly modeled on Allen Ginsberg; **It was only when Allen . . . his rocker.** Allen Ginsberg to Jack Kerouac, n.d. [early November 1948], Columbia; **Neal's last letter . . . own hollowness.** *As Ever: The Collected Correspondence of Allen Ginsberg and Neal Cassady* (Berkeley: Creative Arts, 1977), pp. 35–36, 376; **By the time Allen . . . him look ugly.** Allen Ginsberg to Jack Kerouac, n.d. [early November 1948], Columbia; **After Jack left . . . he had seen.** Allen Ginsberg to Jack Kerouac, n.d. [late November 1948], Columbia; **It was only weeks afterward . . . wished him luck.** Allen Ginsberg to Jack Kerouac, n.d. [early November 1948], Columbia; **To them all, "Little Allen" . . . of life experience.** John Clellon Holmes, "The Consciousness Widener," original ms., p. 20, Stanford.

SHE SITS IN THE AIR INDIA OFFICE: **Instead, she is paralyzed by indecision.** Hope Savage to Jerry and Robbie Madden, April 8, 1960. Author's note: Hope's letters are to "Jerry," which was his given name; he later changed it to David in honor of the composer David Van Vactor, who took a serious interest in him as a young man and subsidized his education. All Savage's letters to David and Robbie Madden are privately held; **late 1936,** according to a close relation; **She had set her sights on . . . in four days.** Hope Savage to Jerry and Robbie Madden, April 30, 1960; **Playing the LP at top volume . . . phonograph.** Interview with David Madden; **When he had ventured . . . when would she return.** Hope Savage to Jerry Madden, n.d. [1955]; **She had long ago found America . . . she still had to try.** Hope Savage to Jerry and Robbie Madden, April 8, 1960; **From Darjeeling en route . . . final decision.** Hope Savage to Jerry and Robbie Madden, April 30, 1960.

JACK KEROUAC DIDN'T BELIEVE IN PLOTS: **Life has no plot . . . Simple as that.** Unpublished Kerouac interview, July 14, 1964, Northport, Long Island, Stanford.

THE FIRST EXTENDED DESCRIPTION: **"I began noticing in every corner . . . blue hand itself."** *Spontaneous Mind,* p. 37; **All spring he had read . . . of their minds.** Allen Ginsberg to Jack Kerouac, n.d. [late May 1948], Columbia; **As he walked past the new Columbia library . . . gone too far."** *Spontaneous Mind,* pp. 35–44; **While Ginsberg had sworn . . . presented itself.** Allen Ginsberg to Howard Shulman, October 16, 1961, Columbia.

WHEN HE WAS A TOOTHLESS OLD MAN: **If the proprietor . . . on his way out.** Interview with Robert Wilson; **"his enabler and co-dependent."** "The Funeral" by Roger Richards; *Long Shot: Corso Remembered,* vol. 24, p. 68; **He was born in 1930 . . . left prison, he did.** *Accidental Autobiography,* pp. 117–126.

ALLEN GINSBERG'S ARRIVAL: **"If I did not have faith . . . were everywhere."** Allen Ginsberg to Jack Kerouac, n.d. [end November 1948], Columbia; **Allen, forever hopeful . . . "roar of a general."** "The Consciousness Widener," p. 5, Stanford; **This time, instead of emptying . . . Bill and Joan.** Allen Ginsberg, "The Fall," unpublished ms., p. 27, Stanford.

SHORTLY BEFORE HIS DEATH: **Not long after the death . . . prefrontal lobotomy.** Allen Ginsberg, *Collected Poems* (New York: HarperCollins, 1984), see "Howl," p. 130; **"A lunatic is a man . . . human honor."** Susan Sontag (ed. and introduction), *Antonin Artaud: Selected Writings* (Berkeley: University of California Press, 1988), p. 485; all Solomon quotes in this section are from Carl Solomon's *More Mishaps* (San Francisco: City Lights, 1968), pp. 113–115.

THE PONY STABLE WASN'T A HIGH-PROFILE ESTABLISHMENT: **"Consummatum est! . . ."** "The Consciousness Widener," p. 6, Stanford; **"Thin air and solid objects,"** Ibid., p. 5, Stanford; **On those nights . . . imagine it was him.** *Ginsberg: A Biography,* p. 133; **"Are you suggesting . . . still a neglected poet."** Gregory Corso, unpublished autobiographical writings, Berg.

HOPE WAS SEATED BY HERSELF: Interview with David Madden.

GINSBERG CAME UPON JOAN: This description of Allen's dream of Joan and the provenance of his poem about her is from Allen Ginsberg's *Journals: Early Fifties, Early Sixties*, Gordon Ball (ed.) (New York: Grove, 1977), p. 63. See also "Siesta in Xbalba," *Collected Poems*, p. 104; **"there is an inner/anterior image . . . O future, unimaginable God."** *Collected Poems*, p. 106, and *Journals: Early Fifties, Early Sixties*, p. 59; **"a dead hand waiting to slip over his like a glove."** William S. Burroughs, *The Word Virus: The William S. Burroughs Reader* (New York: Grove, 2000), p . 93; **Take away the "sawdust of reason" . . .** Gordon Ball (ed.), *Allen Ginsberg, Journals Mid-Fifties 1954–1958* (Harper-Collins: New York, 1995), pp. 136–142.

"THE WAR DID HIM IN": **"The war did him in . . . you boys knew."** Kate Orlovsky to Peter Orlovsky, December 6, 1961, Texas; **In late 1954 . . . the Korean War.** Interview with Peter Orlovsky; **"The first time in life I feel evil. . . ."** *Journals, Mid-Fifties*, p. 73; **"I haven't met your mother at any of the dances."** Carl Solomon to Allen Ginsberg, October 11, 1955, Stanford; poetry excerpt is from "Howl," in *Collected Poems*, pp. 126, 128.

IT WAS A REAL ANCESTRAL MANSION: Interview with David Madden.

SHE MET HIM ONE LAST TIME: Interview with David Madden and two undated letters from Hope Savage to Jerry Madden [New York City].

NAGENDRA NATH LEFT KHULNA: Ashoke Sarkar to Allen Ginsberg, February 24, 1977, Stanford; details on description of Tantric practices from Shashibhusan Dasgupta, *Obscure Religious Cults* (Calcutta: Firma KLM Ltd., 1976), pp. 124–125.

"YES, I'VE STROLLED THROUGH THE DEW-SPARKLED": **"Yes, I've strolled . . . of the Taj Mahal . . ."** Terry Southern and Mason Hoffenberg, *Candy* (New York: G. P. Putnam's & Sons, 1958), pp. 9–10; the information in the rest of this section is from two undated letters by Hope Savage to Jerry Madden and a contemporary photograph.

IF GREGORY CORSO LOOKED OUT: **When the cats inexplicably disappeared . . . paid for it.** *An Accidental Autobiography*, pp. 3–4; **"met a beautiful Shelley . . . in her twentieth year."** *Ibid.*, p. 6; and photocopies of Corso's journals at Ginsberg Trust.

IN HOPE'S EYES, IT WAS NOT THE BIRDS: **The hipster revolt . . . behind them.** Hope Savage to Jerry and Robbie Madden, November 9, 1956; **Though she still signed . . . in America, she decided.** Hope Savage to Jerry Madden, n.d. [fragment]; **Finding Gregory reluctant . . . their last conversation.** Hope Savage to Jerry Madden, October 7, 1955; **While American communism . . . visiting revolutionaries.** Hope Savage to Gregory Corso, Labor Day 1956, Texas; **Blake's "Revolution . . . which way was it?** Hope Savage to Jerry Madden, October 31, 1955; **Her prophecies smacked . . . for herself.** Hope Savage to Jerry Madden, n.d. [New York City, 1954]; **After a performance of . . . she to continue?** Hope Savage to Jerry Madden, December 22, 1955.

JUST WHERE SHE WAS TO GO: **While she was there . . . safekeeping.** Hope Savage to Jerry and Robbie Madden, November 9, 1956; **In September, she attended . . . Arabic.** Hope Savage to Jerry and Robbie Madden, September 26, 1956; **She told him fairy tales . . . loved him unreservedly.** Hope Savage to Gregory Corso, n.d., Texas; **Robert Duncan said . . . Frank Sinatra.** Clipping announcing October 21, 1957, reading on Telegraph Hill, Ginsberg Trust; **Suddenly bells were ringing . . . word of God.** Hope Savage to Jerry Madden, n.d.

THOUGH HE FOUND THEM HARD TO RESIST: **As it was, Gregory . . . New York City.** *An Accidental Autobiography,* p. 16, and Gregory Corso to Randall Jarrell, n.d., Berg; **"beat train."** Jack Kerouac to Allen Ginsberg, December 26, 1956, Columbia; **For Christmas . . . fountain pen.** *An Accidental Autobiography,* p. 25; **If he managed to secure . . . idea of home.** Hope Savage to Jerry and Robbie Madden, November 9, 1956; **"But I have never seen** *anything . . . human face."* **Candy,** p. 11; **At least that was the tale . . . clean of junk.** Interview with Sam Merrill, *Playboy,* November 1973.

FOR THREE YEARS, INDIA HOVERED: **"a necessary light."** In "A Letter to Hersch, June 1958," *Long Shot: Corso Remembered,* vol. 24, p. 11; **"more than poetry is needed."** *An Accidental Autobiography,* p. 209; **"Hope Savage is there."** Ibid., p. 216; **Peter was often sick from junk withdrawal.** Allen Ginsberg to Gregory Corso, March 3, 1961, Ginsberg Trust; **"You are much too fine . . . my entire being."** Herbert Huncke to Peter Orlovsky, n.d. [ca. 1960], Stanford; **"dreadful little volume."** John Hollander, *Partisan Review* 24, no. 2 (Spring 1957): 296–298; **"all the cornbelt Donnes."** Kenneth Rexroth, "San Francisco Letter," *Evergreen Review* 1, no. 2 (Summer 1957): 5–14; **Beat had now become fashion spreads . . . let in Tangier.** James Campbell, *This Is the Beat Generation* (London: Secker & Warburg, 1999); **Even J. Edgar Hoover . . . facing the country.** Gerald Nicosia, *Memory Babe: A Critical Biography of Jack Kerouac* (New York: Grove Press, 1983), p. 602; **Typically, Gregory had bought . . . and Bill, too.** *An Accidental Autobiography,* p. 248; **"I remember your saying . . . Death."** Oliver Harris (ed.), *William Burroughs and Allen Ginsberg: The Yage Letters Redux* (San Francisco: City Lights, 2006), pp. 60–64; **"Take the enclosed copy . . . is permitted."** Ibid., p. 70; **Allen thought Bill . . . bereft.** Allen Ginsberg to Lawrence Ferlinghetti, June 11, 1963, Columbia; **"You don't mess with people."** Allen Ginsberg to William Burroughs and Gregory Corso, n.d., Ginsberg Trust; **"But India may have lost its way."** Pupul Jayakar, "Encounters with Allen Ginsberg," in *Children of Barren Women* (Delhi: Penguin, 1994), pp. 164–165.

ONCE OR TWICE A WEEK: The source for this section is Buddhadev Bose's *Deshantar* (Calcutta: M. C. Sarker & Son, 1964). First published in 1961 in *Desh,* the Bengali literary monthly, this English-language version was translated from Bengali by Jyotimiroy Datta and reworked by the author. Copyright © Jyotimiroy Datta. Used by permission.

THREE DAYS LATER, A CONTINGENT OF FAMILY: **For some time . . . clinched it.** Brenda Knight, *Women of the Beat Generation* (San Francisco: Conari, 1998), p. 142: **To Jack, who'd said good-bye . . . another planet.** Allen Ginsberg to Jack Kerouac, May 11, 1962, Columbia.

THE FARTHER EAST HOPE TRAVELED: Hope Savage to Jerry and Robbie Madden, August 16, 1959 [misdated 1960].

PART II: THE MANDALA IN THE CLOUDS
FIFTEEN MONTHS BEFORE: **Then she went south . . . And there she stopped.** Hope Savage to Jerry Madden, n.d. [November 1957]; **After a brief visit with . . . older brother.** Interview with Davey Van Vactor; **Six months earlier, her . . . asking about her.** Hope Savage to Jerry Madden, n.d. [November 1957]; **When Jerry stuck his hand . . . with a gun.** Interview with David Madden; **To Jerry, Hope had . . . earthly choices.** Hope Savage to Jerry Madden, April 21, 1958; **Hope had been . . . to relive it.** Hope Savage to Jerry Madden, November 13, 1957; **"Jean wanted to come to America . . . in the movies."** Interview with David Madden; **"has studied Chinese and is really a pure angelic mind."** Gregory Corso to

Gary Snyder, August 12, 1958, Davis; **"she talks, with that mad Carolina ... seen her again."** Gary Snyder to Gregory Corso, October 2, 1958, Ginsberg Trust.

THOREAU WROTE THAT TO BE TRULY FREE: **Under the sponsorship of a local Methodist ... Cambridge, Massachusetts."** Henry Savage Jr., *Seeds of Time: The Background of Southern Thinking* (New York: Henry Holt, 1959), pp. 275–276.

JOANNE KYGER WAS A NEARLY PERFECT: **Yet it was hardly a straight line ... in her own right."** Gary Snyder to Allen Ginsberg, January 1, 1959, Stanford; **Of the two-thousand-some koans, Gary had answered forty.** Allen Ginsberg to Jack Kerouac, May 11, 1962, Columbia; **Allen claimed that William ... left wide open.** Allen Ginsberg to Gary Snyder, n.d. [end August 1961], Davis; **Non-Western cultures ... "mind of words."** Gary Snyder to Allen Ginsberg, September 4, 1961, Stanford; **"Don't you want to study ... to obtain one?"** Joanne Kyger, *Strange Big Moon: The Japan and India Journals: 1960–1964* (Berkeley: North Atlantic Books, 2000), p. xii; **Gary explained to Allen that ... permanently.** Gary Snyder to Allen Ginsberg, September 4, 1961, Stanford; **Initially, at least, Kyger ... short-changed her.** *Strange Big Moon,* p. 11; **Even more unsettling ... solicitous nurse.** Ibid., p. 20; **"It seems to me ... or identity?"** Ibid., p. 30; **"Is the woman who waits the woman who weaves?"** Ibid., p. 32; **She asked her husband ... loneliness inside her.** Ibid., p. 33; **"I'm sure / you can see me better / than I can."** Joanne Kyger, "Iliad: Achilles Does Not Die," from Michael Rothenberg (ed.), *As Ever: Selected Poems* (New York: Penguin, 2002), p. 21, copyright © 2002 by Joanne Kyger. Used by permission of Penguin, a division of the Penguin Group (USA), Inc.

HE STAGGERED FROM ONE END: **"where I can get junk, live with it and for it from here on out."** *William Burroughs, Letters to Allen Ginsberg* (New York: Full Court Press, 1982), pp. 104–105; **Yet his reticence was such ... in his life.** Paul Bowles, "Burroughs in Tangier," *Big Table,* vol. 1, 1960, p. 42. The entire opening description of Burroughs is taken from this Bowles essay, but also questioned; **Gregory had briefly suffered ... fearsome, Catholic one.** *An Accidental Autobiography,* p. 254; **They were guests of a wealthy addict ... not yet ready.** Barry Miles, *The Beat Hotel: Ginsberg, Burroughs and Corso in Paris, 1957–1963* (New York: Grove Press, 2000), p. 119; **There were rich meals ending ... get any girls."** Peter Orlovsky journals, Texas; **What they were reading ... hard to keep up.** Barry Gifford and Lawrence Lee, *Jack's Book: An Oral Biography of Jack Kerouac* (New York: St. Martin's Press, 1994), p. 194; **He had taken Janine's virginity, ... emerged sobbing.** Interview with Janine Pommy Vega; **Next time, Peter vowed ... white silk suit.** Peter Orlovsky journals, Texas; **"What if we cut up Peter?"** *Ginsberg: A Biography,* pp. 286–287; **July 6, 1961, Peter wrote ...** *him,* **he told Jack.** Peter Orlovsky to Jack Kerouac, May 11, 1962, Texas; **"And if I don't know Bill ... his previous identity."** Ginsberg to Howard Shulman, October 16, 1961, Columbia; **He'd written his new publisher ... a year in Yemen.** *An Accidental Autobiography,* p. 287; **"clean of past"** Ibid., p. 299; **She had overpowered him ... he told Allen.** Ibid., p. 216; **"What can cut-up the true ... what science?"** Ibid., p. 287.

TRAVELING ON ALONE TO GREECE: Allen Ginsberg to Howard Shulman, October 16, 1961, Columbia.

THE EARLY 1920s FOUND NAGENDRA NATH: Ashoke Sarkar to Allen Ginsberg, February 16, 1977, Stanford.

THOUGH GARY SNYDER'S INDIA ITINERARY: **Gary expected to not ... the monsoons.** Gary Snyder to Allen Ginsberg, October 17, 1961, Stanford; **Perhaps they could join ... Allen suggested.** Allen Ginsberg to Gary Snyder, n.d. [Israel], Davis; **Bowles found him ... unnatural sweetness.** Paul Bowles to Ruth Fainlight and Alan Sillitoe, July 26, 1961. *In Touch: The Letters of Paul Bowles* (New York: Farrar, Straus & Giroux, 1995); **Ceylon was boring ... night with sleepers."** Paul Bowles to Allen Ginsberg, May 1962. Ibid., p. 337; **When traveling in the North African ... in the evening.** Michelle Green, *The Dream at the End of the World* (New York: HarperCollins, 1991), p. 21; **After studying the weather tables ... mystery to him.** Gary Snyder to Allen Ginsberg, May 12, 1959, Stanford; **His *roshi* would say ... "change stinks."** Gary Snyder and Joanne Kyger to Allen Ginsberg, September 4, 1961, Stanford.

ALLEN HAD DREAMED OF BOMBAY: **"A ratty looking Bronx ... last dollar on a taxi.** Allen Ginsberg to Jack Kerouac, May 11, 1962, Columbia; **At night, gangs ... atop each building.** Interview with Peter Orlovsky; **After a preamble relating ... Taj Mahal Hotel,"** Allen Ginsberg to Paul Bowles, n.d., Texas.

A WOMAN MARRIED IN A RED-AND-GOLD: Description of Tibetans' arrival in India from "Stories from the Tibetan Diaspora," www.Khagyun.org. Snyder's encounter with lama and Gandhian from Gary Snyder, *Passage through India* (San Francisco: Gray Fox Press, 1972), p. 49.

THE OLD MAN HELD THE COTTON BATTING: **"This is an Ellora *charkha*. Gandhiji named it. He used it a lot."** *Passage through India*, p. 52; **"It is not truly monistic ... Gnosticism, Catharites."** Ibid., p. 19; **"Another big Indian thing,"** Ibid., pp. 20–22; **"They all believe ... step in human evolution."** Gary Snyder to Allen Ginsberg, January 8, 1962; **Gary's initial enthusiasm ... sinister place.** Allen Ginsberg to John Kelley, June 26, 1962, Columbia; **Meditation seemed ... quarter of an hour.** *Strange Big Moon*, p. 157; **And despite ... of the doctrine.** *Passage through India*, p. 22; **In his 1939 introduction ... give it credence.** Carl Jung, *The Spiritual Teachings of Ramana Maharshi* (Boston: Shambhala, 1972), Foreword; **"existentially bugged."** *Passage through India*, p. 24; **His enlightenment ... subtleties of the self.** Ibid., p. 27; **"I should hope so."** *Passage through India*, p. 35; **To Allen he wrote ... the human spirit.** Gary Snyder to Allen Ginsberg, January 31, 1962, Stanford; **There, he wrote ... all stripes.** Gary Snyder to Allen Ginsberg, October 17, 1962, Stanford; **"refused to be human."** *Passage through India*, p. 57; **Tired and dirty ... decking the driver.** *Strange Big Moon*, p. 176; **Gary was eventually ... with money.** *Passage through India*, p. 57; **Despite the fact ... second-class carriages.** *Strange Big Moon*, p. 176; **Gary hated the fact ... he hadn't paid for.** Ibid., p. 174.

ALMOST IN SPITE OF HIMSELF: **Krishnaji had often teased ... and beauty and desire.** *The Children of Barren Women*, p. 179; **The old man stopped ... no consolation.** Ibid., p. 182; **"I have been spinning ... you spin?"** *Passage through India*, p. 52. **Fortuitously, an article ... life afterward?** *Strange Big Moon*, p. 102; these reservations are posed in her own voice, but I hear Snyder behind them; **"Some Americans ... threw Gandhi away."** *Passage through India*, p. 52.

THERE WAS A RETINUE OF LAMAS: **"It really is another Dimension of time-history here,"** Allen Ginsberg to Jack Kerouac, May 11, 1962, Columbia; **Yet while Peter ... the vow itself.** Allen Ginsberg to Paul Bowles, n.d., Texas; **"You see, you**

must not . . . saffron robes. Allen Ginsberg to Jack Kerouac, May 11, 1962, Columbia; description of Jain beliefs from Heinrich Zimmer's *Myths and Symbols in Indian Art and Civilization* (Princeton: Bollingen Series, Princeton University Press, 1946), pp. 55, 166; **"for cocksmen-cayote types."** Allen Ginsberg to Jack Kerouac, May 11, 1962, Columbia; **"Silence would be good for America."** Allen Ginsberg to Jack Kerouac, May 11, 1962, Columbia.

SHIVA SITS IN SPLENDID ISOLATION: Shiva description from *Myths and Symbols in Indian Art and Civilization,* pp. 115–116; **"Holy Hindu town"** . . . **"It stinks."** *Strange Big Moon,* p. 176; **Gary, somewhat defensively, . . . vivid display.** *Passage through India,* p. 56, and *Strange Big Moon,* p.176; **Eventually, Gary was . . . meet their standards.** *Passage through India,* p. 59; **"Attention Manager . . . therefore leaving."** *Strange Big Moon,* p. 177; **It was an emotional . . . to the city.** *Passage through India,* p. 61.

RISHIKESH WAS THE GATEWAY TO HEAVEN: **In the audience hall . . . proper meditation posture.** *Passage through India,* p. 63; **Orthodox Hindus . . . language of God.** Alain Danielou, *Way to the Labyrinth: Memories of East and West* (New York: New Directions, 1987), p. 212; **"nothing could be sounder, except perhaps Buddhism."** *Passage through India,* p. 64; **"A sorry bunch of psychic retreaters from the dubious human journey."** *Letters to Allen Ginsberg,* p. 57; **Shiva's devotees know . . . Half Woman.** *Myths and Symbols in Indian Art and Civilization,* p.127; **"None . . . dangerous."** *Passage through India,* p. 64; **Joanne found herself . . . yonilike mouth.** *Strange Big Moon,* p. 181; **Peter, silently appraising . . . for yoga.** *Passage through India,* p. 65; **Their rooms were . . . their posture.** Allen Ginsberg to Jack Kerouac, May 11, 1962, Columbia; **"Which brought home . . . most Westerners."** *Passage through India,* p. 65; **Unlike more genial . . . force of arms.** Jamini Sahid and Mohan Ghosh, *Sannyasi and Fakir Raiders in Bengal* (Calcutta: Bengal Civil Service Bengal Secretariat Book Department, 1930); **Gary made note . . . over again.** *Passage through India,* p. 67; **After the austerity . . . message cheered him.** Allen Ginsberg to Jack Kerouac, May 11, 1962, Columbia; **That night, Joanne . . . she wrote.** *Strange Big Moon,* p. 179; **The sight of the . . . Dharamasala.** *Passage through India,* p. 68; **The three sadhus sitting . . . forests and caves.** Allen Ginsberg to Jack Kerouac, May 11, 1962, Columbia; **"a super southern californian longhair beat vegetarian hepcat."** Allen Ginsberg to LeRoi Jones, March 17, 1962, Columbia; **"Just how old . . . eating bananas!"** *Passage through India,* pp. 65, 66.

THE MORPHINE DREAM BEGAN: Dream recounted in excised portion of Indian journal, from typescript at Columbia, also at Stanford, pp. 4–7. **"Only because," she wrote, "I think of manners and control."** *Strange Big Moon,* p. 191; **After eating opium . . . early start.** Ibid., p. 163.

"FRANKLY, I'M AFRAID SHE'S GOING TO HELL FAST": **"First the health goes . . . dew of the dawn."** Kate Orlovsky to Peter Orlovsky, July 3, 1961, Texas; **"Am I dead? . . . before it is too late."** Marie Orlovsky to Peter Orlovsky, May 29, 1961, and Kate Orlovsky to Peter Orlovsky, September 29, 1961, Texas; **Since drugs were . . . some sedatives.** Kate Orlovsky to Peter Orlovsky, August 31, 1961, Texas; **"salad sandwich."** Kate Orlovsky to Peter Orlovsky, July 20, 1961, Texas; **"The things he says! . . . drink of water."** Kate Orlovsky to Peter Orlovsky, July 30, 1961, Texas; **"Death allways seems beautifull . . . police arrived.** Kate Orlovsky to Peter Orlovsky, September 29, 1961, Texas.

But it wasn't Lafcadio Orlovsky: **"Go where there is hope . . . in a family."** Excised portion of Indian journal, pp. 4–7, Columbia; **Rishikesh and Almora . . . only more spiritual.** Allen Ginsberg to John Kelley, June 26, 1962, Stanford; **"You will be OK."** Excised portion of Indian journal, pp. 4–7, Columbia; **In the months after . . . shopping bags.** Joyce Johnson, *Door Wide Open: A Beat Love Affair in Letters* (New York: Viking, 2000), p. 172; **While interned . . . enemy bombers.** Allen Ginsberg to Dorothy Norman, n.d. [May 1962], Beinecke; **Her parents moved her . . . no note.** *Women of the Beat Generation*, p. 143; **Allen's cafeteria dream . . . track of the time.** Excised portion of Indian journal, pp. 4–7, Columbia; **"Jai Ram!"** *Passage through India*, pp. 71–72.

That same morning: Description of Jackie Kennedy's visit is based on John Kenneth Galbraith's account in *Ambassador's Journal* (Boston: Houghton Mifflin, 1968), pp. 276, 285, 289. **The final trip . . . three in Pakistan.** *Time*, March 9, 1962. **In expectation . . . at his palace.** *Time*, March 23, 1962; **Lord Bertrand Russell . . . Nehru had demurred.** Calcutta *Statesman*, April 23, 1962; **(she noted that one of its peacock feathers was crushed).** Interview with Nicholas Vreeland.

Lying on his charpoy: **It had been his idea . . . most famous poet.** *Strange Big Moon*, p. 185; **Ted Wilentz . . . royalty checks.** Ted Wilentz to Allen Ginsberg, August 10, 1952, Virginia; **In his letter . . . Boy, here comes a live one."** *An Accidental Autobiography*, p. 307; **"Do inquire around . . . Love, Gregory."** Ibid., p. 308; **"but to say . . . into the reader's mind."** *Time*, March 9, 1962; **"unnecessarily vicious."** *Strange Big Moon*, p. 192; **"What's to be done . . . after the movies?"** *Indian Journals*, pp. 9–11; **"Too much in my hair."** Excised portion of Indian journal, p. 16, Columbia.

Dharamsala was an old hill station: Description of Dharamsala and the Dalai Lama is based on Thomas Merton's account in *Asian Journals* (New York: New Directions, 1975), pp. 92, 96, 101–102. **Gary Snyder had grown . . . You had to try.** Gary Snyder, *The Gary Snyder Reader: Poetry, Prose and Translations* (New York: Counterpoint, 1999), pp. 91–92, 103.

Later in the day: "A brief account of Mr. Sonam T. Kazi's experience in Tibet before the invasion," London, September 13, 1994, www.tibet.com/status/kazi.html; **Dudjom had anticipated . . . station at Kalimpong.** Interview with Nicholas Vreeland; **Dudjom Rinpoche's own root . . . original translations.** Dudjom Rinpoche, translated by Padmakara Translation Group, *Counsels from My Heart* (San Francisco: Shambhala, 2001), p. 45; **"If you take LSD, can you see what's in that briefcase?"** *Indian Journals*, p. 3; account of conversation and exchanges with Dalai Lama based on *Passage through India*, p. 84, and *Strange Big Moon*, p. 194.

Earlier that morning: **Not far out into the snowfield . . . had once sat.** *Passage through India*, p. 82.

Joanne stayed behind to wash: Quotations from letter to "Nemi" in *Strange Big Moon*, p. 193; **"tibetan-noh play sepulchral voice."** Allen Ginsberg to Jack Kerouac, May 11, 1962, Columbia; **After six weeks of traveling . . . impressive insecurity.** *Strange Big Moon*, p. 190; **"Sounds like a simple, persevering . . . elephant on a mouse."** Allen Ginsberg to Jack Kerouac, May 11, 1962, Columbia.

Not long after their marriage: **"And when you read this Joanne Kyger, as you certainly will."** *Strange Big Moon*, p. 9; **Now she took . . . giving up.** Ibid., pp. 194–195; **She was married to a man . . . most likely was.** Ibid., p. 20; **"The Indians . . . seem to adore him."** Ibid., p. 195; **I look at Joann . . . Will do.** Ibid., p. 191; **"But what about me?"** Ibid., pp. 197–198; Description of Allen Ginsberg's reception in Bombay and the joint rooftop poetry reading taken from R. Parthasarathy, *Writers' Workshop Miscellany* (Calcutta: Writers Workshop, 1962), unpaginated; **Instead, she had fixed Allen . . . Everything just stopped.** *Strange Big Moon,* pp. 197–198; poetry excerpt from "The Maze," *As Ever: Selected Poems,* p. 1, copyright © 2002 by Joanne Kyger. Used by permission of Penguin, a division of the Penguin Group (USA), Inc. **"The difficulty is Ego . . . swallow it into myself."** *Strange Big Moon,* pp. 197–198.

FOR MANY YEARS, THE YOUNG ASOKE: Asoke Sarkar to Allen Ginsberg, January 24, 1985, Stanford, and S. C. Chakravarti, *Philosophical Foundation of Bengal Vaishnavism* (Calcutta: Munshiram Manoharlal, 1975), p. 35.

SIPPING PERCOLATED COFFEE AT A TABLE: **He and Peter were assumed . . . Western holy men.** Allen Ginsberg to Dorothy Norman [May 1962], Beinecke; **"There is plenty of . . . Don't disturb me."** *Illustrated Weekly of India,* April 1962; Description of Ellora cave dream in excised portion of Indian journal, pp. 26, 28–30, Stanford; final passage translation is from Thich Nhat Hanh's version of *The Sutra of the Perfection of Wisdom of the Diamond That Cuts Through Illusion* (Berkeley: Parallax Press, 1992); **In a postcard . . . dreams themselves.** Allen Ginsberg to Leo Skir, reproduced in *Women of the Beat Generation,* p. 144; **"the subjective result . . . desire for god."** Allen Ginsberg to Jack Kerouac, May 11, 1962, Columbia.

"IMAGINE THE BEAUTIFUL DRAMA": Allen Ginsberg to Gregory Corso, April 19, 1962, Ginsberg Trust.

PART III: A BLUE HAND

IN MARCH 1962: **"Seems she had been in Aden, Ethiopia, Iran, and then back to India."** *Passage through India,* p. 78; **Allen's rushed prose was illiterate, she complained to Gregory;** Gregory Corso to Hope Savage, Ginsberg Trust. This letter was among the letters and photographs that he sent to her in Camden for safekeeping in the summer of 1956; **Gary speculated in his journal that she was, perhaps, a little crazy.** *Passage through India,* p. 78; **Hope next appeared . . . shawl and barefoot.** Ibid., p. 95; **Bit by bit . . . she told them.** Ibid., p. 78; **In a shipboard letter . . . everyone else.** Gary Snyder and Joanne Kyger to Allen Ginsberg, May 6, 1962, Stanford; **In a curious aside . . . but Iranian.** *Passage through India,* p. 78; **"Winters in . . . first-class cuisine.** Allen Ginsberg to Gregory Corso, April 19, 1962, Ginsberg Trust; **Within two weeks . . . going to India.** Ted Wilentz to Allen Ginsberg, May 1, 1962, Virginia; **"Everything here paradisal . . . okay, love, Allen."** Allen Ginsberg to Gregory Corso, late April 1962, Ginsberg Trust.

THE HINDU PANTHEON: **All too often, strikes paralyzed the city.** Calcutta *Statesman,* June 26, 1962; *Basic Development Plan for the Calcutta Metropolitan District 1966–86,* published under the sponsorship of the Ford Foundation. Other sources on Calcutta include Geoffrey Moorehouse's *Calcutta* (London: Phoenix House, 1971); **Allen had watched him perform in New York in 1944.** From 1971 Ginsberg journal, Stanford; description of Bengal renaissance from Sunil Ganguly's *Ardhak Jeevan* [*Half a Life*] (Calcutta: Ananda, 2000), p. 156; **Though Buddhadev Bose . . . vied for Tagore's mantle.** Buddhadeva Bose, *An Acre of Green Grass* (Calcutta: Papyrus, 1982), p. 13; **"Main thing we do . . . hunt them down."** Peter Orlovsky to Lucien Carr,

May 29, 1962, Virginia; **"The English used in India . . . American Negro English."** *Writers' Workshop Miscellany*; **"twinkle eye smile."** Peter Orlovsky to Allen Ginsberg, June 6, 1962, Stanford. When I asked Peter Orlovsky about Hope Savage, he told me that while Allen may have met her, he never had. When I told him he had met her many times, he was astonished. By then the myth of Hope Savage had outstripped his memory of her; **"Seems the gandhi sperit . . . because ya kissed a girl."** Peter Orlovsky to Lucien Carr, May 29, 1962, Virginia.

"Behold, this is the Universe": Swami Prabhavananda and Christopher Isherwood (trans.), *The Bhagavad Gita* (Hollywood: Vedanta Press, 1944), p. 115. Oppenheimer knew Sanskrit, and his quotation reflected his own understanding of the text; **"We have grown into a classic . . . vehicle of my devotion."** Timothy Leary to Allen Ginsberg, undated 1962 letters from Copenhagen and Mexico, Stanford; **"Apparently lots of boy love in the yellow hat monastery."** Allen Ginsberg to Peter Orlovsky, June 6, 1962, Columbia. "Entering any orifice of oneself or another," though doubtless common in any monastic community, would in fact constitute a major infraction of one's vows, and one would no longer be a monk, according to Nicholas Vreeland, a monk of the Yellow Hat school. The lama in question was perhaps a man named Sangharakshita (born Dennis Lingwood in south London) who, like Lama Govinda, whom Allen also met, was ordained in a Theravadan country—though his ordination was eventually questioned. Allen did not accept his offer of the boy and, indeed, didn't touch anyone but Peter in his time in India; **"You get this wang . . . a long journey."** Allen Ginsberg to Peter Orlovsky, June 6, 1962, Columbia; **"to cover the real pain . . . the task of preparing to die."** Allen Ginsberg to Robert LaVigne, June 30, 1962, Columbia; **"Terrible with fangs . . . Doomsday morning."** *The Bhagavad Gita*, p. 116; **"the hosts of Rheumatism & Cancer."** *Indian Journals*, p. 51; **"When will I be ready to die? . . . figures of daily India?"** *Indian Journals*, p. 29.

Bengali intellectuals with more time: Interview with Sunil Ganguly and his memoir, *Half a Life*. I am grateful to Chaitali Basu for her translation, which I have drawn upon heavily.

It was a relief to travel outside: **Locally, the cholera outbreak . . . commented upon.** Calcutta *Statesman,* June 27, 1963; **"local pious opinion . . . really dug."** Allen Ginsberg to John Kelley, June 26, 1962, Columbia. Interviews with Sunil Ganguly for description of how Ginsberg appeared to the *Krittibas* group, also *Half a Life,* p. 207.

In the dream, Allen retrieved: Interview with Jyoti Datta; **Satori could not be achieved . . . on koan study.** Gary Snyder to Allen Ginsberg, November 11, 1962, Stanford; **Jyoti's father-in-law . . . with Peter Orlovsky.** Buddhadeva Bose to daughter Damayanti from Calcutta, December 7, 1962, translated by Jyoti Datta, private collection; description of dinner party from *Blitz,* September 19, 1964; **Even worse, Peter . . . terrorizing the family maidservant.** Interview with Meenakshi Datta; **One pundit, writing . . . "their real nature."** Anjisnu Bhattacharya, "Beat Poets in Calcutta," *Swadhinata,* August 19, 1962, Stanford; description of Sunil's and Shakti's LSD experience from interviews with Sunil Ganguly and Tarapada Roy and Jyoti Datta.

After hunkering down: **In Calcutta, the jhola bag and kolhapuri sandals were the badge of the intellectual.** This ensemble, along with cheap Indian bedspreads, brass incense holders, and marijuana accessories, would later be imported wholesale by American hippies—a boon for India's hard-currency reserves and a feather in Pupul Jayakar's cap; description of Manjula Mitra from interview with Utpal Kumar Basu.

MUCH LIKE HIS FATHER, NAGENDRA NATH: **The radiant orange robes . . . Massage & Bath Clinic, Ltd.** Ashoke Sarkar to Allen Ginsberg, January 24, 1977, Stanford; **Four years later . . . two children with her.** Ashoke Sarkar to Allen Ginsberg, October 22, 1989, Stanford; **He thought nothing . . . Raj Bhavan.** Interview with Jyoti Datta; **He made a practice . . . was perfect.** Interview with Malay Roy Choudhury; **In Arabic, *faqir* . . . to God alone.** Seyyed Hossein Nasr, *Islam: Religion, History, Civilization* (San Francisco: HarperSanFrancisco, 2003), p. 84; **"the Reformation of Humanity."** Asoke Sarkar to Allen Ginsberg, January 24, 1977, Stanford; **"The difference is 1926 and 1925 . . . pleasure and passion."** Asoke Fakir to Allen Ginsberg, September 6, 1962, Stanford.

"HARI BOL," THE MEN CRIED: For the scene at Nimtola, I have drawn on interviews with Sarat Kumar Mukhopadhyay, Utpal Kumar Basu, and Sunil Ganguly; **"When I was young . . . Dear Blake, come back."** *Indian Journals,* p. 58; **That night he dreamed . . . as ever.** Excised portion, Indian journals, Stanford; **"It isn't enough for yr heart . . . everybody's heart is broken now."** *Indian Journals,* p. 52.

"IF I THOUGHT HIS FIGURES & REASONING": **I would be inclined to do something.** Allen Ginsberg to Louis Ginsberg, September 25, 1962, Columbia; **Wouldn't it be better . . . cold war psychosis?** Allen Ginsberg to Bertrand Russell, September 5, 1962, Columbia; **"Act or Perish."** Bertrand Russell to Allen Ginsberg, September 14, 1962, Columbia; **"I'm not sure he's exaggerating . . . what you think?"** Allen Ginsberg to Louis Ginsberg, October 14, 1962, Columbia; **Allen wrote similar . . . their opinion.** Allen Ginsberg to Jack Kerouac, September 9, 1962, Texas; **Gary replied . . . get into trouble.** Gary Snyder to Allen Ginsberg, November 15, 1962, Davis; **"To be or not to be,"** Allen Ginsberg to Louis Ginsberg, September 25, 1962, Columbia; **"damn thing about the missus of destruction."** *An Accidental Autobiography,* p. 314. **"gentle homeless on-the-road teaheads."** *City Lights Journal* #1 (San Francisco: City Lights, 1962), p. 1; scene at Tarapith from *Indian Journals,* pp. 85–88. For background on Tarapith as a pilgrimage site, the myth of Tara, and the story of Bamakshepa, I am indebted to the following works: E. A. Morinis, *Pilgrimage in the Hindu Tradition: A Case Study of West Bengal* (Bombay, Calcutta, and Madras: Oxford University Press, 1984), pp. 166–167, quoting oral sources, and pp. 167, 182; Sushil Kumar Bandopadhyaya (trans.), *Sri Sri Bamakshepa* (Calcutta: Tarapith Bhairab, n.d.), unpaginated; and David R. Kingsley, *Tantric Visions of the Divine Feminine: The Ten Mahavidyas* (Berkeley and Los Angeles: University of California Press, 1997), p. 111. Lines quoted from "Kaddish" (including his letter from Naomi) in *Collected Poems,* p. 221, 224.

THEY WERE KNOWN AS HOLY FOOLS: **"They are born Bauls . . . friendship and dharma will arrive."** Asoke Fakir to Allen Ginsberg, April 8, 1967, Stanford; **"O blue dressed woman . . . Radha Radha Radha."** *Indian Journals,* p. 89.

THE DAY AFTER ALLEN: Description of America's and India's responses to the India-China war drawn from *Ambassador's Journal,* pp. 374, 387, 388, 396, 411–412, and interview with Sunil Ganguly. **In Delhi, people began digging trenches.** Allen Ginsberg to Lawrence Ferlinghetti, March 15, 1963, Columbia; **Shakti was even more . . . inadvertently committed.** Sunil Ganguly to Allen Ginsberg, January 1, 1963, Stanford; **What was really needed . . . universal bliss.** Allen Ginsberg to Ted Wilentz, November 3, 1962, Virginia, and Allen Ginsberg to Robert LaVigne, November 3, 1962, Stanford.

LIKE THE REST OF THE NATION: *Children of Barren Women,* p. 182.

"ENCLOSED PICTURE OF HOPE": Allen Ginsberg to Gregory Corso, October 11, 1962, Ginsberg Trust; **"First time I've seen her sociable to a companion like girls should be."** Allen Ginsberg to Gregory Corso, August 26, 1962, Ginsberg Trust; **Nearly every time Sunil . . . manner toward her.** Interview with Sunil Ganguly; **"All very ladylike . . . married?"** Allen Ginsberg to Gregory Corso, October 11, 1962, Ginsberg Trust; **He worried that . . . Zeus and his minions.** *An Accidental Autobiography,* p. 314; **"First you say . . . I feel great."** Allen Ginsberg to Gregory Corso, n.d., Ginsberg Trust; **"ideal revolutionary."** *An Accidental Autobiography,* p. 315; **"He's trying to flatter me . . . trying this approach."** Allen Ginsberg to Gregory Corso, May 26, 1962, Ginsberg Trust; **"She still be my angel . . . such a long time."** *An Accidental Autobiography,* p. 319; **Allen continued to . . . anxieties.** Allen Ginsberg to Gregory Corso, July 25, 1962, Ginsberg Trust; **"I love her . . . my undying love."** *An Accidental Autobiography,* pp. 341–343.

"THE LAST TIME I SAW HOPE": **"How like Russian . . . from a long line . . ."** Untitled ms. by Gregory Corso, n.d., Texas; **"Went thru one year of complete hell . . . hell to be heaven."** *An Accidental Autobiography,* p. 239. **A fine small jewel of a book."** Lisa Brinker to Gary Snyder, November 13 [early 1970s], Davis; **"I need not . . . no body's business."** Gregory Corso, unpublished ms., n.d. [ca. 1965], "These pages, my biographical remembrances of my first true love," Texas; **"I have known Almighty Kindness Herself! . . . Her confidence!"** "But I Do Not Need Kindness," excerpt from Gregory Corso, *Mindfield: New and Selected Poems,* pp. 32–33, copyright © 1958 by Gregory Corso. Reprinted by permission of City Lights Books; **While they were living . . . name was Hope Savage.** Interview with Gus Reininger; **She claimed . . . shock treatment.** *An Accidental Autobiography,* p. 78; **This had stolen something . . . in 1953.** While Hope Savage's purported shock treatments have been published as uncontested fact elsewhere, I can neither attest that she said this nor confirm that if she said this, it is, in fact, a true statement; **"I don't know what they took away . . . and therefore I feel I could never do anything perfect or complete."** Gregory Corso, interview with Michael Andre in *Unmuzzled Ox* 6.2, no. 22 (Winter 1981): 123–158; **"But when the conquered spirit . . . take care of the cats?"** "Dear Girl," excerpt from Gregory Corso, *Mindfield: New and Selected Poems,* p. 104, copyright © 1959 by Gregory Corso. Reprinted by permission of the New Directions Corporation; **"The priest cut open . . . Where's your soul?"** From "But I Do Not Need Kindness," from *Mindfield: New and Selected Poems,* pp. 32–33, copyright © 1958 by Gregory Corso. Reprinted by permission of City Light Books; **Confession, he knew . . . had run away.** Gregory Corso, unpublished ms. "These pages, my biographical remembrances . . ." Texas; **"I ran to Kindness . . . I wept. I wept."** "But I Do Not Need Kindness," excerpt from *Mindfield: New and Selected Poems,* pp. 32–33, © 1958 by Gregory Corso. Reprinted by permission of City Lights Books.

ALL THE PITS WERE AFLAME: Interview with Sunil Ganguly.

"I KNOW HER TO BE A GREAT LADY": **"Of all people . . . such crap."** Allen Ginsberg to Jyoti Datta, December 16, 1962, private collection; **Ginsberg had shown up . . . apologize to his wife.** Interview with Elaine Steele. For this account of the arrest under Howrah bridge, I am grateful to Derek Boshier, an English painter who was there that evening. He couldn't remember who made the remark about blowing it up, but it seems typical of Peter's offbeat, seemingly innocent, humor; **"a willful blind-**

ness . . . what the hell." *As Ever: The Collected Correspondence of Allen Ginsberg and Neal Cassady*, p. 89; **Peter felt the same . . . for a foreign fellowship.** Manjula Mitra to Peter Orlovsky, December 23, 1962, Texas; **"Should I get married? . . . underwear."** "Marriage," from *Mindfield: New and Selected Poems*, pp. 62–64, © 1960 by Gregory Corso. Reprinted by permission of New Directions Publishing Corporation; **"keep her free."** *Indian Journals*, p. 119; **"My god! . . . ladies home journal."** *As Ever: The Collected Correspondence of Allen Ginsberg and Neal Cassady*, p. 89.

LIKE VENICE IN THE OFF-SEASON: **After Nimtola, he found the scene tame.** Allen Ginsberg to Jyoti Datta, private collection; **"sleazy."** Excised from Indian journal, "shame to be uttering, writing such vague number of sleazy images to my own book I've never read them beginning to end myself," Stanford; **"They're all mad."** *Indian Journals*, pp. 131–137.

HE DIDN'T HAVE A WATCH: Quotes on Mira Bai from Bankey Behari's *The Story of Mira Bai* (Gorakpur: Gita Press, 2002). Account of Brindaban pilgrimage drawn from David L. Haberman's *Journey Through the Twelve Forests* (New York: Oxford University Press, 1994), pp. 204–205; **"Best oriental wisdom . . . to find out."** Allen Ginsberg to Lucien Carr, n.d. [January 1963], Virginia.

"WHAT DOES WRITERS' WORKSHOP": Sunil Ganguly to Allen Ginsberg, March 15, 1963, Stanford; **"costly alcohol."** Sunil Ganguly to Allen Ginsberg, n.d., Stanford; **Shakti, it was rumored . . . scholarship.** Manjula Mitra to Allen Ginsberg, April 11, 1963, Texas; **Where Shakti's Bengali . . . received them?** Sandeepan Chatterjee to Allen Ginsberg, March 6, 1963, and p.c. April 3, 1963, Stanford; **"to undo the done-for world and start afresh from chaos."** *Time,* November 20, 1964; **At Allen's suggestion . . . published it.** Malay Roy Choudhury to Allen Ginsberg, May 8, 1963, Stanford; **Shakti was meant . . . think of it?** Sandeepan Chatterjee to Allen Ginsberg, February 23, 1963, Stanford; "How can I earn money . . . love that isn't anywhere." Asoke Fakir to Allen Ginsberg, March 1, 1963, Stanford; **After a period . . . talk to them.** Sunil Ganguly to Allen Ginsberg, March 15, 1963, Stanford; **Of his entire circle . . . his poetry.** Sunil Ganguly to Allen Ginsberg, February 5, 1963, Stanford; **Shakti was writing . . . plans to write.** Sunil Ganguly to Allen Ginsberg, January 1, 1963, Stanford; **"Quit Colonial Aesthetics" . . . backseat to cant.** "Poetry should convey the brutal sound of the breaking values and startling tremors of the rebelious [sic] soul of the artist himself, with words stripped of their usual meaning and used contrapuntally," Malay Roy Choudhury, "Manifesto on Hungryalistic Poetry," Haradhon, n.d.; **"Take Off Your Mask."** Malay Roy Choudhury, "The Hungry Generation Movement," in *The Peripheral Window* (Santiniketan, 2004); **In his letters . . . on the cover.** Sunil Ganguly to Allen Ginsberg, March 15, 1963, Stanford; **[Allen] didn't belong in *Krittibas*.** Interview with Jyoti Datta.

"WHY DOES THIS GIRL": Quotes from the encounter with the CID are from Allen Ginsberg's February 27, 1963, account of CID investigation, Stanford; **At the coffeehouse, there were already rumors she was pregnant;** interview with Utpal Kumar Basu; **"The circle we have got here . . . ready to do anything."** Manjula Mitra to Allen Ginsberg, April 11, 1963, Texas; quotes from Allen's visit to Delhi are from *Children of Barren Women,* p. 170; **Allen had never participated . . . entire journey.** *Spontaneous Mind,* p. 10. His second demonstration was upon his return to the United States, at the Sheraton Hotel in San Francisco, protesting the presence of Madame Nhu; **"If God wills."** *Indian Journals,* p. 188; **"person-to-person calm."** From Ginsberg letter, quoted in *Children of Barren Women,* p. 171; **"I only wish people . . . how much there is to revolt against."** Allen Ginsberg to Louis Ginsberg, March 18, 1963, Columbia.

ALLEN FIRST HEARD IT FROM HIS ROOM: **"That Buchenwald look."** Allen Ginsberg to Gregory Corso, May 5, 1963, Ginsberg Trust; **Days later, he'd find . . . overcome his fears.** Excised part of Indian journal, p. 102 of typescript, Stanford; **In Calcutta . . . the dying.** Interview with Peter Orlovsky; **"I was so surprised . . . above her hip woe."** Peter Orlovsky, "Lepers Cry," in *Clean Asshole Poems & Smiling Vegetable Songs* (Orono, Maine: Northern Lights, 1993), pp. 105–110, copyright © Peter Orlovsky. Reprinted by permission of the author; **"the thought of the skeleton lying under the tree in street."** Allen Ginsberg to Gregory Corso, May 5, 1963, Ginsberg Trust; **"whispering . . . the same nowhere to go."** Allen Ginsberg to Jack Kerouac, May 8, 1963, Columbia; for the visit to Devraha Baba, I have drawn on this letter as well as in Francisco Clemente's *Evening Ragas and Paradiso* (New York: Gagosian Gallery, 1992), p. 9, and an interview with Peter Orlovsky; dream of waiting for the bus described in excised portion of Indian journal, Columbia; **The flat began to fill up . . . little time for Allen.** Allen Ginsberg to Gregory Corso, March 21, 1963, Ginsberg Trust and Peter Orlovsky's notebooks, Texas; **"Oh! . . . How wounded, how wounded!"** Allen Ginsberg to Jack Kerouac, May 8, 1963, Texas, and also *Indian Journals,* p. 3.

THE MUTE UNDER THE PEEPUL TREE: **"I want to go to my house where my family . . . I want my bed and clothes."** Allen Ginsberg to A. S. Raman, September 27, 1963, Stanford; **"Everybody afraid to bother for fear of . . . insoluable problem."** Allen Ginsberg to Paul Bowles, n.d. [April 1963], Stanford.

"I WANT YOU BACK": **silly goodly Peter, too.** *An Accidental Autobiography,* pp. 352–353; **With the help . . . the letter then.** Manjula Mitra to Allen Ginsberg, December 23, 1962, and Manjula Mitra to Peter Orlovsky, July 29, 1963, Texas; **"see the situation . . . long hair and beard."** Allen Ginsberg to Gregory Corso, March 21, 1963, Ginsberg Trust.

"FROM A CERTAIN POINT": **"case history."** Manjula Mitra to Peter Orlovsky, May 29, 1963, Texas; **If she realized . . . jumbled.** Manjula Mitra to Peter Orlovsky, June 10, 1963, Texas; **"Miscellaneous, 1963."** Or perhaps an early hippie relic; **"Dear Gregory . . . am grateful, Sam Savage."** Sam Savage to Gregory Corso, May 2, 1963, Stanford, reprinted by permission of the copyright holder; **Gregory received the note . . . pending fatherhood.** *An Accidental Autobiography,* p. 359; **Another day I leave India . . . the years have to offer?** Excised part of Indian journal, p. 147 of typescript, Stanford.

ALLEN GINSBERG IMAGINED: **"the sweetness of all those Gurus . . . so nice to me."** Allen Ginsberg to Jack Kerouac, October 6, 1963, Texas; poetry excerpt is from "The Change," *Collected Poems,* p. 330.

EPILOGUE: JESSORE ROAD

THE LOW RUMBLE OF THEIR TAXI: Quotes from car and rickshaw on Jessore Road in this section and throughout epilogue are taken from audiocassette labeled "71D1/024 A 'C' September 2, 1971, Calcutta Salt Lake refugee camp. September 4 with Mustapha guide of Bangladesh; Laxman Das, Shanbinbetan [Shantiniketan]-September 6, 1971," Stanford.

On September 9, 1971: **"You know Robert Fraser . . . not sure about Mick."** William S. Burroughs to Allen Ginsberg, August 20, 1971, Stanford; **Jan Wenner . . . Fraser replied.** From interview with James Harris in San Francisco, August 21, 1971, Columbia; **In the end, Burroughs . . . 188 bottles of pickles.** From interview with Frank Tedesco, *Berkeley Barb,* June 4–10, 1971, Columbia; **During the Chicago riots . . . work on that, too.** *Spontaneous Mind,* p. 178; **"How many lifetimes ago?"** Allen Ginsberg unpublished journal, labeled "October 31–September 1, 1971," Columbia.

At the entrance to the Ramakrishna: "These people are not scared of flood, because Bangladesh is full of water." Typescript of Jessore Road notebook, p. 18. The rest of the dialogue is from cassette tape.

Allen Ginsberg started it all: **"He succeeded in doing the heretofore . . . Like crazy, man."** Paul Engle to George, July 22, 1963, Iowa; **"1. God is Shit."** Malay Roy Choudhury, "Religious Manifesto of the Hungry Generation," Columbia; **Though Allen wanted . . . New York the long way.** September 15 and 16, 1963, drafts of telegrams in Peter Orlovsky Papers, Texas; **"This was unimaginable . . . fare from you."** Sunil Ganguly to Allen Ginsberg, n.d., Stanford; **"I am nearly ruined . . . willingness-to-oblige."** Utpal K. Basu to Allen Ginsberg, September 23, 1964, Stanford; **Sunil, hearing of . . . city's real problems.** Paul Engle to Allen Ginsberg, December 24, 1964, Stanford; **Malay, believing himself . . . felt abandoned and betrayed.** Malay Roy Choudhury to Allen Ginsberg, January 29, 1965, Stanford; **"I think I am the only person . . . is INDIA."** Malay Roy Choudhury to Allen Ginsberg, October 8, 1964, Columbia.

It wasn't until Allen: Interview with Sunil Ganguly.

Two days after he arrived: **"Gregory's old 'Revolution Is the Solution'– uttering girlfriend."** Ginsberg notebook typescript, September 3, 1971, p. 2, Stanford; **"pure, holy, Gandhian poverty."** Interview with Jyoti Datta; **On the roof of his hut . . . "wife and baby family."** Unpublished journal, September 1971, Stanford.

The Loka Dharma Mahashram: Interview with Sally Grossman and letters from Asoke Sarkar to Allen Ginsberg, February 16, 1965, August 9, 1965, [April 1967], June 27, 1967, December 18, 1967, January 1, 1968, May 19, 1974, February 24, 1977, Stanford; **Tim described himself as like . . . ruins of the old.** Asoke Sarkar, clipping, "Tim Leary: Psychedelic Pioneer in Vancouver," Stanford.

Every year on his birthday: Ashok Sarkar to Allen Ginsberg, July 3, 1974, April 23, 1975, May 19, 1974, March 3, 1980, October 22, 1989, Stanford.

Acknowledgment is made for permission to reprint excerpts from the following works:

"But I Do Not Need Kindness" from *Gasoline* by Gregory Corso. Copyright © 1957 by Gregory Corso. Reprinted by permission of City Lights Books.

"Dear Girl" from *Long Live Man* by Gregory Corso. Copyright © 1962 by Gregory Corso. Reprinted by permission of New Directions Publishing Corporation.

"Howl," "Kaddish," and "The Change" from *Collected Poems 1947–1980* by Allen Ginsberg. Copyright © 1984 by Allen Ginsberg. Reprinted by permission of HarperCollins Publishers.

"Iliad: Achilles Does Not Die" and "The Maze" from *As Ever: Selected Poems* by Joanne Kyger, edited by Michael Rothenberg. Copyright © Joanne Kyger, 2002. Used by permission of Penguin Books, a member of Penguin Group (USA) Inc.

The author is grateful to the curators at the following institutions for permission to cite from their collections: The Papers of Paul Engle, The University of Iowa Libraries, Iowa City, Iowa; the Papers of Allen Ginsberg, MSS 7883, 7883-a, Clifton Waller Barrett Library of American Literature, Special Collections, University of Virginia Library; the papers of Peter Orlovsky and Gregory Corso, the Harry Ransom Humanities Research Center, The University of Texas at Austin; letters and journals of Allen Ginsberg, Rare Book and Manuscript Library, Columbia University; unpublished letters from Allen Ginsberg and Gregory Corso to Gary Snyder in the Gary Snyder Collection at Special Collections, University of California Library, Davis; unpublished letters and manuscripts from the Allen Ginsberg Papers at Stanford University. She would also like to thank the following individuals and executors for permission to quote from unpublished letters and manuscripts: for Allen Ginsberg's unpublished manuscript and letters, The Ginsberg Trust, © Allen Ginsberg Estate; quotations from Gary Snyder's unpublished letters, Gary Snyder; quotations from Joanne Kyger's unpublished letters, Joanne Kyger; quotation from an unpublished letter by Carl Solomon, Elaine Friedman;

Peter Orlovsky's unpublished letters and journals and the unpublished letters of Kate Orlovsky, Peter Orlovsky Trust; translation of Buddhadeva Bose's account of his visit to Greenwich Village, Jyotimiroy Datta; quotations from an unpublished letter by Paul Engle, Hua-Ling Engle; quotations from unpublished letters by Asoke Fakir, Ashok Sarkar; selections from unpublished manuscript by Gregory Corso, Sheri Baird, executor of the Corso Estate; letter from Sam Savage to Gregory Corso, Sam Savage.

PHOTO CAPTIONS AND CREDITS

PART I

Hal Chase, Jack Kerouac, Allen Ginsberg, and William Burroughs on Morningside Heights. © Allen Ginsberg Estate.

Ginsberg at work. © Allen Ginsberg Estate.

Hope Savage in Greenwich Village. Courtesy of David Madden.

Gregory Corso in Paris garret wearing Hope's cloak. © Allen Ginsberg Estate.

Peter Orlovsky, Burroughs, Alan Ansen, Corso, Paul Bowles, and Ginsberg in Tangier. © Allen Ginsberg Estate.

PART II

Hope Savage, Jean, and Robbie Madden in mountains of Boone, North Carolina. Courtesy of David Madden.

Meditating sadhu in Rishikesh. © Allen Ginsberg Estate.

Joanne Kyger, Gary Snyder, and Peter Orlovsky in Kausani. © Allen Ginsberg Estate.

Triund Forest Lodge outside Dharamsala. © Allen Ginsberg Estate.

Peter Orlovsky and cow. © Allen Ginsberg Estate.

PART III

Hope Savage, looking like a spy in Tehran. © Allen Ginsberg Estate.

College Street Coffee House with *Krittibas* group.

Asoke Fakir. © Allen Ginsberg Estate.

Manjula Mitra in Jodhpur Park flat with Peter's guitar. © Allen Ginsberg Estate.

Peter Orlovsky with Shakti Chattopadhyay, Sunil Gangopadhyay, and Sandeepan Chatterjee on Amjadia rooftop. © Allen Ginsberg Estate.

Shiva worshipper in Benares. © Allen Ginsberg Estate.

Allen Ginsberg in front of Taj Mahal. © Allen Ginsberg Estate.

EPILOGUE

Baul singer in a *pied gauri,* Calcutta street corner. © Allen Ginsberg Estate.

Jenny Saville
Neil Jenney
De Kooning
Malcolm Morley